10-30

# *READINGS IN EASTERN RELIGIOUS THOUGHT*
## BUDDHISM

# READINGS IN EASTERN RELIGIOUS THOUGHT

## Volume II
# BUDDHISM

*Edited by*
Allie M. Frazier

THE WESTMINSTER PRESS
PHILADELPHIA

STANDARD BOOK No. 664-24847-0

LIBRARY OF CONGRESS CATALOG CARD No. 69-14197

BOOK DESIGN BY
DOROTHY ALDEN SMITH

PUBLISHED BY THE WESTMINSTER PRESS ®
PHILADELPHIA, PENNSYLVANIA

PRINTED IN THE UNITED STATES OF AMERICA

*To*
*Charles Arthur Campbell*

# Preface

This book of readings on Buddhist religious thought and practice brings together in one volume both interpretative essays on the Buddhist tradition and selections from the sacred literature of Buddhism. The volume is designed to aid college students and readers in general who may be approaching Buddhism for the first time. Westerners who genuinely desire to comprehend Eastern religions must immerse themselves in the original sources of those traditions; they must come to grips with the sacred literature without the constant assistance of detailed commentary and interpretation. The beginning student of Eastern religion, however, requires a guide that can trace for him a viable path through the complicated and bewildering scriptures and religious movements of the East. Such guidance is provided in this volume by the expert commentaries upon Buddhism spaced throughout the selection of primary sources. These commentaries function as maps, indicating the main thoroughfares through the Buddhist tradition, as well as the byways, detours, and uncharted territory.

In an introductory volume, a full representation of the scope of the Buddhist tradition is not possible. The principle governing the selection of materials for this volume has always been to include those original sources and commentaries which illuminate the fundamental themes of Buddhist thought and experience.

I would like to express my appreciation to Mrs. Leslie Seyfried Roberts, who greatly assisted me in the final stages of the preparation of the manuscript. My wife, Ruth, aided me at every stage in the preparation of this volume; she read early drafts, offered valuable critical advice, and helped me in ways too numerous to mention. Finally, I owe a debt of gratitude to Hollins College and its students, who have given me every encouragement in my work on this project.

A. M. F.

*Hollins College*
*Hollins College, Virginia*

# Contents

# Introduction

The adventure of studying non-Western religions is undertaken with the assumption that it is possible to comprehend a religious tradition other than one's own. If this assumption is unwarranted, then the whole project of the Westerner's study of Eastern religions might just as well be canceled. Of course, we can have information about Eastern religious thought and practice by merely describing them in an encyclopedic fashion, but we should recognize that knowing the "facts" about Eastern beliefs and practice is not equivalent to comprehending their significance and meaning.

For example, how adequate is our comprehension of human language if our sole understanding of it is derived from the study of words and their meanings as cataloged in a dictionary? Not until we have some grasp of the use of words, of their function in communication, their capacity to bemuse us, mystify us, befuddle us, delight us, and, finally, to use us as their architects and instruments, do we discover the complex meaning of the phenomenon of language. It is just so with the comprehension of Eastern religious thought. Its living content is not apprehended solely in the husks of externality, the "facts" of *what* beliefs, *what* practices. An adequate understanding of Eastern religious thought requires that we appropriate its human significance.

The discovery of the human significance of a foreign religious tradition does not require that we adopt its basic beliefs, nor does it impose upon us any necessity to accept its fundamental myths. One does not have to be a Buddhist to understand Buddhism. Buddhism is a religion of man and, as such, expresses the hopes, aspirations, and basic value commitments of religious persons. The externals of various religions—their myths, beliefs, rituals—must be interpreted in order to be understood. An effort must be made to find out what these externals mean to those who respond to them, produce them, and participate in them.

However, the discovery of the human significance of non-Western religions is not a simple task. The difficulties of the enterprise are many and subtle and continue to require our best scholarship and our most imaginative thought. In short, the effort to penetrate to the personal meaning of Eastern religions is a task of such magnitude that only the person who has the time and the discipline to think seriously should undertake it. Yet no more rewarding adventure confronts the Western mind than the uncovering and interpretation of Eastern religious thought.

The obstacles which lie in the path of such an adventurer should not be minimized. It is only by sustained effort that we manage to isolate and define the basic categories by which our experience is structured and made intelligible. The basic principles by which the mind orders its experience are so much a part of the fabric of experience that they escape our critical notice unless we submit them to careful scrutiny. In this respect, they are similar to eyeglasses. Eyeglasses sit on our noses in the most intimate proximity, yet the more we become habituated to them, the more remote they become. How much more difficult is it to understand a tradition that does not share our basic assumptions?

However, the reward for serious study of non-Western religious thought is a considerable enrichment of personal consciousness. Not only will one's own religious life be clarified in the course of such a comparative study, but one will also see old religious problems and indeed the whole human predicament in new perspectives. Regardless of the particular stand that a Westerner takes toward religion, an introduction to the general spirit of Eastern religious thought can have a liberating effect. Such a study frees him from accepting doctrines as established facts and allows him the opportunity to understand his own religious beliefs and experiences more completely.

## CHAPTER I

# The Dialogue in Myth of East and West

JOSEPH CAMPBELL

## THE DIALOGUE

The myth of eternal return, which is still basic to Oriental life, displays an order of fixed forms that appear and reappear through all time. The daily round of the sun, the waning and waxing moon, the cycle of the year, and the rhythm of organic birth, death, and new birth, represent a miracle of continuous arising that is fundamental to the nature of the universe. We all know the archaic myth of the four ages of gold, silver, bronze, and iron, where the world is shown declining, growing ever worse. It will disintegrate presently in chaos, only to burst forth again, fresh as a flower, to recommence spontaneously the inevitable course. There never was a time when time was not. Nor will there be a time when this kaleidoscopic play of eternity in time will have ceased.

There is therefore nothing to be gained, either for the universe or for man, through individual originality and effort. Those who have identified themselves with the mortal body and its affections will necessarily find that all is painful, since everything—for them —must end. But for those who have found the still point of eternity, around which all—including themselves—revolves, everything is acceptable as it is; indeed, can even be experienced as glorious and wonderful. The first duty of the individual, consequently, is simply to play his given role—as do the sun and moon, the various animal and plant species, the waters, the rocks, and the stars—without resistance, without fault; and then, if possible, so to order his mind as to identify its consciousness with the inhabiting principle of the whole.

The dreamlike spell of this contemplative, metaphysically oriented tradition, where light and darkness dance together in a world-creating cosmic shadow play, carries into modern times an image that is of incalculable age. In its primitive form it is widely known among the jungle villages of the broad equatorial zone that extends from Africa eastward, through India, Southeast Asia, and Oceania, to Brazil, where the basic myth is of a dreamlike age of the beginning, when there was neither death nor birth, which, however, terminated when a murder was committed. The body of the victim was cut up and buried. And not only did the food plants on which the community lives arise from those buried parts, but on all who ate of their fruit the organs of reproduction appeared; so that death, which had come into the world through a killing, was countered by its opposite, generation, and the self-consuming thing that is life, which lives on life, began its interminable course.

Throughout the dark green jungles of the world there abound not only dreadful animal scenes of tooth and claw, but also terrible human rites of cannibal communion, dramatically representing—with the force of an initiatory shock—the murder scene, sexual act, and festival meal of the beginning, when life and death became two, which had been one, and the sexes became two, which also had been one. Creatures come into being, live on the death of others, die, and become the food of others, continuing, thus, into and through the transformations of time, the timeless archetype of the mythological beginning; and the individual matters no more than a fallen leaf. Psychologically, the effect of the enactment of such a rite is to shift the focus of the mind from the individual (who perishes) to the everlasting group. Magically, it is to reinforce the ever-living life in all lives, which appears to be many but is really one; so that the growth is stimulated of the yams, coconuts, pigs, moon, and breadfruits, and of the human community as well.

Sir James G. Frazer, in *The Golden Bough,* has shown that in the early city states of the nuclear Near East, from which center all of the high civilizations of the world have been derived, god-kings were sacrificed in the way of this jungle rite, and Sir Leonard Woolley's excavation of the Royal Tombs of Ur, in which whole courts had been ceremonially interred alive, revealed that in Sumer such practices continued until as late as c. 2350 B.C. We know, furthermore, that in India, in the sixteenth century A.D., kings were observed ceremoniously slicing themselves to bits, and in the temples of the Black Goddess Kali, the terrible one of many names, "difficult of approach" (*durgā*), whose stomach is a void and so can never be filled and whose womb is giving birth forever to all things, a river of blood has been pouring continuously for millenniums, from beheaded offerings, through channels carved to return it, still living, to its divine source.

To this day seven or eight hundred goats are slaughtered in three days in the Kalighat, the principal temple of the goddess in Calcutta, during her autumn festival, the Durga Puja. The heads are piled before the image, and the bodies go to the devotees, to be consumed in contemplative communion. Water buffalo, sheep, pigs, and fowl, likewise, are immolated lavishly in her worship, and before the prohibition of human sacrifice in 1835, she received from every part of the land even richer fare. In the towering Shiva temple of Tanjore a male child was beheaded before the altar of the goddess every Friday at the holy hour of twilight. In the year 1830, a petty monarch of Bastar, desiring her grace, offered on one occasion twenty-five men at her altar in Danteshvari, and in the sixteenth century a king of Cooch Behar immolated a hundred and fifty in that place.

In the Jaintia hills of Assam it was the custom of a certain royal house to offer one human victim at the Durga Puja every year. After having bathed and purified himself, the sacrifice was dressed in new attire, daubed with red sandalwood and vermilion, arrayed with garlands, and, thus bedecked, installed upon a raised dais before the image, where he spent some time in meditation, repeating sacred sounds, and, when ready, made a sign with his finger. The executioner, likewise pronouncing sacred syllables, having elevated the sword, thereupon struck off the man's head, which was immediately presented to the goddess on a golden plate. The lungs, being cooked, were consumed by yogis, and the royal family partook of a small quantity of rice steeped in the sacrificial blood. Those offered in this sacrifice were normally volunteers. However, when such were lacking, victims were kidnaped from outside the little state; and so it chanced, in 1832, that four men disappeared from the British domain, of whom one escaped to tell his tale, and the following year the kingdom was annexed—without its custom.

"By one human sacrifice with proper rites, the goddess remains gratified for a thousand years," we read in the Kalika Purana, a Hindu scripture of about the tenth century A.D.; "and by the sacrifice of three men, one hundred thousand. Shiva, in his terrific aspect, as the consort of the goddess, is appeased for three thousand years by an offering of human flesh. For blood, if immediately consecrated, becomes ambrosia, and since the head and body are extremely gratifying, these should be presented in the worship of the goddess. The wise would do well to add such flesh, free from hair, to their offerings of food."

In the garden of innocence where such rites can be enacted with perfect equanimity, both the victim and the sacrificial priest are able to identify their consciousness, and thereby their reality, with the inhabiting principle of the whole. They can truly say and truly feel, in the words of the Indian Bhagavad Gita, that "even as worn out clothes are cast off and others put on that are new, so worn out bodies are cast off by the dweller in the body and others put on that are new."

For the West, however, the possibility of such an egoless return to a state of soul antecedent to the birth of individuality has long since passed away; and the first important stage in the branching off can be seen to have occurred in that very part of the nuclear Near East where the earliest god-kings and their courts had been for centuries ritually entombed: namely Sumer, where a new sense of the separation of the spheres of god and man began to be represented in myth and ritual about 2350 B.C. The king, then, was no longer a god, but a servant of the god, his Tenant Farmer, supervisor of the race of human slaves created to serve the gods with unremitting toil. And no longer identity, but relationship, was the paramount concern. Man had been made not to *be* God but to know, honor, and serve him; so that even the king, who, according to the earlier mythological view, had been the chief embodiment of divinity on earth, was now but a priest offering sacrifice in tendance to One above—not a god returning himself in sacrifice to Himself.

In the course of the following centuries, the new sense of separation led to a counter-yearning for return—not to identity, for such was no longer possible of conception (creator and creature were not the same), but to the presence and vision of the forfeited god. Hence the new mythology brought forth, in due time, a development away from the earlier static view of returning cycles. A progressive, temporally oriented mythology arose, of a creation, once and for all, at the beginning of time, a subsequent fall, and a work of restoration, still in progress. The world no longer was to be known as a mere showing in time of the paradigms of eternity, but as a field of unprecedented cosmic conflict between two powers, one light and one dark.

The earliest prophet of this mythology of cosmic restoration was, apparently, the Persian Zoroaster, whose dates, however, have not been securely established. They have been variously placed between c. 1200 and c. 550 B.C., so that, like Homer (of about the same span of years), he should perhaps be regarded rather as symbolic of a tradition than as specifically, or solely, one man. The system associated with his name is based on the idea of a conflict between the wise lord, Ahura Mazda, "first father of the Righteous Order, who gave to the sun and stars their path," and an independent evil principle, Angra Mainyu, the Deceiver, principle of the lie, who, when all had been excellently made, entered into it in every particle. The world, consequently, is a compound wherein good and evil, light and dark, wisdom and violence, are contending for a victory. And the privilege and duty of each man—who, himself, as a part of creation, is a compound of good and evil—is to elect, voluntarily, to engage in the battle in the interest of the light. It is supposed that with the birth of Zoroaster, twelve thousand years following the creation of the world, a decisive turn was given the conflict in favor of the good, and that when he returns, after another twelve millennia, in the person of the messiah Saoshyant, there will take place a final battle and cosmic conflagration, through which the principle of darkness and the lie will be undone. Whereafter, all will be light, there will be no further history, and the Kingdom of God (Ahura Mazda) will have been established in its pristine form forever.

It is obvious that a potent mythical formula for the reorientation of the human spirit is here supplied—pitching it forward along the way of time, summoning man to an assumption of autonomous responsibility for the renovation of the universe in God's name, and thus fostering a new, potentially political (not finally contemplative) philosophy of holy war. "May we be such," runs a Persian prayer, "as those who bring on this renovation and make this world progressive, till its perfection shall have been achieved."

The first historic manifestation of the force of this new mythic view was in the Achaemenian empire of Cyrus the Great (died 529 B.C.) and Darius I (reigned c. 521–486 B.C.), which in a few decades extended its domain from India to Greece, and under the protection of which the post-exilic Hebrews both rebuilt their temple (Ezra 1:1–11) and reconstructed their traditional inheritance. The second historic manifestation was in the Hebrew application of its universal message to themselves; the next was in the world mission of Christianity; and the fourth, in that of Islam.

"Enlarge the place of your tent, and let the curtains of your habitations be stretched out; hold not back, lengthen your cords and strengthen your stakes. For you will spread abroad to the right and to the left, and your descendants will possess the nations and will people the desolate cities" (Isaiah 54:2–3; c. 546–536 B.C.).

"And this gospel of the kingdom will be preached throughout the whole world as a testimony to all nations; and then the end will come" (Matthew 24:14; c. 90 A.D.).

"And slay them wherever you catch them, and turn them out from where they have turned you out; for tumult and oppression are worse than slaughter. . . . And fight them on until there is no more tumult or oppression and there prevail justice and faith in Allah; but if they cease, let there be no hostility except to those who practice oppression" (Koran 2:191, 193; c. 632 A.D.).

Two completely opposed mythologies of the destiny and virtue of man, therefore, have come together in the modern world. And they are contributing in discord to whatever new society may be in the process of formation. For, of the tree that grows in the garden where God walks in the cool of the day, the wise men westward of Iran have partaken of the fruit of the knowledge of good and evil, whereas those on the other side of that cultural divide, in India and the Far East, have relished only the fruit of eternal life. However, the two limbs, we are informed, come together in the center of the garden, where they form a single tree at the base, branching out when they reach a certain height. Likewise, the two mythologies spring from one base in the Near East. And if man should taste of both fruits he would become, we have been told, as God himself (Genesis 3:22)—which is the boon that the meeting of East and West today is offering to us all.

## THE SHARED MYTH OF THE ONE THAT BECAME TWO

The extent to which the mythologies—and therewith psychologies—of the Orient and Occident diverged in the course of the period between the dawn of civilization in the Near East and the present age of mutual rediscovery appears in their opposed versions of the shared mythological image of the first being, who was originally one but became two.

"In the beginning," states an Indian example of c. 700 B.C., preserved in the Brihadaranyaka Upanishad,

this universe was nothing but the Self in the form of a man. It looked around and saw that there was nothing but itself, whereupon its first shout was, "It is I!"; whence the concept "I" arose. (And that is why, even now, when addressed, one answers first, "It is I!" only then giving the other name that one bears.)

Then he was afraid. (That is why anyone alone is afraid.) But he considered: "Since there is no one here but myself, what is there to fear?" Whereupon the fear departed. (For what should have been feared? It is only to a second that fear refers.)

However, he still lacked delight (therefore, we lack delight when alone) and desired a second. He was exactly as large as a man and woman embracing. This Self then divided itself in two parts; and with that, there were a master and a mistress. (Therefore this body, by itself, as the sage Yajnavalkya declares, is like half of a split pea. And that is why, indeed, this space is filled by a woman.)

The male embraced the female, and from that the human race arose. She, however, reflected: "How can he unite with me, who am produced from himself? Well then, let me hide!" She became a cow, he a bull and united with her; and from that cattle arose. She became a mare, he a stallion; she an ass, he a donkey and united with her; and from that solid-hoofed animals arose. She became a goat, he a buck; she a sheep, he a ram and united with her; and from that goats and sheep arose. Thus he poured forth all pairing things, down to the ants. Then he realized: "I, actually, am creation; for I have poured forth all this." Whence arose the concept "Creation" [Sanskrit *sṛṣṭiḥ:* "what is poured forth"].

Anyone understanding this becomes, truly, himself a creator in this creation.

The best-known Occidental example of this image of the first being, split in two, which seem to be two but are actually one, is, of course, that of the Book of Genesis, second chapter, where it is turned, however, to a different sense. For the couple is separated here by a superior being, who, as we are told, caused a deep sleep to fall upon the man and, while he slept, took one of his ribs. In the Indian version it is the god himself that divides and becomes not man alone but all creation; so that everything is a manifestation of that single inhabiting divine substance: there is no other; whereas in the Bible, God and man, from the beginning, are distinct. Man is made in the image of God, indeed, and the breath of God has been breathed into his nostrils; yet his being, his self, is not that of God, nor is it one with the universe. The fashioning of the world, of the animals, and of Adam (who then became Adam and Eve) was accomplished not within the sphere of divinity but outside of it. There is, consequently, an *intrinsic*, not merely *formal*, separation. And the goal of knowledge cannot be to *see* God here and now in all things; for God is not in things. God is transcendent. God is beheld only by the dead. The goal of knowledge has to be, rather, to know the *relationship* of God to his creation, or, more specifically, to man, and through such knowledge, by God's grace, to link one's own will back to that of the Creator.

Moreover, according to the biblical version of this myth, it was only after creation that man fell, whereas in the Indian example creation itself was a fall—the fragmentation of a god. And the god is not condemned. Rather, his creation, his "pouring forth" (*sṛṣṭiḥ*), is described as an act of voluntary, dynamic will-to-be-more, which anteceded creation and has, therefore, a metaphysical, symbolical, not literal, historical meaning. The fall of Adam and Eve was an event within the already created frame of time and space, an accident that should not have taken place. The myth of the Self in the form of a man, on the other hand, who looked around and saw nothing but himself, said "I," felt fear, and then desired to be two, tells of an intrinsic, not errant, factor in the manifold of being, the correction or undoing of which would not improve, but dissolve, creation. The Indian point of view is metaphysical, poetical; the biblical, ethical and historical.

Adam's fall and exile from the garden was thus in no sense a metaphysical departure of divine substance from itself, but an event only in the history, or pre-history, of man. And this event in the created world has been followed throughout the remainder of the book by the record of man's linkage and failures of linkage back to God—again, historically conceived. For, as we next hear, God himself, at a certain point in the course of time, out of his own volition, moved toward man, instituting a new law in the form of a covenant with a certain people. And these became, therewith, a priestly race, unique in the world. God's reconciliation with man, of whose creation he had repented (Genesis 6:6), was to be achieved only by virtue of this particular community— in time: for in time there should take place the realization of the Lord God's kingdom on earth, when the heathen monarchies would crumble and Israel be saved, when men would "cast forth their idols of silver and their idols of gold, which they made to themselves to worship, to the moles and to the bats."

> Be broken, you peoples, and be dismayed;
>    give ear, all you far countries;
> gird yourselves and be dismayed;
>    gird yourselves and be dismayed.
> Take counsel together, but it will come to nought;
>    speak a word, but it will not stand,
>    for God is with us.

In the Indian view, on the contrary, what is divine here is divine there also; nor has anyone to wait—or even to hope—for a "day of the Lord." For what has been lost is in each his very self (*ātman*), here and now, requiring only to be sought. Or, as they say: "Only when men shall roll up space like a piece of leather will there be an end of sorrow apart from knowing God."

The question arises (again historical) in the world dominated by the Bible, as to the identity of the favored community, and three are well known to have developed claims: the Jewish, the Christian, and the Moslem, each supposing itself to have been authorized by a particular revelation. God, that is to say, though conceived as outside of history and not himself its substance (transcendent: not immanent), is supposed to have engaged himself miraculously in the enterprise of restoring fallen man through a covenant, sacrament, or revealed book, with a view to a general, communal experience of fulfillment yet to come. The world is corrupt and man a sinner; the individual, however, through engagement along with God in the destiny of the only authorized community, participates in the coming glory of the kingdom of righteousness, when "the glory of the Lord shall be revealed, and all flesh shall see it together."

In the experience and vision of India, on the other hand, although the holy mystery and power have been understood to be indeed transcendent ("other than the known; moreover, above the unknown"), they are also, at the same time, immanent ("like a razor in a razorcase, like fire in tinder"). It is not that the divine is every*where:* it is that the divine is every*thing.* So that one does not require any outside reference, revelation, sacrament, or authorized community to return to it. One has but to alter one's psychological orientation and recognize (re-cognize) what is within. Deprived of this recognition, we are removed from our own reality by a cerebral shortsightedness which is called in Sanskrit *māyā,* "delusion" (from the verbal root *mā,* "to measure, measure out, to form, to build," denoting, in the first place, the power of a god or demon to produce illusory effects, to change form, and to appear under deceiving masks; in the second place, "magic," the production of illusions and, in warfare, camouflage, deceptive tactics; and finally, in philosophical discourse, the illusion superimposed upon reality as an effect of ignorance). Instead of the biblical exile from a geographically, historically conceived garden wherein God walked in the cool of the day, we have in India, therefore, already c. 700 B.C. (some three hundred years before the putting together of the Pentateuch), a *psychological* reading of the great theme.

The shared myth of the primal androgyne is applied in the two traditions to the same task—the exposition of man's distance, in his normal secular life, from the divine Alpha and Omega. Yet the arguments radically differ, and therefore support two radically different civilizations. For, if man has been removed from the divine through a historical event, it will be a historical event that leads him back, whereas if it has been by some sort of psychological displacement that he has been blocked, psychology will be his vehicle of return. And so it is that in India the final focus of concern is not the community (though, as we shall see, the idea of the holy community plays a formidable role as a disciplinary force), but yoga.

## THE TWO VIEWS OF EGO

The Indian term *yoga* is derived from the Sanskrit verbal root *yuj,* "to link, join, or unite," which is related etymologically to "yoke," a yoke of oxen, and is in sense analogous to the word "religion" (Latin *re-ligio*), "to link back, or bind." Man, the creature, is by religion bound back to God. However, religion, *religio,* refers to a linking historically conditioned by way of a covenant, sacrament, or Koran, whereas yoga is the psychological linking of the mind to that superordinated principle "by which the mind knows." Furthermore, in yoga what is linked is finally the self to itself, consciousness to consciousness; for what had seemed, through *māyā,* to be two are in reality not so; whereas in religion what are linked are God and man, which are not the same.

It is of course true that in the popular religions of the Orient the gods are worshiped as though external to their devotees, and all the rules and rites of a covenanted relationship are observed. Nevertheless, the ultimate realization, which the sages have celebrated, is that the god worshiped as though without is in reality a reflex of the same mystery as oneself. As long as an illusion of ego remains, the commensurate illusion of a separate deity also will be there; and vice versa, as long as the idea of a separate deity is cherished, an illusion of ego, related to it in love, fear, worship, exile, or atonement, will also be there. But precisely that illusion of duality is the trick of *māyā.* "Thou art that" (*tat tvam asi*) is the proper thought for the first step to wisdom.

In the beginning, as we have read, there was only the Self; but it said "I" (Sanskrit *aham*) and immediately felt fear, after which, desire.

It is to be remarked that in this view of the instant of creation (presented from within the sphere of the psyche of the creative being itself) the same two basic motivations are identified as the leading modern schools of depth analysis have indicated for the *human* psyche: aggression and desire. Carl G. Jung, in his early paper on *The Unconscious in Normal and Pathological Psychology* (1916), wrote of two psychological types: the introvert, harried by fear, and the extrovert, driven by desire. Sigmund Freud also, in his *Beyond the Pleasure Principle* (1920), wrote of "the death wish" and "the life wish": on the one hand, the will to violence and the fear of it (*thanatos, destruo*), and, on the other hand, the need and desire to love and be loved (*eros, libido*). Both spring spontaneously from the deep dark source of the energies of the psyche, the *id,* and are governed, therefore, by the self-centered "pleasure principle": *I* want: *I* am afraid. Comparably, in the Indian myth, as soon as the self said "I" (*aham*), it knew first fear, and then desire.

But now—and here, I believe, is a point of fundamental importance for our reading of the basic difference between the Oriental and Occidental approaches to the cultivation of the soul—in the Indian myth the principle of ego, "I" (*aham*), is identified completely with the pleasure principle, whereas in the psychologies of both Freud and Jung its proper function is to know and relate to external reality (Freud's "reality principle"): not the reality of the metaphysical but that of the physical, empirical sphere of time and space. In other words, spiritual maturity, as understood in the modern Occident, requires a differentiation of *ego* from *id,* whereas in the Orient, throughout the history at least of every teaching that has stemmed from India, ego (*ahaṁ-kāra:* "the making of the sound 'I' ") is impugned as the principle of libidinous delusion, to be dissolved.

Let us glance at the wonderful story of the Buddha in the episode of his attainment of the goal of all goals beneath the "tree of awakening," the Bo- or Bodhi-tree (*bodhi,* "awakening").

The Blessed One, alone, accompanied only by his own resolve, with his mind fixed only on attainment, rose up like a lion at nightfall, at the time when flowers close, and, proceeding along a road that the gods had hung with banners, strode toward the

Bodhi-tree. Snakes, gnomes, birds, divine musicians, and other beings of numerous variety did him worship with perfumes, flowers, and other offerings, while the choirs of the heavens poured forth celestial music; so that the ten thousand worlds were filled with delightful scents, garlands, and shouts of acclaim.

And there happened to come, just then, from the opposite direction, a grass-cutter named Sotthiya, bearing a burden of cut grass, and when he saw the Great Being, that he was a holy man, he presented to him eight handfuls. Whereafter, coming to the Bodhi-tree, the one who was about to become the Buddha stood on the southern side and faced north. Instantly the southern half of the world sank until it seemed to touch the lowest hell, while the northern rose to the highest heaven.

"Methinks," then said the Buddha-to-be, "this cannot be the place for the attainment of supreme wisdom"; and walking round the tree with his right side toward it, he came to the western side and faced east. Thereupon, the western half of the world sank until it seemed to touch the lowest hell, while the eastern half rose to the highest heaven. Indeed, wherever the Blessed One stood, the broad earth rose and fell, as though it were a huge cartwheel lying on its hub and someone were treading on the rim.

"Methinks," said the Buddha-to-be, "this also cannot be the place for the attainment of supreme wisdom"; and walking further, with his right side toward the tree, he came to the northern side and faced south. Then the northern half of the world sank until it seemed to touch the lowest hell, while the southern half rose to the highest heaven.

"Methinks," said the Buddha-to-be, "this also cannot be the place for the attainment of supreme wisdom"; and walking round the tree with his right side toward it, he came to the eastern side and faced west.

Now it is on the eastern side of their Bodhi-trees that all the Buddhas have sat down, cross-legged, and that side neither trembles nor quakes.

Then the Great Being saying to himself, "This is the Immovable Spot on which all the Buddhas have established themselves:

this is the place for destroying passion's net," he took hold of his handful of grass by one end and shook it out there. And straightway the blades of grass formed themselves into a seat fourteen cubits long, of such symmetry of shape as not even the most skillful painter or carver could design.

The Buddha-to-be, turning his back to the trunk of the Bodhi-tree, faced east, and making the mighty resolution, "Let my skin, sinews, and bones become dry, and welcome; and let all the flesh and blood of my body dry up; but never from this seat will I stir until I have attained the supreme and absolute wisdom!" he sat himself down cross-legged in an unconquerable position, from which not even the descent of a hundred thunderbolts at once could have dislodged him.

Having departed from his palace, wife, and child some years before, to seek the knowledge that should release all beings from sorrow, the prince Gautama Shakyamuni had come thus at last to the midpoint, the supporting point, of the universe—which is described here in mythological terms, lest it should be taken for a physical place to be sought somewhere on earth. For its location is psychological. It is that point of balance in the mind from which the universe can be perfectly regarded: the still-standing point of disengagement around which all things turn. To man's secular view, things appear to move in time and to be in their final character concrete. I am here, you are there: right and left; up, down; life and death. The pairs of opposites are all around, and the wheel of the world, the wheel of time, is ever revolving, with our lives engaged in its round. However, there is an all-supporting midpoint, a hub where the opposites come together, like the spokes of a wheel, in emptiness. And it is there, facing east (the world direction of the new day), that the Buddhas of past, present, and future—who are of one Buddhahood, though manifest in series in the mode of time—are said to have experienced absolute illumination.

The prince Gautama Shakyamuni, established in his mind in that spot and about to penetrate the last mystery of being, was now to be assailed by the lord of the life illusion: that same self-

in-the-form-of-a-man who, before the beginning of time, looked
around and saw nothing but himself, said "I," and immediately
experienced first fear, and then desire. Mythologically represented, this same Being of all beings appeared before the Buddha-
to-be, first as a prince, bearing a flowery bow, in his character as
Eros, Desire (Sanskrit *kāma*), and then as a frightening maharaja
of demons, charging on a bellowing war-elephant, King Thanatos
(Sanskrit *māra*), King Death.

"The one who is called in the world the Lord Desire," we read
in a celebrated Sanskrit version of the Buddha-Life, composed by
one of the earliest masters of the so-called "poetic" (*kāvya*) style
of literary composition, a learned Brahmin who had been con-
verted to the Buddhist Order, Ashvaghosha by name (fl. c.
100 A.D.),

the owner of the flowery shafts who is also called the Lord Death and
is the final foe of spiritual disengagement, summoning before himself
his three attractive sons, namely, Mental-Confusion, Gaiety, and Pride,
and his voluptuous daughters, Lust, Delight, and Pining, sent them
before the Blessed One. Taking up his flowery bow and his five infatuating arrows, which are named Exciter of the Paroxysm of Desire,
Gladdener, Infatuator, Parcher, and Carrier of Death, he followed
his brood to the foot of the tree where the Great Being was sitting.
Toying with an arrow, the god showed himself and addressed the
calm seer who was there making the ferry passage to the farther
shore of the ocean of being.

"Up, up, O noble prince!" he ordered, with a voice of divine authority. "Recall the duties of your caste and abandon this dissolute
quest for disengagement. The mendicant life is ill suited for anyone
born of a noble house; but rather, by devotion to the duties of your
caste, you are to serve the order of the good society, maintain the laws
of the revealed religion, combat wickedness in the world, and merit
thereby a residence in the highest heaven as a god."

The Blessed One failed to move.

"You will not rise?" then said the god. He fixed an arrow to his
bow. "If you are stubborn, stiff-necked, and abide by your resolve,
this arrow that I am notching to my string, which has already inflamed the sun itself, shall be let fly. It is already darting out its

tongue at you, like a serpent." And, threatening, without result, he released the shaft—without result.

For the Blessed One, by virtue of innumerable acts of boundless giving throughout innumerable lifetimes, had dissolved within his mind the concept "I" (*aham*), and along with it the correlative experience of any "thou" (*tvam*). In the void of the Immovable Spot, beneath the tree of the knowledge beyond the pairs-of-opposites beyond life and death, good and evil, as well as beyond I and thou, had he so much as thought "I" he would have felt "they," and, beholding the voluptuous daughters of the god who were displaying themselves attractively before him as objects in the field of a subject, he would have been, to say the least, required to control himself. However, there being no "I" present to his mind, there was no "they" there either. Absolutely unmoved, because himself absolutely not there, perfectly established on the Immovable Spot in the unconquerable (psychological) position of all the Buddhas, the Blessed One was impervious to the sharp shaft.

And the god, perceiving that his flowery stroke had failed, said to himself: "He does not notice even the arrow that set the sun aflame! Can he be destitute of sense? He is worthy neither of my flowery shaft, nor of my daughters: let me send against him my army."

And immediately putting off his infatuating aspect as the Lord Desire, that great god became the Lord Death, and around him an army of demonic forms crystallized, wearing frightening shapes and bearing in their hands bows and arrows, darts, clubs, swords, trees, and even blazing mountains; having the visages of boars, fish, horses, camels, asses, tigers, bears, lions and elephants; one-eyed, multi-faced, three-headed, pot-bellied, and with speckled bellies; equipped with claws, equipped with tusks, some bearing headless bodies in their hands, many with half-mutilated faces, monstrous mouths, knobby knees, and the reek of goats; copper red, some clothed in leather, others wearing nothing at all, with fiery or smoke-colored hair, many with long, pendulous ears, having half their faces white, others having half their bodies green; red and smoke-colored, yellow and black; with arms longer than the reach of serpents, their girdles jingling with bells: some as tall as palms, bearing spears, some of a child's size with projecting teeth; some with the bodies of birds and faces of rams, or men's bodies and the faces of cats; with disheveled hair, with topknots, or half bald; with frowning or triumphant faces, wasting one's strength or fascinating one's mind. Some sported in the sky, others went along the tops of trees; many danced upon each other, more leaped about wildly on the ground. One, dancing, shook a trident; another crashed his club; one like a bull bounded for joy; another blazed out flames from every hair. And then there were some who stood around to frighten him with many lolling tongues, many mouths, savage, sharply pointed teeth, upright ears, like spikes, and eyes like the disk of the sun. Others, leaping into the sky, flung rocks, trees, and axes, blazing straw as voluminous as mountain peaks, showers of embers, serpents of fire, showers of stones. And all the time, a naked woman bearing in her hand a skull flittered about, unsettled, staying not in any spot, like the mind of a distracted student over sacred texts.

But lo! amidst all these terrors, sights, sounds, and odors, the mind of the Blessed One was no more shaken than the wits of Garuda, the golden-feathered sun-bird, among crows. And a voice cried from the sky: "O Mara, take not upon thyself this vain fatigue! Put aside thy malice and go in peace! For though fire may one day give up its heat, water its fluidity, earth solidity; never will this Great Being, who acquired the merit that brought him to this tree through many lifetimes in unnumbered eons, abandon his resolution."

And the god, Mara, discomfited, together with his army, disappeared. Heaven, luminous with the light of the full moon, then shone like the smile of a maid, showering flowers, the petals of flowers, bouquets of flowers, freshly wet with dew, on the Blessed One; who, that night, during the remainder of the night, in the first watch of that wonderful night, acquired the knowledge of his previous existence, in the second watch acquired the divine eye, in the last watch fathomed the law of Dependent Origination, and at sunrise attained omniscience.

The earth quaked in its delight, like a woman thrilled. The gods descended from every side to worship the Blessed One that was now the Buddha, the Wake. "O glory to thee, illuminate hero among men," they sang, as they walked around him in reverential sunwise ambulation. And the daemons of the earth, even the sons and daughters of Mara, the deities who roam the sky and those that walk the ground—all arrived. And after worshiping the victor with the various forms of homage suitable to their stations, they returned, radiant with a new rapture, to their sundry abodes.

In sum: the Buddha in his dissolution of the sense of "I" had moved in consciousness back past the motivation of creation—which, however, did not mean that he had ceased to live. Indeed, he was to remain half a century longer within the world of time and space, participating with irony in the void of this manifold, seeing duality yet knowing it to be deceptive, compassionately teaching what cannot be taught to others who were not really other. For there is no way to communicate an experience in words to those who have not already had the experience—or at least something somewhat like it, to be referred to by analogy. Furthermore, where there is no ego, there is no "other"—either to be feared, to be desired, or to be taught.

In the classic Indian doctrine of the four ends for which men are supposed to live and strive—love and pleasure (*kāma*), power and success (*artha*), lawful order and moral virtue (*dharma*), and, finally, release from delusion (*mokṣa*)—we note that the first two are manifestations of what Freud has termed "the pleasure principle," primary urges of the natural man, epitomized in the formula "I want." In the adult, according to the Oriental view, these are to be quelled and checked by the principles of *dharma,* which, in the classic Indian system, are impressed upon the individual by the training of his caste. The infantile "I want" is to be subdued by a "thou shalt," socially applied (not individually determined), which is supposed to be as much a part of the immutable cosmic order as the course of the sun itself.

Now it is to be observed that in the version just presented of the temptation of the Buddha, the Antagonist represents all three of the first triad of ends (the so-called *trivarga:* "aggregate of three"); for in his character as the Lord Desire he personifies the first; as the Lord Death, the aggressive force of the second; while in his summons to the meditating sage to arise and return to the duties of his station in society, he promotes the third. And, indeed, as a manifestation of that Self which not only poured forth but permanently supports the universe, he is the proper incarnation of these ends. For they do, in fact, support the world. And in most of the rites of all religions, this triune god, we may say, in one aspect or another, is the one and only god adored.

However, in the name and achievement of the Buddha, the "Illuminated One," the fourth end is announced: release from delusion. And to the attainment of this, the others are impediments, difficult to remove, yet, for one of purpose, not invincible. Sitting at the world navel, pressing back through the welling creative force that was surging into and through his own being, the Buddha actually broke back into the void beyond, and— ironically—the universe immediately burst into bloom. Such an act of self-noughting is one of individual effort. There can be no question about that. However, an Occidental eye cannot but observe that there is no requirement or expectation anywhere in this Indian system of four ends—neither in the primary two of the natural organism and the impressed third of society, nor in the exalted fourth of release—for a maturation of the personality through intelligent, fresh, individual adjustment to the time-space world round about, creative experimentation with unexplored possibilities, and the assumption of personal responsibility for unprecedented acts performed within the context of the social order. In the Indian tradition all has been perfectly arranged from all eternity. There can be nothing new, nothing to be learned but what the sages have taught from of yore. And finally, when the boredom of this nursery horizon of "I want" against "thou shalt" has become insufferable, the fourth and final aim is all that is offered—of an extinction of the infantile ego altogether: disengagement or release (*mokṣa*) from both "I" and "thou."

In the European West, on the other hand, where the fundamental doctrine of the freedom of the will essentially dissociates each individual from every other, as well as from both the will in nature and the will of God, there is placed upon each the responsibility of coming intelligently, out of his own experience and volition, to some sort of relationship with—not identity with or extinction in—the all, the void, the suchness, the absolute, or whatever the proper term may be for that which is beyond terms. And, in the secular sphere likewise, it is normally expected that an educated ego should have developed away from the simple infantile polarity of the pleasure and obedience principles toward a personal, uncompulsive, sensitive relationship to empirical reality, a certain adventurous attitude toward the unpredictable, and a sense of personal responsibility for decisions. Not life as a good soldier, but life as a developed, unique individual, is the ideal. And we shall search the Orient in vain for anything quite comparable. There the ideal, on the contrary, is the quenching, not development, of ego. That is the formula turned this way and that, up and down the line, throughout the literature: a systematic, steady, continually drumming devaluation of the "I" principle, the reality function—which has remained, consequently, undeveloped, and so, wide open to the seizures of completely uncritical mythic identifications.

CHAPTER II

# The
# Buddhist Tradition

Buddhism appeared in India in the fifth century B.C., the beginning of that period known in Indian history as the Epic age. Its teachings and the manner of its growth reflect the pervasive conditions of human life and experience that characterized Indian society during that period. The Vedic age, ca. 1500–500 B.C., originated with the Aryan invasions of the Indus Valley. Vedic religious history is marked by two significant phases of growth. In the Vedic hymns we discover the primitive religion of the Aryans, a polytheistic nature worship. The Vedic hymns give us a portrait of a people who worshiped the living presence of divine powers in natural events and who responded to such nature deities in prayers of supplication, thanksgiving, and praise. By personifying natural forces, the Aryans expressed their affinity with those natural forces of the world which evoked awe, terror, and dread. Gradually this primitive nature worship gave way to a second phase in the development of Vedic religion, the elaboration of a formal, ceremonial religion over which the Brahmin priests presided. During the formative stages of this ritualized religion, the conviction grew that religious knowledge and power were the sole possessions of a single class of people, the Brahmins. The gods of the Vedic pantheon ceased to operate as independent powers, and it was thought that their activity depended upon the proper performance of sacrificial rites.

The Brahmins, who held the key to sacred ceremony and

formula, almost literally manipulated the gods. The scene for the manifestation of holy powers shifted from natural events, such as rain, wind, storm, fire, and thunder, to the closely guarded secrets of the Vedic formulas, spells, and prayers. By a rudimentary kind of inference, the Aryans reasoned that if the gods depended upon ritual in order to exercise their power, then the rituals themselves must contain the highest form of holy power since both the gods and men depended upon them. Increasingly, the Brahmins, as guardians of the holy powers of ceremony, became a closed, hereditary order exercising immense influence on all phases of life in the emerging Aryan settlements.

The two centuries spanning 800–600 B.C. saw the Aryans engaged in consolidating their position as victors over the Dravidian civilization and in creating small principalities throughout northwestern and southeastern India. Although many dialects were in use, Sanskrit was the principal language. Most Aryan enclaves were organized and regulated according to customs and rules that were later to be codified in the Brahmanas (particularly the laws of Manu). Vestiges of the caste system had already appeared and had the effect of dividing the inhabitants of the Aryan principalities into several broad classes defined by sanctions relating to social function, marriage, and moral duties. What had originated as a division of labor and a natural dominance of victor over vanquished now hardened into more rigid social divisions, supported by religious teaching and stringent moral rules.

There is much evidence indicating the presence of a spirit of speculation and spiritual search during this period. The most ancient Upanishads originated around 600 B.C. Upanishadic literature manifests a deepening spiritual existence among the Indians and a shift in religious focus from the deified natural forces and formal ritual to the inner depths of the self. Supportive of this enhanced spirituality was the growing tradition, among both Brahmins and noblemen, of the vocation of solitary asceticism and contemplation. Earnest seekers after self-purification and spiritual insight renounced worldly occupations and retreated to the forest to discipline themselves by ascetic practices in preparation for intense meditation. This kind of religious commitment provided the religious with an alternative to the typical priestly function of the Brahmin. More importantly, it afforded a novel flow of creative ideas and insights into the changing religious tradition, guaranteeing a constant challenge to the established tradition, thereby enlarging it. Since the insights and speculations of the "forest searchers" were produced in the solitude of their lonely quests, they were not designed to serve the interests of an artificial and arid ceremonialism. Rather, as new and independent ideas, they conflicted with the existing forms of religion and lifted the Indian's vision to higher forms of spiritual and moral life.

While nature worship and elaborate ritualism are most significant to an understanding of the development of Hinduism, they were not the sole currents of religious life and thought during the Vedic age. Actually, these phases were but one line of development in an age that exhibited many conflicting and contradictory movements. The period beginning ca. 600 B.C. was an age of immense ferment, innovation, and change. Ritualism of the most sophisticated variety lived side by side with a popular religion of superstition and magic. Simple nature worship persisted in the same context as lofty, mystical speculation. A demanding moralism and rigorous self-denial were countered by a lack of moral seriousness and the free play of human passions both in war and in social life. While the authority of the Vedic tradition was consolidating its position and strengthening the hand of the Brahmins, it was also, dialectically, generating in noblemen and other independent searchers the refutation of its claims to special religious knowledge and authority.

All the diverse peoples of Indian society during the Epic period suffered from the ambiguity of human life and the arbitrary fates of an unsettled existence. This was an age remarkably lacking in political, religious, moral, and social stability. The harried actors of this scene in Indian history were swirled willy-nilly by the tides of intellectual ferment, intertribal dissension, and perpetual threat of foreign invasion. No one system of ideas or ideals could capture the allegiance of the people. The terrible effects of violence and subjugation, complemented by endemic chaos in social conditions, gave rise to a search for repose and peace. A yearning for deliverance from a world crowded with evil and misery arose in the Indian soul. One way to escape from the world of misery was to renounce all involvement in the world, to retreat from the delusions of this "vale of tears" into the sanctuary of the inner spirit. The mind driven to the border of madness by the ambiguity and uncertainty of human life sought release through a world-renouncing mysticism, or by regressing to a more primitive response in unbridled superstition, or by lapsing into a prehuman bestiality of intoxication and ecstasy. In periods of excessive stress and crisis, humanity dreams its great dreams and is haunted by its most horrendous nightmares. But whether it be the former or the latter, the human imagination unleashes its creative energies and becomes the architect of new worlds and new ideals.

The intellectual ferment and religious aspiration of the sixth century B.C. in India produced two great religious innovators: Mahavira, the inspiration of Jainism, and Gotama, the founder of Buddhism. Curiously, this century was marked by a remarkable upsurge of intellectual and religious creativity throughout much of the civilized world. In Greece, we find the bold speculations of Parmenides and Empedocles, as well as the revolutionary impact of the Dionysian cult, Orphicism, and the Eleusinian mysteries. In China, Lao Tzu initiated the Taoist religion and Confucius offered his sage advice for moral, political, and spiritual reform. Seemingly, a significant proportion of mankind in the sixth century B.C. was seeking a new vision of man's place in the world and was receptive to the harbingers of new wisdom.

## HINAYANA BUDDHISM

Early Buddhism, originating in the fifth century B.C. with the life of Gotama Buddha, must be distinguished from the later forms of Buddhism that began to develop at about the same time as the great systems of Hindu thought in the second century B.C. The founder of Buddhism was a nobleman of the ancient family of Gotama (Gautama). The approximate dates of his life, 560–

480 B.C., make him a contemporary of the historic founder of
Jainism, Mahavira. Like Mahavira, Gotama was of aristocratic
origin and left his home as a young man to seek truth and
emancipation. Unlike Mahavira, he rejected the path of religious
asceticism as the most significant rule for the spiritual life. Rather,
he uncovered a new course of self-discipline which could lead
one beyond the confines of suffering existence to pure bliss.

The title "Buddha" was applied to Gotama only after his enlightenment, for it means "awakened one." Gotama achieved
enlightenment by means of an insight into the source of human
ill and by discovering a path toward emancipation. He came to
realize that the architect of recurring life is desire: desire is the
source of all misery, birth, and death. By realizing that suffering
was more than physical—that it involved the feeling of transience, limitation, frustration, and meaninglessness—he won his
way to the insight that desire is the origin of all misery. The
thralldom of desire binds us to the life process, inevitably tying
us to imperfection, limitation, and emptiness.

The basic premise of Buddha's teaching was that everything's
existence depends upon a cause. Since the life process inevitably
brings suffering, death, old age, and new birth, it must also have
a cause that can be discovered and removed. The Buddha's way
(the Eightfold Path) leads to the obliteration of the causes of
misery and pain, and thence to happiness and bliss. As a result of
these elementary principles, Buddha attacked the sacerdotal ritualism of Vedic religion with great vigor. From his point of view,
elaborate sacrificial rituals, which were performed to invoke divine powers or to appease wrathful deities, were entirely irrelevant to the spiritual malaise of man. Actually, after Buddha and
Mahavira, the old Vedic sacrificial system fell into decay and new
energies of great spirituality were brought into play in Hinduism,
creating its more mature forms of religious faith. Both Buddha
and Mahavira urged that the way to emancipation was open to
all who would walk it and that no special class held the key to
spiritual emancipation.

For almost two centuries following the death of Buddha an

impenetrable curtain of obscurity fell over the historical development of Buddhism. However, in the third century B.C., Buddhism emerged once again to the forefront of religious life in India. This dramatic revival was produced by the great Emperor Asoka (273–232 B.C.), who exercised dominion over vast areas of India. Asoka was a Buddhist, and during his reign Buddhism became a state religion. By his official edicts and practical example, he spread abroad the teaching of the Buddha both within India and beyond its confines to neighboring lands, such as Ceylon, Burma, and other parts of central Asia.

During the reign of Asoka, the needs of the laity for direct participation in religious life emerged as a central concern of Buddhism. While the teaching of Buddha had a decidedly practical orientation, his own life as a "forest searcher" tended to influence his earliest followers to take up a monastic life of solitude seeking Nirvana on their own. Generally speaking, early Buddhism was a product of a very privileged stratum in society. Buddha himself was a nobleman, and because of his devaluation of Brahministic ritual, the noblemen were the first to respond sympathetically to his vision. The Brahmins were the established religious authorities in all matters relating to communal religious life, and this fact inhibited the development of early Buddhism as a religion of the underprivileged and the layman (even though the Buddha is alleged to have spent the last part of his life teaching his discipline to the common man).

With little possibility for developing Buddhist religion among the laity, where Brahminism held sway, the early followers of the Buddha tended to overemphasize certain features of the Buddha's teaching and life, such as the search for Nirvana by the monk who deliberately isolates himself from the mainstream of communal life, to the neglect of others. As a consequence, the doctrine of Arhatship, the achievement of awakened spirituality, was presumed to refer *only* to the life of the mendicant monk seeking salvation on his own. In view of this early emphasis in the Buddhist tradition, it is remarkable that Buddhism ever became a world religion, since any motive for missionary extension

of the faith seems to have been entirely lacking. Moreover, it is
equally baffling that Buddhism emerged as a religion of the laity,
given its early emphasis upon the isolated monk, self-dependent,
seeking his own salvation, without troubling himself with the
release of the souls of other men.

In this context, the importance of the work of Asoka cannot be
overemphasized. The great Buddhist king paid very little attention to those features of Buddha's teachings which strongly emphasized the quest for Nirvana and other esoteric teachings
beyond the range of the common man's understanding. His
propagation of Buddhism focused upon elementary teachings of
the Buddha which the layman could comprehend and apply to
his own life. Through his leadership and example, a long-
neglected aspect of Buddha's teaching was given a central place
in the movement and assumed its proper role in the religious life.
Asoka emphasized those Buddhist principles of morality which
were necessary for happiness in this life both for oneself and for
others. As a result of Asoka's work, a balance was struck in
Buddhism between the austerity of the monks seeking enlightenment on their own and a less stringent discipline for the laymen
which allowed their participation in the circle of the Buddhist
faith. However, a tension did exist between the smaller community of mendicant monks and the greater community of mankind
at large, and this eventually led to a great schism in the Buddhist
tradition between the Hinayana ("the smaller vehicle" or
"career") and the Mahayana ("the greater vehicle" or "career").

Another innovation that dates from the reign of Asoka is the
commitment to writing of the Buddhist oral tradition, already
two and a half centuries old. The earliest writings in the Buddhist tradition are in the Pali dialect, a literary form of Sanskrit.
The ancient Pali literature is divided into three Pitakas, or
baskets, which are conceived as receptacles which convey the Buddhist teaching and tradition. The first Pitaka (in Pali, *Vinaya-
Pitaka*) contains the various rules and ordinances to be observed
by Buddhist monks. It is therefore called the "basket of discipline." For the most part, it is dry, technical reading, in many

ways similar to the Torah of Judaism. The second Pitaka, the *Sutta-Pitaka,* purports to convey the utterances of the Buddha either in prose or verse. A typical form of Buddha's teaching found in this Pitaka is the dialogue. In the dialogues, the opponent or student is led by an extensive chain of argument to the conclusion that the Buddha intends him to reach. The final Pitaka, called the *Abhidhamma,* is probably the most difficult of all. It contains wide-ranging philosophical discussions of the fundamental metaphysics of ancient Buddhism. Regarding all the Pitakas, one thing is clear: they are composites of an oral tradition and probably contain considerable editing and amplification from different periods. Scholars tend to agree, however, that during the reign of Asoka the oral tradition of Buddhism was committed to writing in a fairly complete manner, giving us the Pali literature.

A very ancient form of Pali Buddhism flourishes in modern times in Ceylon, Thailand, and Burma. For the religious peoples of these lands, the Pali literature, interpreted in a literal fashion, remains the authoritative source for the Buddhist faith.

Buddhism changed radically in the centuries following the reign of Asoka and gradually moved away from its native soil in India to China, Japan, Southeast Asia, and other parts of the world. There is a striking parallel between Buddhism and Christianity in their developments as world religions. Growing out of Brahminism, much as Christianity grew out of Judaism, Buddhism achieved its apogee of power and influence in conquering worlds beyond the place of its origin. In the twentieth century, only a minor part of the Indian population are adherents to Buddhism, yet Buddhism is one of the major religions of the modern world!

## MAHAYANA BUDDHISM

Buddhism, which made great advances during the reign of Asoka, was not without its internal problems. Controversy over many matters relating to doctrine and discipline tended to splinter the movement into sects. Tradition informs us that in the third century B.C. there were some eighteen sects within the Buddhist movement. In 247 B.C., Asoka called a great Buddhist council to settle sectarian disputes which had broken out in the ranks of the faithful. The controversy that raged between the conservative, tradition-bound Buddhists (Sthavira-vada) and the more liberal, reforming Buddhists (Mahasanghikas) was characteristic. Followers of the Stahavira-vada insisted upon strict conformity to the discipline of the law, believing that the only valid, authoritative scriptures were the Pali texts, and that the interpretations of Buddha's teaching found in the Pali literature should be accepted without modification. The Mahasanghikas, as their name indicates (maha, "larger"; sanghi, "assembly"), advocated and practiced a wider, more flexible form of Buddhism. They supported enlarging the assembly of faithful Buddhists to include laity, even women, and frowned upon the exclusiveness of the Arhat ideal. They favored a relaxation of the discipline of the Vinaya, but, most importantly, they encouraged flexibility and openness with regard to the question of authoritative scripture. There was a distinct inclination to sever the Buddhist tradition from its absolute dependence upon the historical Buddha. This tendency manifested itself in the Mahasanghikas' desire to move attention away from the mundane affairs of the Buddha's historical life and teaching in order to emphasize the supernatural qualities and powers of the Buddha. Some of their company went so far as to suggest that Buddha represented an ideal of wisdom and a path to salvation that was not restricted to a particular historical age. They argued that the truth of Buddhism can be manifested through other beings (Buddha-beings) and at other times. In these ways, the Mahasanghikas defended novel interpretations as being valid spiritually and worthy of being incorporated into the Buddhist canon. This movement is representative of the forces working for change within Buddhism in the third century B.C.

In the four centuries following Asoka, Mahayana Buddhism sprang up and radically altered the future of the Buddhist movement. Mahayana, the "larger vehicle" or "career," became a highly popular form of Buddhism. It set before the man of religious aspiration the ideal of the Bodhisattva. The term "bodhisattva" occurs in Hinayana texts, usually denoting a person on the verge of becoming enlightened. This term in Mahayana, however, means the highest form of spirituality, the wholly compassionate being who remains on the threshold of Buddhahood in order to deliver all sentient creatures beyond samsara to Nirvana. The Bodhisattva, through selfless love, gives over all merit accumulated in his perfect life to those creatures caught in the wheel of ignorance and rebirth. In sharp contrast to the Arhat (the ideal man of Hinayana), the Bodhisattva vows to create and sustain a love and wisdom that is capable of saving all suffering beings. Mahayana teaches that every man is a potential Bodhisattva, whether he be monk or layman. Because the Bodhisattva exhibits such an immense power to save, he is worshiped as a deity and is invoked continually by the faithful. The Mahayana increasingly came to view the existence of Gotama as but one manifestation of a cosmic principle of salvation that has operated and will continue to operate in many Bodhisattvas and Buddhas eternally.

Mahayana was the wave of the future for Buddhism. Its emotional fervor and compassionate concern made it attractive to a mass of humanity searching for deliverance from a world of misery and violence. The concept of a "larger vehicle" in which all could ride to the farther shores of liberation and enlightenment evidently unleashed the fertile imagination of the Indian mind. The heavens were discovered to be cluttered with past Buddhas and Buddhas-to-be. Mahayana theology, taking seriously the idea that Gotama was only one of several Buddhas, speculated freely about the character, actions, and significance of this plentiful harvest of imaginary Buddhas. One such legendary Buddha who rose to prominence and played a vital role in the Buddhist faith is Amitabha. According to one legend, Amitabha (the Buddha of measureless light) by his mighty acts of virtue created a Pure Land (paradise). Those contemplating the virtues of Amitabha and having faith in him are assured of a home in this happy Buddha-land. About the fifth or sixth century A.D., Amitabha was included, along with four other legendary Buddhas, in a pentad (the Buddhas of contemplation). According to a mature form of Mahayana theology, the five Buddhas of contemplation are evoked in the worshiper's mind by meditation upon the Adi-Buddha, the primal Buddha spirit. In other words, they are but reflexes or emanations of the universal spirit of the Buddha. The tracing of this single thread in the tapestry of Mahayana gives some indication of the extent to which speculative and mythological material was introduced into Buddhism by Mahayana.

Mahayana was tolerant, evolutionary, and accommodating. It achieved great popularity because it transformed the early, austere practice of Buddhism into a matter of warm, human charity. Moreover, in its popular forms, it provided a profusion of sacred beings who were quite accessible to the worshiper, and worshipers could adhere to the Mahayana faith without giving up other religious beliefs and practices.

While this potential for accommodating alien religious forms contributed to the rapid expansion of the Mahayana religion, it is also responsible for its kaleidoscopic transformations. Mahayana Buddhism, then, is not one large vehicle but rather many smaller, connected vehicles constituted of many different forms. When Mahayana spread out from India into the north (China, Korea, Japan, and so on), it assumed different forms in each country. While its spirit of accommodation ensured its popular appeal, it also guaranteed its dilution and diffusion by such things as superstition, magic, animism, and other indigenous religious beliefs and institutions.

## MONASTIC AND LAY BUDDHISM

The institution of monastic life within Buddhism developed early and has survived until the present day, frequently in almost the same form in which it originated. The historical development

of the Buddhist movement indicates that the ideal of the monastic life lies at the core of the Buddhist religion. It witnesses to
the Buddhist realization that the higher life cannot be achieved
in any ordinary societal arrangement. The world of family life
and "business as usual" are not conducive, in the Buddhist view,
to the quest for spiritual freedom and insight. Hence, even
during the Buddha's life a community of mendicant monks was
formed and, following his death, it grew in importance and
power as the focus of religious interest. This community of
monks and hermits was called the Sangha. While it formed only
a small proportion of the Buddhist faithful, as representative of
the highest aspirations of Buddhism it has always constituted a
central part of the Buddhist religion.

Before and during the Buddha's lifetime, the ideal of the
"forest searcher" was a viable option for those men vitally interested in pursuing spiritual truth. Thus, the Sangha arose quite
naturally out of the social conditions prevailing in India at the
time of Buddha. Frequently, the forest hermits undertook, as
did the Buddha at one stage of his quest, a rigorous asceticism
designed to purge themselves of ignorance and wrongdoing and
to prepare themselves for spiritual vision through the discipline
of meditation. In his quest for spiritual enlightenment, the Buddha found that excessive self-mortification and self-denial were
not adequate to produce a state of spiritual perfection. Thus, as a
result of Buddha's teaching, the discipline of the homeless monks
shifted away from the severity of self-mortification toward the
cultivation of a loving heart and a peaceful countenance. The
regulations governing the congregation of monks were designed
to foster those conditions conducive to the emancipation of heart
and mind, and also to the cultivation of benevolence, knowledge,
and tranquillity.

This is not to suggest that the rules of monastic order, set
down in the Vinaya, were not rigorous and demanding, but
rather to indicate that an entirely new spirit seemed to suffuse
monastic Buddhism in contrast to the priestly spirit of Brahminism. For the Buddhists, the exclusiveness, based on birth, and the

arid ceremonialism of Brahminism were offensive, for in the
Buddha's eyes neither birth nor ritual could guarantee spiritual
health. In Hinduism as it existed in Buddha's day, the Brahmin
was the guardian and interpreter of the Vedic truths; he was the
mediator between divine power and the secular community. The
Buddhist Sangha, however, was open to all genuine seekers after
spiritual illumination, and while they manifested the pure spirit
of the law of Buddhism, they neither supervised the laity nor
served as mediators for it.

The rules regulating the Sangha were grounded in three essential principles: poverty, chastity, and inoffensiveness. Monks were
to live a simple unencumbered life, free from the demands and
distractions of family, property, and normal social obligations.
According to the Hinayana interpretation of monastic existence,
the monks were the only real Buddhists, the only first-class citi-
zens of the Buddhist community. The sole path to emancipation
or Arhatship was participation in monastic life. But in the later
stages of Buddhist history, during the period of the Mahayanists,
concessions were made to include all of the laity as were capable
of achieving spiritual perfection, or Bodhisattvahood.

For the primitive Buddhists, members of the Sangha should
be homeless, just as the Buddha had renounced home and temporal power in order to be filled with wisdom. Adherence to this
rule varied greatly even at that early stage in the evolution of the
Monastic institution. Some monks in strict conformity to the
principle of homelessness retired to the depths of the forest and
sought, in solitude, to cultivate the conditions requisite for spiritual liberation. More frequently, in the early days, monks lived
in communities with the laity or in special dwellings such as
temples, sanctuaries, and eventually, monasteries. While even
today the ideal of the forest hermit still survives in Buddhist
lands, the predominant style of monastic life is to live in special
monasteries and temples.

The begging bowl could be considered to be the highest symbol
of Buddhist monastic existence. From the earliest times, Buddhist
monks have relied (in varying degrees) upon begging for those

essentials required for their sustenance. It is commonly said by the Buddhists that the begging bowl is the breeding ground of many virtues, including: independence, control of desire and pride, noninvolvement, withdrawal from the incessant demands of personal desire and social duty, and cultivation of benevolence. Strictly speaking, from the point of view of the beggar, there is no "real" begging, for in depending upon the laity for life's sustenance, the Buddhist monk provides the laity with an opportunity for doing good works and storing up merit. The vow of poverty practiced by the Buddhist monks produces an opportunity for the laity to practice a cardinal virtue of Buddhism, benevolence, and, in turn, creates those conditions of independence and noninvolvement in ordinary society so necessary to the discipline of achieving final liberation. Mahayana places great stress upon the altruistic aspects of begging as a part of its effort to cultivate love for all suffering beings.

The strict vows relating to chastity probably originated in the commonly held opinion in many religions that sexual involvements are serious distractions from the highest form of spiritual life. This attitude is reflected in one Christian authority's statement that "woman is a desirable calamity." The Buddhist stricture against sexual attachment derives from the Buddhist principle that pleasures bind one more closely to the life of desire and the resulting confusions of samsara. Sexuality unleashes one of the most powerful energies of the human being and therefore is fatal to the freedom and detachment of the monk. Moreover, sexual involvements can lead to what Kazantzakis' delightful character Zorba called "the full catastrophe," that is, children, family, the bonds of social responsibility, and all the distractions attendant thereto. Such involvements inhibit the dedication, discipline, and contemplation necessary for achieving perfection. Later, about A.D. 500, with the development of the Tantra form of Buddhism, we see the development of a highly systematized procedure for the participation by monks in sexual life. In Tantra Buddhism, the sexuality of a monk was not thought to lead to self-contamination, nor was it held to be incompatible with the fullest spiritual freedom. Rather, it was considered to be a means for achieving enlightenment. This reflects a central tenet of the Tantric movement in both Hinduism and Buddhism, namely, that men can achieve perfection by means of, and through, nature, rather than by a rejection of nature. The attitude toward sexuality in the Tantric movement preserves the truth that sexuality is not essentially degrading, but under proper circumstances can be instrumental for self-realization and self-transcendence.

The vows of inoffensiveness, or nonviolence, probably have their origin in the Buddhist reaction to the increase in violence and suffering during the ages immediately preceding and even during the rise of Buddhism. At this time, the invention and mastery of the use of iron and bronze created a dramatic escalation of human violence and suffering. The epic literature of the Hindu tradition records a vivid picture of intertribal conflict and the resultant suffering which characterize the years between 1500 and 200 B.C. Not only did the Indo-Aryans fight among themselves, but they engaged in a continuous effort to repell invaders from without. According to the Buddha, the calamity of existence should not be increased by undisciplined thought and deeds, which serve only to increase the woe of mankind. This principle was stringently applied both in the monastic and the lay communities. Monks and laymen should foster within themselves and others a feeling for the kinship of all sentient creatures. Humans are all in the same situation, subject to the conditioning factors of ignorance and pain and to the inevitability of rebirth. Under these circumstances, all Buddhists should practice the principle of noninjury. This ethical principle is closely associated in Buddhism with the concepts of nonego and of emptiness (sunyata).

Hinayana Buddhism insisted upon the transience of all things, including the person. The human being was composed of a conglomeration of dharmas (elements functioning in a lawlike manner) and really had no intrinsic unity. The discipline of the law enjoined a detachment from the feeling of individuality which was generated by those desires and passions which occupied one's mind. One procedure for attaining the wisdom of nonego was by an introverted discipline which sought the contraction of selfhood by eliminating or controlling those functions of the psychic apparatus which created selfishness. Another path, aiming at the same goal, was the unlimited expansion of the self by identifying it with the Unlimited, Emptiness (Sunyata). This latter was achieved by exploding the boundaries of the self through the widening effects of universal love and sympathy. Such practice of love and sympathy had the effect of breaking down all false barriers between beings and destroying those distinctions generating the evil of samsara. As one transcends finite limitations through love, one comes to meditate upon, and eventually to realize, the Unlimited Reality, void of all differentiations and distinctions. The truth of all reality, Emptiness, is realized. The practice of altruism and universal benevolence by monastic and lay communities was a humanizing force in those societies in which Buddhism functioned as a vital religious force.

Those followers of the law of Buddha who were not members of the monastic orders were to live a life modeled on the monks' existence, but the discipline of lay life was less rigorous. After all, the layman must remain in fruitful contact with society and his obligations must be supportive of social order. Achieving independence and detachment is nearly impossible in ordinary social life, so that the Buddhist laity could not achieve perfect spiritual emancipation. The heart of the Buddhist recommendations regarding lay existence resides in the ethical commands of Buddha's teaching. Buddhist principles enjoined for all laymen a life of good conduct, love, respect for the monastic institution, and moderation in the search for, and enjoyment of, pleasures. Indicative of the tremendous respect held by adherents of Buddhism for their monastic communities are the numerous festivals and holy days when the laity live a modified monastic life. On these special religious days, faithful Buddhists fast, abstain from sexual involvements, and meditate upon Buddhist virtues. Such attempts to approximate the monk's existence are thought to lead to increased spiritual vitality and health. The goal of the faithful

Buddhist outside the monastic institution is to foster the cardinal virtues of Buddhist ethics in their community life. Temperance, moderation, love, and storing up of merit can lead to a rebirth in an enhanced sphere of existence, a Buddhist heaven.

The rich interplay between the two communities in Buddhism continues to the present day. The monastic style of existence has undergone very little significant change over the centuries. Like any institution in changing conditions, it has alternately relaxed or tightened its rules and ideals. However, the spirit that brought it into existence has remained a vital force in its preservation through the two thousand years of its existence.

## EXTENSION OF BUDDHISM BEYOND INDIA

Hinayana Buddhism, under the auspices of Asoka, extended the range of its influence beyond the confines of India to the countries of Ceylon, Burma, and Thailand. Only in these countries to the east and south of India has the Hinayana form of Buddhism survived to the modern age. The Buddhism of Ceylon, called Sinhalese, is an uncorrupted form of Hinayana which has exhibited little development over the centuries and still reflects the state of doctrine and canon in the Hinayana church of Asoka's day (third century B.C.). Although the Sinhalese tradition traces its origin to a personal visit by Buddha, all evidence indicates that Asoka's missionaries introduced Buddhism to Ceylon and Burma. When Hinayana ceased to be a vital religious force in India, Ceylon became the center of this ancient form of Buddhism. While the history of Burmese and Siamese Buddhism is quite obscure, all signs indicate that Buddhist development in Burma and Thailand derived from and depended upon the Buddhism of Ceylon.

Mahayana Buddhism spread to the north and flourished in such countries as China, Korea, Japan, and Tibet. The task of tracing the complex growth of Mahayana in these countries cannot be undertaken here. As previously indicated, Mahayana was an amazingly flexible faith and was capable of multiple metamorphoses as it interacted with different cultures and assimilated itself to alien religious forms. A brief discussion of the development of Buddhism in China, Tibet, and Japan will indicate the broad outline of the development of Mahayana beyond the confines of India.

Buddhism entered China as early as A.D. 62 and it made its entrance by several avenues. Missionaries brought both the Hinayana and the Mahayana doctrines into China, but only the Mahayana thrived and exerted a significant influence upon Chinese culture. A second path that Buddhism took in invading China was through returning pilgrims and sages sent to India by Chinese imperial courts to study Indian spirituality. Between the second and fourth century A.D., China and India enjoyed the fruits of a productive cultural exchange. Teachers and monks of the Buddhist and Hindu faiths were welcome at the Chinese royal courts. There they gave religious instruction and discoursed on man's spiritual destiny. Because of royal patronage, Mahayana Buddhism soon gained a foothold in aristocratic circles, and in a very short time it spread to outlying provinces and throughout the country.

An event of singular importance for the development of Chinese Buddhism occurred in A.D. 520 with the coming of Bodhidharma to China. Bodhidharma, considered a patriarch of Buddhism, had a dramatic effect upon the future course of development in Chinese Buddhism. His principal teachings were that salvation did not lie in good works and that wisdom did not lie in sacred literature. Only intuition or insight could bring salvation and wisdom. He founded the Dhyana or Meditation School of Mahayana which was to have great success in China and Japan. Many interesting legends have grown up about this great religious saint. One legend tells us that he earned the popular name given him, Wall-gazer, by sitting for nine years staring at a wall. Another records the encounter of Bodhidharma with a learned Chinese emperor. Bodhidharma informed this famous patron of Buddhism that building temples and encouraging the translation of Buddhist scriptures would bring him no merit.

The offended ruler then desired to know from the great saint which Buddhist doctrine was most important. To this, Bodhidharma replied: "When all is emptiness, there is no important doctrine."

Although the Bodhidharma's teachings were not immediately successful, eventually they became the foundation of the Ch'an school of Buddhism which has been an exceptionally powerful force in Chinese religious history. The Ch'an school of Chinese Buddhism, when it was carried into Japan, was known there as Zen Buddhism. Much of the success of the Bodhidharma's teaching in China can be attributed to the fact that it harmonized with Taoism. The doctrines of Taoism and meditative Buddhism were so closely meshed that one could study Buddhism by reading Taoist scriptures and vice versa. It was this capacity of Mahayana Buddhism to align itself with the mainstream of a culture which enabled it to succeed so rapidly and dramatically in diverse countries.

The Buddhism of Tibet, known as Lamaism, is a radical transformation of Buddhist doctrine and practice, even for a form of Mahayana Buddhism. Buddhism was introduced into Tibet at a relatively late period, approximately 747 B.C., when the Lamaist church was founded. The founder of Lamaism, Padma Sambhava, an Indian sage, was thought to be a great excorcist, capable of dispelling evil spirits and effecting miraculous cures. Lamaism is a curious combination of nationalized Buddhism, demonology, deification of humans, and profuse multiplication of deities, Bodhisattvas, and Buddhas. It is a magical form of Buddhism, specifically conforming to the peculiar interests of the Tibetans. They desire to control the multitude of demons and furies which their superstitions and imaginations have produced to taunt and terrify them. The icons of the Lama tradition frequently bear the countenances of fiends and monsters—masks which allow the holy powers to strike fear in the hosts of evil. All forms of religious magic, art, and ritual are enlisted by the Tibetans in their struggle to protect themselves against the terrible forces of evil that rage around them.

Another typical characteristic of Lamaism was its practice of deifying human beings, particularly distinguished visiting teachers and high officials of the Tibetan monasteries. Evidently, the Tibetans had a very low tolerance for asceticism, discipline, and speculation and, thus, de-emphasized these aspects of Mahayana. They accepted the general Eastern tendency to view spiritual saints as manifestations of divinity and made it the basic principle of organization for their church and their country. Civic power became identified with the Buddhist institutions, whose leaders were seen to be incarnate deities. A Tibetan form of Lamaism flourished for a short time in northern China, but it never achieved a permanent footing in China.

The accepted date for the appearance of Buddhism in Japan is A.D. 552. Chinese Buddhism was carried into Japan from Korea, but the Japanese initiated many interesting and beautiful variations of the Mahayana faith. Several important sects of Mahayana Buddhism continue to thrive in Japan, including the Tendai, Shingon, Jodo, Shinshu, Nichiren, and Zen. Buddhism in Japan has shown a remarkable tendency to divide itself, almost indefinitely, into subsects within the framework of these larger classifications indicated above.

# CHAPTER III

# Introduction to Buddhism

## EDWARD CONZE

### BUDDHISM AS A RELIGION

Buddhism is an Eastern form of spirituality. Its doctrine, in its basic assumptions, is identical with many other teachings all over the world, teachings which may be called 'mystical.' The essence of this philosophy of life has been explained with great force and clarity by Thomas a Kempis, in his *Imitation of Christ*. What is known as 'Buddhism' is a part of the common human heritage of wisdom, by which men have succeeded in overcoming this world, and in gaining immortality, or a deathless life.

During the last two centuries, spiritual interests have in Europe been relegated into the background by preoccupations with economic and social problems. The word 'spiritual' seems vague nowadays. It is, indeed, not easy to define. It is easier to state by what means one gets to the spiritual realm than to say what it is in itself. Three avenues of approach to the spiritual are, I think, handed down by the almost universal tradition of the sages:

to regard sensory experience as relatively unimportant;
to try to renounce what one is attached to;
to try to treat all people alike—whatever their looks,
intelligence, colour, smell, education, etc.

The collective effort of the European races during the last centuries has gone into channels which by this definition are not 'spiritual.'

Reprinted from Edward Conze, *Buddhism: Its Essence and Development* (Oxford: Bruno Cassirer, Ltd., 1951; New York: Harper & Row, Publishers, Inc., 1959), pages 11-26. Used by permission of Bruno Cassirer, Ltd., and Harper & Row, Publishers, Inc.

It is often assumed that there is some fundamental and essential difference between East and West, between Europe and Asia, in their attitude to life, in their sense of values, and in the functioning of their souls. Christians who regard Buddhism as unsuitable for European conditions forget the Asiatic origin of their own religion, and of all religions for that matter. A religion is an organisation of spiritual aspirations, which reject the sensory world and negate the impulses which bind us to it. For 3,000 years Asia alone has been creative of spiritual ideas and methods. The Europeans have in these matters borrowed from Asia, have adapted Asiatic ideas, and, often, coarsened them. One could not, I think, point to any *spiritual* creation in Europe which is not secondary, which does not have its ultimate impulse in the East. European thought has excelled in the elaboration of *social* law and organisation, especially in Rome and England, and in the *scientific* understanding and control of sensory phenomena. The indigenous tradition of Europe is inclined to affirm the will to live, and to turn actively towards the world of the senses. The spiritual tradition of mankind is based on the negation of the will to live, and is turned away from the world of the senses. All European spirituality has had to be periodically renewed by an influx from the East, from the time of Pythagoras and Parmenides onwards. Take away the Oriental elements in Greek philosophy, take away Jesus Christ, Saint Paul, Dionysius Areopagita, and Arabic thought—and European spiritual thinking during the last 2,000 years becomes unthinkable. About a century ago the thought of India had begun to exert its influence on Europe, and it will help to revivify the languishing remnants of European spirituality.

Some features distinguish Buddhism from other forms of wisdom. They are of two kinds:

> Much of what has been handed down as 'Buddhism' is due not to the exercise of wisdom, but to the social conditions in which the Buddhist community existed, to the language employed, and to the science and mythology in vogue

among the people who adopted it. One must throughout distinguish the exotic curiosities from the essentials of a holy life.

There are a number of methods for winning salvation by meditation, of which Buddhist tradition gives a clearer and fuller account than I have found elsewhere. This is, however, largely a matter of temperament.

Properly studied, the literature of the Jains, of the Sufis, of the Christian monks of the Egyptian desert, and of what the Catholic Church calls 'ascetical' or 'mystical' theology, yields much of the same kind.

To a person who is thoroughly disillusioned with the contemporary world, and with himself, Buddhism may offer many points of attraction—in the transcending sublimity of the fairy land of its subtle thoughts, in the splendour of its works of art, in the magnificence of its hold over vast populations, and in the determined heroism and quiet refinement of those who are steeped into it. Although one may originally be attracted by its remoteness, one can appreciate the real value of Buddhism only when one judges it by the results it produces in one's own life from day to day.

The rules of wholesome conduct which are recommended in the Buddhist Scriptures are grouped under three headings: *Morality, Contemplation* and *Wisdom*. Much of what is included under *Morality* and *Contemplation* is the common property of all those Indian religious movements which sought salvation in a life apart from ordinary everyday society. There we have, in addition to rules of conduct for the laity, regulations for the life of the homeless brotherhood of monks; many Yoga practices—rhythmical and mindful breathing, the restraint of the senses, methods for inducing trance by staring at coloured circles, stages of ecstasis, the cultivation of unlimited friendliness, compassion, sympathetic joy and even-mindedness. Further, meditations of a generally edifying character, which could be found in any mystical religion, such as meditation on death, on the repulsiveness of the functions of this material body, on the Trinity of the Buddha, the Dharma (Truth), and the Samgha (Brotherhood). Few could be expected to practise all those methods in one life-time. There are many roads to emancipation. What is common to all of them is that they aim at the extinction of the belief in individuality.

When taken in its present-day vagueness, the word 'individuality' does, however, fail to convey the Buddha's meaning. According to Buddhist teaching, as we shall see in more detail later on, man, with all his possible belongings, consists of five 'heaps,' technically known as *Skandhas*. They are:

> The Body
> Feelings
> Perceptions
> Impulses and Emotions
> Acts of Consciousness.

Anything a person may grasp at, or lean on, or appropriate, must fall within one of those five groups, which make up the *stuff* of 'individuality.' The *belief* in individuality is said to arise from the invention of a 'self' over and above those five heaps. The belief expresses itself in the assumption that any of this is 'mine,' or that 'I am' any of this, or that any of this 'is myself.' Or, in other words, in the belief that 'I am this,' or that 'I have this,' or that 'this is in me,' or that 'I am in this.' The fact of individuality disappears with the belief in it, since it is no more than a gratuitous imagination. When the individual, as constituted by an arbitrary lump taken from those five heaps, ceases to exist, the result is Nirvana—the goal of Buddhism. If one wishes to express this by saying that one has found one's 'true individuality,' the word 'individuality,' as understood at present, is elastic and vague enough to permit this. The Buddhist Scriptures do, however, distinctly avoid this, or any equivalent, expression.

The various schools of Buddhism spring, as I will try to show, from differences in the approach to the Buddhist goal. Already in the early Order, men of different temperament and endowment are reported to have reached the goal by different roads. Sariputra was renowned for his wisdom, Ananda for his faith and devotion, Maudgalyayana for his magical potency. In later times, different-minded people formed different schools, and, in addition, the spread of the doctrine led to geographical separation and to separate organisations. Some of the methods for achieving de-individualisation, which we shall discuss in the later chapters of this book, are not mentioned at all in the oldest strata of the tradition as it has come down to us, or are no more than dimly foreshadowed. But, as many of the later Buddhists would have argued, in his love for beings the Buddha would have excluded nothing that could help anyone who wanted the right thing. A great deal of this book will be devoted to explaining what each of the chief schools stood for, what method it chose as its own particular way, how it can be thought to lead to the same goal as the others, and how it fared in the world of history.

## BUDDHISM AS A PHILOSOPHY

Philosophy, as we understand it in Europe, is a creation of the Greeks. It is unknown to Buddhist tradition, which would regard the enquiry into reality, for the mere purpose of knowing more about it, as a waste of valuable time. The Buddha's teaching is exclusively concerned with showing the way to salvation. Any 'philosophy' there may be in the works of Buddhist authors is quite incidental. In the ample vocabulary of Buddhism we find no word to correspond to our term 'philosophy.' An analogy may clarify the position. The Chinese language, as the Chinese understood it, did not contain any grammar, and it was taught in China without any grammatical instructions. Some European philologists, on the model of our Latin grammatical categories, have constructed a 'grammar' for the Chinese language. It does not fit particularly well, and the Chinese continue to dispense with it. The Latin-style grammar, with its familiar categories, may, however, help some Europeans to learn the Chinese language more easily. In a similar way, an attempt to define Bud-

dhist thought in the philosophical terminology current in Europe
may facilitate the approach to it. Buddhism, as a 'philosophy'
could then be described as a 'dialectical pragmatism' with a 'psychological' turn. Let us consider these three items one by one.

In its origin and intention a doctrine of salvation, Buddhism
has always been marked by its intensely practical attitude. Speculation on matters irrelevant to salvation is discouraged. Suffering
is the basic fact of life. If a man were struck by an arrow, he
would not refuse to have it extricated before he knew who shot
the arrow, whether that man was married or not, tall or small,
fair or dark. All he would want, would be to be rid of the arrow.
The Buddha's last injunction to his disciples ran: *All conditioned
things are impermanent. Work out your salvation with diligence.*
In their long history, the Buddhists have never lost this practical
bent. Innumerable misunderstandings would have been avoided
if one had seen that the statements of Buddhist writers are not
meant to be propositions about the nature of reality, but advice
on how to act, statements about modes of behaviour, and the experiences connected with them. 'If you want to get there, then
you must do this.' 'If you do this, you will experience this.'

We can, therefore, say with some truth that Buddhist thinking
tends in the direction of what we call *Pragmatism.* The value of
a thought is to be judged by what you can do with it, by
the quality of the life which results from it. Wherever one
finds evidence of such qualities as detachment, kindness, serene
self-confidence, etc., one would be inclined to believe that the
'philosophy' behind such an attitude had much to say in its
favour. *Of whatever teachings you can assure yourself that they
conduce to dispassion, and not to passions; to detachment and
not to bondage; to decrease of worldly gains, and not to their
increase; to frugality and not to covetousness; to content and not
to discontent; to solitude and not to company; to energy and
not to sluggishness; to delight in good and not to delight in evil,
of such teachings you may with certainty affirm: This is the
Norm. This is the Discipline. This is the Master's Message.*

As Buddhism developed, its pragmatism became even more

explicit. One came to see that anything one may say is ultimately false—false by the mere fact that one says it. *Those who say do not know; those who know do not say.* The *Aryan silence* alone did not violate the Truth. If one says something—and it is astonishing to find how much the supporters of the Aryan silence had to say—it is justified only by what they called 'skill in means.' In other words, one says it because it may help other people at a certain stage of their spiritual progress. The holy doctrine is primarily a medicine. The Buddha is like a physician. Just as a doctor must know the diagnosis of the different kinds of illness, must know their causes, the antidotes and remedies, and must be able to apply them, so also the Buddha has taught the *Four Holy Truths,* which indicate the range of suffering, its origin, its cessation, and the way which leads to its cessation. If one, however, isolates the Buddha's statements from the task they intend to perform, then they become quite meaningless, and lose all their force.

Meditation is in Buddhism easily the chief means of salvation. The stress is throughout far less on 'doing something' by overt action, than on contemplation and mental discipline. What one aims at is the control of mental processes by meditating on them. In consequence, Buddhist thought is impregnated with what we call *Psychology*. It mixes metaphysics and psychology in a way to which we have no parallel in the West.

In addition to pragmatism and psychological emphasis, Buddhist thought is inclined to what we may call *Dialectics*. Dialectics is a form of logic, associated in Europe with such names as Zenon of Elea and Hegel. It stands for the belief that, if you think properly and deeply on anything, you arrive at contradictions, i.e. at statements which to some extent cancel each other out. Buddhist thinkers loved paradox and contradiction. I may illustrate this by two quotations from the *Diamond Sutra,* a treatise written probably about 350 A.D., which has had more readers than any other metaphysical work. There the Buddha says: *"'Beings,' 'beings,' O Subhuti, as 'no-beings' have they been taught by the Tathagata. Therefore are they called 'beings.'"* Or again: *"As many beings as there are in these world systems, of them I know, in my wisdom, the manifold trends of thought. And why? 'Trends of thought,' 'trends of thought,' O Subhuti, as 'no-trends' have they been taught by the Tathagata. Therefore are they called 'trends of thought.' And why? Past thought is not got at; future thought is not got at; present thought is not got at."*

By defeating thought, contradictions are set free. Another fetter of existence has been cast off, and the vastness of the unlimited space of truth opens itself up. In a more secular way, some people get a similar feeling from reading nonsense literature. In Buddhism, the ordinary rules of logic are defied in the name of the freedom of the Spirit which transcends them. In addition, it is the introduction of the notion of the Absolute which here, as also with Zenon, Nicholas of Cusa and Hegel, makes self-contradictory statements appear permissible.

## SELF-EXTINCTION, AND THE DOCTRINE OF NOT SELF

The specific contribution of Buddhism to religious thought lies in its insistence on the doctrine of *'not-self'* (*an-attā* in Pali, *anātman* in Sanskrit). The belief in a 'self' is considered by all Buddhists as an indispensable condition to the emergence of suffering. We conjure up such ideas as 'I' and 'mine,' and many most undesirable states result. We would be perfectly happy, quite blissfully happy, as happy as, according to some psychologists, the child is in the womb, if we first could get rid of ourselves. The assertion that one can be really happy only after one is no longer there, is one of the dialectical paradoxes which to the man in the street must appear just as plain nonsense. In any case, it is fairly obvious that unhappiness requires that I should identify myself with other things, in the sense that I think that what happens to them happens to me. If there is a tooth, and there is decay in that tooth, this is a process in the tooth, and in the nerve attached to it. If now my 'I' reaches out to the tooth, convinces itself that this is 'my' tooth—and it sometimes does not seem to need very much convincing—and believes that what happens to the tooth is bound to affect *me,* a certain disturbance of thought is likely to result. The Buddhist sees it like this: Here is the idea of 'I,' a mere figment of the imagination, with nothing real to correspond to it. There are all sorts of processes going on in the world. Now I conjure up another figment of the imagination, the idea of 'belonging,' and come to the conclusion that some, not particularly well defined, portion of this world 'belongs' to that 'I,' or to 'me.' In this approach Buddhism greatly differs from some of our traditions in the West. In the philosophy of Aristotle, for instance, this idea of 'belonging' (hyparkhein) is quite uncritically treated as an ultimate datum of experience, and the entire logic and ontology of Aristotle is built upon it.

This doctrine of Anatta is very deep. One assumes that it will need more than one life-time to get to the bottom of it. As it is handed down by Buddhist tradition, it really comprises two statements. The two propositions which we must distinguish are:

It is claimed that nothing in reality corresponds to such words or ideas as 'I,' 'mine,' 'belonging,' etc. In other words, the self is not a fact.

We are urged to consider that nothing in our empirical self is worthy of being regarded as the real self.

The second of these propositions will become clearer in the course of this book. We must now have a look at the first one.

We are urged to struggle against the intellectual conviction that there is such a thing as a 'self,' or a 'soul,' or a 'substance,' or such relations as 'belonging' or 'owning.' It is not denied that the self, etc., are data of the world as it appears to common sense. But as facts of ultimate reality, we must reject the 'self,' and all kindred ideas. This step has an important corollary. If there is no such thing as a 'self,' there is also no such thing as a 'person.' For a 'person' is something which is organised round a supposed inner core, a central growing point, a 'self.'

In my book, *Contradiction and Reality,* I have attempted to re-state in modern terms the Buddhist arguments against the objective validity of the notion of 'self.' Their repetition would lead us too far here. Whatever arguments there may be against the idea of 'self,' it is obvious that we habitually speak of it, and find it difficult to dispense with the word. In England, Hume's denial of the existence of the ego, as an entity distinct from mental processes, comes very near the Anatta-doctrine. From the purely theoretical point of view Buddhism has in this respect little to teach that one cannot find as well, and probably in a more congenial form, in Hume and kindred thinkers, like William James. The difference between the Buddhist and the European and American philosophers lies in what they do with a philosophical proposition once they have arrived at it. In Europe, we have become accustomed to an almost complete gap between the theory of philosophers and their practice, between their views on the nature of the universe and their mode of life. Schopenhauer and Herbert Spencer, for instance, at once come to mind as particularly striking examples. If a philosopher here has proved that there is no ego, he is apt to leave it at that, and to behave very much as if there were one. His greed, hate and attachment remain practically untouched by his philosophical arguments. He is judged by the consistency of his views, not with his life, but with themselves, by his style, his erudition—in short, by purely intellectual standards. It just would not do to 'refute' a philosopher by pointing out that he is insufferably rude to his wife, envies his more fortunate colleagues, and gets flustered when contradicted. In Buddhism, on the contrary, the entire stress lies on the mode of living, on the saintliness of life, on the removal of attachment to this world. A merely theoretical proposition, such as 'there is no ego' would be regarded as utterly sterile, and useless. Thought is no more than a tool and its justification lies in its products.

Not content with the intellectual conviction that there is no ego, a Buddhist aims at an entirely new attitude to life. Day in, day out, in all the many functions and bothers of daily life, he must learn to behave as if there were no ego. Those who look to Buddhism for startlingly new and unheard-of ideas on the problem of self, will find little. Those who look to it for advice on how to lead a self-less life, may learn a great deal. The great contribution of Buddhist 'philosophy' lies in the methods it worked out to impress the truth of not-self on our reluctant minds, it lies in the discipline which the Buddhists imposed upon themselves in order to make this truth into a part of their own being.

The other side of the Anatta-doctrine, which consists in the repudiation of everything which constitutes or attracts the empirical self, has earned for Buddhism the reputation of being a 'pessimistic' faith. It is true that this world, i.e. everything conditioned and impermanent, is emphatically regarded as wholly ill, as wholly pervaded with suffering, as something to be rejected totally, abandoned totally, for the one goal of Nirvana. I am not quite sure, however, that 'radical pessimism' is really a good word for this attitude to the world. Observers of such Buddhist countries as Burma and Tibet record that their inhabitants are spontaneously cheerful, and even gay—laymen and monks alike. It is rather puzzling that the pessimistic gloom which one reads into the Buddhist doctrine of universal suffering should reflect itself in a cheerful countenance. This world may be a vale of tears, but there is joy in shedding its burden. It must be renounced. But if there is a kingdom of God to win by renouncing it, the gain infinitely outweighs the loss. In any case, the best thing we can do with such a word as 'pessimism' is to discard it and look the problem straight in the face.

The negative attitude of Buddhist thinkers to this world is obviously bound up with the question of the meaning of life, and the problem of the destiny of man. However difficult this problem may be, however unscientific it may be to concern ourselves with it, we must come to a decision on it, because the entire happiness and fruitfulness of our lives depends on the answer. The views on the nature and destiny of man, or the meaning of human existence, fall roughly into two classes. According to some, man is a product of the earth. The earth is his home. His task is to make himself at home on the earth. Self-preservation is the highest law, and even duty, of man. Others, however, believe that man is a spirit ill at ease, a soul fallen from heaven, a stranger on this earth. His task is to regain the state of perfection which was his before he fell into this world. Self-denial is the highest law and duty of man.

Our modern civilisation favours the first view-point, Buddhism the second. It would, of course, be futile to contend that such issues can be decided by argument alone. In all decisions on values one must be careful not to exalt one's own personal tastes, temperament, and preferences to the dignity of an objective and natural law. One should only define one's position, and not coerce others into it. The Buddhist point of view will appeal only to those people who are completely disillusioned with the world as it is, and with themselves, who are extremely sensitive to pain, suffering, and any kind of turmoil, who have an extreme desire for happiness, and a considerable capacity for renunciation. No Buddhist would assume that all men are either able or willing to understand his doctrine.

The Buddhist seeks for a total happiness beyond this world. Why should he be so ambitious? Why not be content with getting as much happiness out of this world as we can, however little it may be? The answer is that in actual practice we are seen not to be content. If increase in physical comfort and earthly satisfactions would make us content, then the inhabitants of the suburbs of London should be immeasurably more radiant and contented than Chinese coolies or Spanish peasants. The exact opposite is the case. Our human nature, according to the Buddhist contention, is so constituted that we are content with nothing but complete permanence, complete ease, complete security. And none of that can we ever find in this shifting world.

The discoveries which philosophers and psychologists have made in recent years about the central importance of anxiety at the very core of our being, have quite a Buddhist ring about them. According to the views elaborated by Scheler, Freud, Heidegger and Jaspers, there is in the core of our being a basic anxiety, a little empty hole from which all other forms of anxiety and unease draw their strength. In its pure form, this anxiety is experienced only by people with an introspective and philosophical turn of mind, and even then only rarely. If one has never felt it oneself, no amount of explanation will convince. If one has felt it, one will never forget, however much one may try. It may come upon you when you have been asleep, withdrawn from the world; you wake up in the middle of the night and feel a kind of astonishment at being there, which then gives way to a fear and horror at the mere fact of being there. It is then that you catch yourself by yourself, just for a moment, against the background of a kind of nothingness all around you, and with a gnawing sense of your powerlessness, your utter helplessness in the face of this astonishing fact that you are there at all. Usually, we avoid this experience as much as we possibly can, because it is so shattering and painful. Usually, I am very careful not to have myself by myself, but the I plus all sorts of other experiences. People who are busy all the time, who must always think of something, who must always be doing something, are incessantly running away from this experience of the *basic* or *original* anxiety. What we usually do is to lean and to rely on something else than this empty centre of ourselves. The Buddhist contention is that we will never be at ease before we have overcome this basic anxiety, and that we can do that only by relying on nothing at all.

## IMMORTALITY

With their exalted view of the nature of man, Buddhists regard it as a reasonable and sensible thing for us to strive for immortality. The aim of Buddhism, like that of many other religions, is to gain immortality, a deathless life. The Buddha, after he had become enlightened, claimed to have opened up the *doors to the Undying*. It is obvious that there is a great difference between the perpetuation of this individuality on the one side and immortality on the other. Immortality is just the opposite of this life, which is bound up with death, and inseparable from it. We start dying the moment we are born. The rate of metabolism in our bodies begins to slow down immediately after conception. Birth is the cause of death. All the circumstances which may bring about actual death are but its occasions. The act of birth, or conception, to be more accurate, is the decisive cause which makes death inevitable. I sometimes believe that the English persist in the gentle habit of executing criminals by hanging, because this form of execution affords such a close parallel to the course of human life. At the moment of conception we jump, as it were, off a board, with a noose round our necks. In due course, we will be strangled—it is only a matter of sooner or later. We are all the time aware of our perilous condition, whether we dare face it or not. How *can* one be at one's ease in the interval? Immortality is therefore not a desire to perpetuate an individuality which is bought at the price of inevitable decay, but a transcending of this individuality.

Now suppose that Mr. John Smith is fed up with this state of affairs in which everything is just produced for a short time in order to be destroyed again. Suppose he wishes to become immortal. Then he has no choice but to deny himself throughout the whole length and breadth of his being. Anything impermanent in himself he has to get rid of. Just try to think of what is left of Mr. Smith after he has become immortal. His body would obviously be gone. With the body his instincts would have disappeared—since they are bound up with his glands, with the needs of his tissues, in short with the body. His mind also, as he knows it, would have to be sacrificed. Because this mind of ours is bound up with bodily processes, its operations are based on the data provided by the bodily organs of sense, and it reveals its impermanence by incessantly and restlessly jumping from one thing to another. With the mind would go his sense of logical consistency. As a matter of fact, Mr. John Smith, turned immortal, would not recognise himself at all. He would have lost everything that made him recognisable to himself and to others.

And he could be born anew only if he had learned to deny all that clutters up the immortal side of his being—which lies, as the Buddhists would put it, outside his five skandhas—if he would deny all that constitutes his dear little self. Buddhist training consists, indeed, in systematically weakening our hold on those things in us which keep us from regaining the immortality which we lost when we were born. The body is subdued, the instincts are weakened, the mind is calmed, logical thinking is baffled and exhausted by absurdities, and sensory facts are thought little of, the eye of faith and the eye of wisdom replacing the eyes of the body. It comes really to the same as the precept of John Wesley, when he urged a disciple of his *to kill himself by inches*.

But, as I have said, it all depends on one's view on the nature of man. Those who regard man as a creature of the earth only, will be inclined to compare this Buddhist yearning for immortality with the snail which leaves its house in order to go on a flying expedition. Those who regard man as an essentially spiritual being will prefer the Buddhist simile of the mountain swans who, when they have left their mountain lake, go from puddle to puddle, without making their home anywhere, until they are back to their true home in the clear waters of the mountain lake.

## Survival Values

How ever eloquent the sages may be on this issue, common sense cannot help feeling that this kind of unworldliness is all very well and noble, but certainly quite unsuitable for anyone who has to live in this world, and on this earth. We are all of us nowadays unconscious Darwinians, and the survival value of an unworldly doctrine seems to be fearfully small. How could it ever keep its footing on the earth? Historical facts, however, are rather disconcerting to common sense. The Buddhist community is the oldest institution of mankind. It has survived longer than any other institution, except the kindred sect of the Jains. Here you have the big bullying empires of history, guarded by hosts of soldiers, ships and magistrates. Scarcely one of them lasted

of an organist striking different notes as he pleases, Buddhists outspokenly deny the existence of such a fabulous being. To postulate an independent âtman outside a combination of the five Skandhas,[1] of which an individual being is supposed by Buddhists to consist, is to unreservedly welcome egoism with all its pernicious corollaries. And what distinguishes Buddhism most characteristically and emphatically from all other religions is the doctrine of non-âtman or non-ego, exactly opposite to the postulate of a soul-substance which is cherished by most religious enthusiasts. In this sense, Buddhism is undoubtedly a religion without the soul.

To make these points clearer in a general way, let us briefly treat in this chapter of such principal tenets of Buddhism as Karma, Âtman, Avidyâ, Nirvâna, Dharmakâya, etc. Some of these doctrines being the common property of the two schools of Buddhism, Hînayânism and Mahâyânism, their brief, comprehensive exposition here will furnish our readers with a general notion about the constitution of Buddhism, and will also prepare them to pursue a further specific exposition of the Mahâyâna doctrine which follows.

## KARMA

One of the most fundamental doctrines established by Buddha is that nothing in this world comes from a single cause, that the existence of a universe is the result of a combination of several causes (*hetu*) and conditions (*pratyaya*), and is at the same time an active force contributing to the production of an effect in the future. As far as phenomenal existences are concerned, this law of cause and effect holds universally valid. Nothing, even God, can interfere with the course of things thus regulated, materially as well as morally. If a God really exists and has some concern about our worldly affairs, he must first conform himself to the law of causation. Because the principle of karma, which is the

---

[1] They are: (1) form or materiality, (2) sensation, (3) conception, (4) action or deeds, and (5) consciousness.

Buddhist term for causation morally conceived, holds supreme everywhere and all the time.

The conception of karma plays the most important rôle in Buddhist ethics. Karma is the formative principle of the universe. It determines the course of events and the destiny of our existence. The reason why we cannot change our present state of things as we may will, is that it has already been determined by the karma that was performed in our previous lives, not only individually but collectively. But, for this same reason, we shall be able to work out our destiny in the future, which is nothing but the resultant of several factors that are working and that are being worked by ourselves in this life.

Therefore, says Buddha:

> "By self alone is evil done,
> By self is one disgraced;
> By self is evil left undone,
> By self alone is he purified;
> Purity and impurity belong to self:
> No one can purify another."[2]

Again,

> "Not in the sky
> Nor in the midst of the sea,
> Nor entering a cleft of the mountains,
> Is found that realm on earth
> Where one may stand and be
> From an evil deed absolved."[3]

This doctrine of karma may be regarded as an application in our ethical realm of the theory of the conservation of energy. Everything done is done once for all; its footprints on the sand of our moral and social evolution are forever left; nay, more than left, they are generative, good or evil, and waiting for further development under favorable conditions. In the physical world,

---

[2] *The Dhammapada*, v. 165. Tr. by A. J. Edmunds.
[3] *The Dhammapada*, v. 127.

even the slightest possible movement of our limbs cannot but affect the general cosmic motion of the earth, however infinitesimal it be; and if we had a proper instrument, we could surely measure its precise extent of effect. So is it even with our deeds. A deed once performed, together with its subjective motives, can never vanish without leaving some impressions either on the individual consciousness or on the supra-individual, i.e., social consciousness.

We need not further state that the conception of karma in its general aspect is scientifically verified. In our moral and material life, where the law of relativity rules supreme, the doctrine of karma must be considered thoroughly valid. And as long as its validity is admitted in this field, we can live our phenomenal life without resorting to the hypothesis of a personal God, as declared by Lamarck when his significant work on evolution was presented to Emperor Napoleon.

But it will do injustice to Buddhism if we designate it agnosticism or naturalism, denying or ignoring the existence of the ultimate, unifying principle, in which all contradictions are obliterated. Dharmakâya is the name given by Buddhists to this highest principle, viewed not only from the philosophical but also from the religious standpoint. In the Dharmakâya, Buddhists find the ultimate significance of life, which, when seen from its phenomenal aspect, cannot escape the bondage of karma and its irrefragable laws.

## AVIDYÂ

What claims our attention next is the problem of nescience, which is one of the most essential features of Buddhism. Buddhists think, nescience (in Sanskrit *avidyâ*) is the subjective aspect of karma, involving us in a series of rebirths. Rebirth, considered by itself, is no moral evil, but rather a necessary condition of progress toward perfection, if perfection ever be attainable here. It is an evil only when it is the outcome of ignorance,—ignorance as to the true meaning of our earthly existence.

Ignorant are they who do not recognise the evanescence of worldly things and who tenaciously cleave to them as final realities; who madly struggle to shun the misery brought about by their own folly; who savagely cling to the self against the will of God, as Christians would say; who take particulars as final existences and ignore one pervading reality which underlies them all; who build up an adamantine wall between the mine and thine: in a word, ignorant are those who do not understand that there is no such thing as an ego-soul, and that all individual existences are unified in the system of Dharmakâya. Buddhism, therefore, most emphatically maintains that to attain the bliss of Nirvana we must radically dispel this illusion, this ignorance, this root of all evil and suffering in this life.

The doctrine of nescience or ignorance is technically expressed in the following formula, which is commonly called the Twelve Nidânas or Pratyayasamutpada, that is to say Chains of Dependence:

(1) There is Ignorance (*avidyâ*) in the beginning; (2) from Ignorance Action (*sanskâra*) comes forth; (3) from Action Consciousness (*vijñâna*) comes forth; (4) from Consciousness Name-and-Form (*nâmarûpa*) comes forth; (5) from Name-and-Form the Six Organs (*ṣadâyâtana*) come forth; (6) from the Six Organs Touch (*sparça*) comes forth; (7) from Touch Sensation (*vedanâ*) comes forth; (8) from Sensation Desire (*tṛṣnâ*) comes forth; (9) from Desire Clinging (*upâdâna*) comes forth; (10) from Clinging Being (*bhâva*) comes forth; (11) from Being Birth (*jati*) comes forth; and (12) from Birth Pain (*duḥkha*) comes forth.

According to Vasubandhu's *Abhidharmakoça,* the formula is explained as follows: Being ignorant in our previous life as to the significance of our existence, we let loose our desires and act wantonly. Owing to this karma, we are destined in the present life to be endowed with consciousness (*vijñâna*), name-and-form (*nâmarûpa*), the six organs of sense (*ṣadâyâtana*), and sensation (*vedanâ*). By the exercise of these faculties, we now desire for, hanker after, cling to, these illusive existences which have no ultimate reality whatever. In consequence of this "Will to Live" we potentially accumulate or make up the karma that will lead us to further metempsychosis of birth and death.

The formula is by no means logical, nor is it exhaustive, but the fundamental notion that life started in ignorance or blind will remains veritable.

## Non-Atman

The problem of nescience naturally leads to the doctrine usually known as that of of non-atman, i.e., non-ego, to which allusion was made at the beginning of this chapter. This doctrine of Buddhism is one of the subjects that has caused much criticism by Christian scholars. Its thesis runs: There is no such thing as ego-soul, which, according to the vulgar interpretation, is the agent of our mental activities. And this is the reason why Buddhism is sometimes called a religion without the soul, as aforesaid.

This Buddhist negation of the ego-soul is perhaps startling to the people, who, having no speculative power, blindly accept the traditional, materialistic view of the soul. They think, they are very spiritual in endorsing the dualism of soul and flesh, and in making the soul something like a corporeal entity, though far more ethereal than an ordinary object of the senses. They think of the soul as being more in the form of an angel, when they teach that it ascends to heaven immediately after its release from the material imprisonment.

They further imagine that the soul, because of its imprisonment in the body, groans in pain for its liberty, not being able to bear its mundane limitations. The immortality of the soul is a continuation after the dismemberment of material elements of this ethereal, astral, ghost-like entity,—very much resembling the Samkhyan *Lingham* or the Vedantic *sûksama-çârîra*. Self-consciousness will not a whit suffer in its continued activity, as it is the essential function of the soul. Brothers and sisters, parents and sons and daughters, wives and husbands, all transfigured and sublimated, will meet again in the celestial abode, and perpetuate

their home life much after the manner of their earthly one.
People who take this view of the soul and its immortality must
feel a great disappointment or even resentment, when they are
asked to recognise the Buddhist theory of non-âtman.

The absurdity of ascribing to the soul a sort of astral existence
taught by some theosophists is due to the confusion of the name
and the object corresponding to it. The soul, or what is tanta-
mount according to the vulgar notion, the ego, is a name given
to a certain coördination of mental activities. Abstract names are
invented by us to economise our intellectual labors, and of course
have no corresponding realities as particular presences in the
concrete objective world. Vulgar minds have forgotten the history of the formation of abstract names. Being accustomed always
to find certain objective realities or concrete individuals answer-
ing to certain names, they—those naïve realists—imagine that all
names, irrespective of their nature, must have their concrete individual equivalents in the sensual world. Their idealism or spirit-
ualism, so called, is in fact a gross form of materialism, in spite
of their unfounded fear of the latter as atheistic and even immoral;—curse of ignorance!

The non-âtman theory does not deny that there is a coördination or unification of various mental operations. Buddhism calls
this system of coördination vijñâna, not âtman. Vijñâna is consciousness, while âtman is the ego conceived as a concrete entity,
—a hypostatic agent which, abiding in the deepest recess of the
mind, directs all subjective activities according to its own discre-
tion. This view is radically rejected by Buddhism.

A familiar analogy illustrating the doctrine of non-âtman is
the notion of a wheel or that of a house. Wheel is the name given
to a combination in a fixed form of the spokes, axle, tire, hub,
rim, etc.; house is that given to a combination of roofs, pillars,
windows, floors, walls, etc., after a certain model and for a certain
purpose. Now, take all these parts independently, and where is
the house or the wheel to be found? House or wheel is merely
the name designating a certain form in which parts are systematically and definitely disposed. What an absurdity, then, it

must be to insist on the independent existence of the wheel or of the house as an agent behind the combination of certain parts thus definitely arranged!

It is wonderful that Buddhism clearly anticipated the outcome of modern psychological researches at the time when all other religious and philosophical systems were eagerly cherishing dogmatic superstitions concerning the nature of the ego. The refusal of modern psychology to have soul mean anything more than the sum-total of all mental experiences, such as sensations, ideas, feelings, decisions, etc., is precisely a rehearsal of the Buddhist doctrine of non-âtman. It does not deny that there is a unity of consciousness, for to deny this is to doubt our everyday experiences, but it refuses to assert that this unity is absolute, unconditioned, and independent. Everything in this phenomenal phase of existence, is a combination of certain causes (*hetu*) and conditions (*pratyaya*) brought together according to the principle of karma; and everything that is compound is finite and subject to dissolution, and, therefore, always limited by something else. Even the soul-life, as far as its phenomenality goes, is no exception to this universal law. To maintain the existence of a soul-substance which is supposed to lie hidden behind the phenomena of consciousness, is not only misleading, but harmful and productive of some morally dangerous conclusions. The supposition that there is something where there is really nothing, makes us cling to this chimerical form, with no other result than subjecting ourselves to an eternal series of sufferings. So we read in the *Lankâvatâra Sûtra*, III:

> "A flower in the air, or a hare with horns,
> Or a pregnant maid of stone:
> To take what is not for what is,
> 'Tis called a judgment false.

> "In a combination of causes,
> The vulgar seek the reality of self.
> As truth they understand not,
> From birth to birth they transmigrate."

## THE NON-ATMAN-NESS OF THINGS

Mahâyânism has gone a step further than Hînayânism in the
development of the doctrine of non-âtman, for it expressly dis-
avows, besides the denial of the existence of the ego-substance, a
noumenal conception of things, i.e., the conception of particulars
as having something absolute in them. Hînayânism, indeed, also
disfavors this conception of thinginess, but it does so only im-
plicitly. It is Mahâyânism that definitely insists on the non-
existence of a personal (*pudgala*) as well as a thingish (*dharma*)
ego.

According to the vulgar view, particular existences are real,
they have permanent substantial entities, remaining forever as
such. They think, therefore, that organic matter remains forever
organic just as much as inorganic matter remains inorganic;
that, as they are essentially different, there is no mutual transformation between them. The human soul is different from that of
the lower animals and sentient beings from non-sentient beings;
the difference being well-defined and permanent, there is no
bridge over which one can cross to the other. We may call this
view naturalistic egoism.

Mahâyânism, against this egoistic conception of the world, extends its theory of non-âtman to the realm lying outside us. It
maintains that there is no irreducible reality in particular existences, so long as they are combinations of several causes and
conditions brought together by the principle of karma. Things
are here because they are sustained by karma. As soon as its force
is exhausted, the conditions that made their existence possible
lose efficiency and dissolve, and in their places will follow other
conditions and existences. Therefore, what is organic to-day, may
be inorganic to-morrow, and *vice versa*. Carbon, for instance,
which is stored within the earth appears in the form of coal or
graphite or diamond; but that which exists on its surface is found
sometimes combined with other elements in the form of an animal or a vegetable, sometimes in its free elementary state. It is
the same carbon everywhere; it becomes inorganic or organic,

according to its karma, it has no âtman in itself which directs its transformation by its own self-determining will. Mutual transformation is everywhere observable; there is a constant shifting of forces, an eternal transmigration of the elements,—all of which tend to show the transitoriness and non-âtman-ness of individual existences. The universe is moving like a whirl-wind, nothing in it proving to be stationary, nothing in it rigidly adhering to its own form of existence.

Suppose, on the other hand, there were an âtman behind every particular being; suppose, too, it were absolute and permanent and self-acting; and this phenomenal world would then come to a standstill, and life be forever gone. For is not changeability the most essential feature and condition of life, and also the strongest evidence for the non-existence of individual things as realities? The physical sciences recognise this universal fact of mutual transformation in its positive aspect and call it the law of the conservation of energy and of matter. Mahâyânism, recognising its negative side, proposes the doctrine of the non-âtman-ness of things, that is to say, the impermanency of all particular existences. Therefore, it is said, *"Sarvam anityam, sarvam çûnyam, sarvam anâtman."* (All is transitory, all is void, all is without ego.)

Mahâyânists condemn the vulgar view that denies the consubstantiality and reciprocal transformation of all beings, not only because it is scientifically untenable, but mainly because, ethically and religiously considered, it is fraught with extremely dangerous ideas,—ideas which finally may lead a "brother to deliver up the brother to death and the father the child," and, again, it may constrain "the children to rise up against their parents and cause them to be put to death." Why? Because this view, born of egoism, would dry up the well of human love and sympathy, and transform us into creatures of bestial selfishness; because this view is not capable of inspiring us with the sense of mutuality and commiseration and of making us disinterestedly feel for our fellow-beings. Then, all fine religious and humane sentiments would depart from our hearts, and we should be nothing less than rigid, lifeless corpses, no pulse beating, no blood running.

And how many victims are offered every day on this altar of egoism! They are not necessarily immoral by nature, but blindly led by the false conception of life and the world, they have been rendered incapable of seeing their own spiritual doubles in their neighbors. Being ever controlled by their sensual impulses, they sin against humanity, against nature, and against themselves.

We read in the *Mahâyâna-abhisamaya Sûtra* (Nanjo, no. 196):

> "Empty and calm and devoid of ego
> Is the nature of all things:
> There is no individual being
> That in reality exists.

> "Nor end nor beginning having
> Nor any middle course,
> All is a sham, here's no reality whatever:
> It is like unto a vision and a dream.

> "It is like unto clouds and lightning,
> It is like unto gossamer or bubbles floating,
> It is like unto fiery revolving wheel,
> It is like unto water-splashing.

> "Because of causes and conditions things are here:
> In them there's no self-nature [i.e., âtman]:
> All things that move and work,
> Know them as such.

> "Ignorance and thirsty desire,
> The source of birth and death they are:
> Right contemplation and discipline by heart,
> Desire and ignorance obliterate.

> "All beings in the world,
> Beyond words they are and expressions:
> Their ultimate nature, pure and true,
> Is like unto vacuity of space."[4]

---

[4] This last passage should not be understood in the sense of a total abnegation of existence. It means simply the transcendentality of the highest principle.

## THE DHARMAKÂYA

The Dharmakâya, which literally means "body or system of being," is, according to the Mahâyânists, the ultimate reality that underlies all particular phenomena; it is that which makes the existence of individuals possible; it is the *raison d'être* of the universe; it is the norm of being, which regulates the course of events and thoughts. The conception of Dharmakâya is peculiarly Mahâyânistic, for the Hînayâna school did not go so far as to formulate the ultimate principle of the universe; its adherents stopped short at a positivistic interpretation of Buddhism. The Dharmakâya remained for them to be the Body of the Law, or the Buddha's personality as embodied in the truth taught by him.

The Dharmakâya may be compared in one sense to the God of Christianity and in another sense to the Brahmin or Paramât-man of Vedantism. It is different, however, from the former in that it does not stand transcendentally above the universe, which, according to the Christian view, was created by God, but which is, according to Mahâyânism, a manifestation of the Dharmakâya himself. It is also different from Brahman in that it is not absolutely impersonal, nor is it a mere being. The Dharmakâya, on the contrary, is capable of willing and reflecting, or, to use Buddhist phraseology, it is *Karunâ* (love) and *Bodhi* (intelligence), and not the mere state of being.

This pantheistic and at the same time entheistic Dharmakâya is working in every sentient being, for sentient beings are nothing but a self-manifestation of the Dharmakâya. Individuals are not isolated existences, as imagined by most people. If isolated, they are nothing, they are so many soap-bubbles which vanish one after another in the vacuity of space. All particular existences acquire their meaning only when they are thought of in their oneness in the Dharmakâya. The veil of Mâya, i.e., subjective ignorance may temporally throw an obstacle to our perceiving the universal light of Dharmakâya, in which we are all one. But when our Bodhi or intellect, which is by the way a reflection of the Dharmakâya in the human mind, is so fully enlightened, we

no more build the artificial barrier of egoism before our spiritual
eye; the distinction between the *meum* and *teum* is obliterated,
no dualism throws the nets of entanglement over us; I recognise
myself in you and you recognise yourself in me; *tat tvam asi*. Or,

> "What is here, that is there;
> What is there, that is here:
> Who sees duality here,
> From death to death goes he."

This state of enlightenment may be called the spiritual expansion of the ego, or, negatively, the ideal annihilation of the ego.
A never-drying stream of sympathy and love which is the life of
religion will now spontaneously flow out of the fountainhead
of Dharmakâya.

The doctrine of non-ego teaches us that there is no reality in
individual existences, that we do not have any transcendental
entity called ego-substance. The doctrine of Dharmakâya, to
supplement this, teaches us that we all are one in the System of
Being and only as such are immortal. The one shows us the folly
of clinging to individual existences and of coveting the immortality of the ego-soul; the other convinces us of the truth that we
are saved by living into the unity of Dharmakâya. The doctrine
of non-âtman liberates us from the shackle of unfounded egoism;
but as mere liberation does not mean anything positive and may
perchance lead us to asceticism, we apply the energy thus released
to the execution of the will of Dharmakâya.

The questions: "Why have we to love our neighbors as ourselves? Why have we to do to others all things whatsoever we
would that they should do to us?" are answered thus by Buddhists: "It is because we are all one in the Dharmakâya, because
when the clouds of ignorance and egoism are totally dispersed,
the light of universal love and intelligence cannot help but shine
in all its glory. And, enveloped in this glory, we do not see any
enemy, nor neighbor, we are not even conscious of whether we
are one in the Dharmakâya. There is no 'my will' here, but only
'thy will,' the will of Dharmakâya, in which we live and move
and have our being."

The Apostle Paul says: "For as in Adam all die, even so in Christ shall all be made alive." Why? Buddhists would answer, "because Adam asserted his egoism in giving himself up to ignorance, (the tree of knowledge is in truth the tree of ignorance, for from it comes the duality of me and thee); while Christ on the contrary surrendered his egoistic assertion to the intelligence of the universal Dharmakâya. That is why we die in the former and are made alive in the latter."

## Nirvâna

The meaning of Nirvâna has been variously interpreted by non-Buddhist students from the philological and the historical standpoint; but it matters little what conclusions they have reached, as we are not going to recapitulate them here; nor do they at all affect our presentation of the Buddhists' own view as below. For it is the latter that concerns us here most and constitutes the all-important part of the problem. We have had too much of non-Buddhist speculation on the question at issue. The majority of the critics, while claiming to be fair and impartial, have, by some preconceived ideas, been led to a conclusion, which is not at all acceptable to intelligent Buddhists. Further, the fact has escaped their notice that Pâli literature from which they chiefly derive their information on the subject represents the views of one of the many sects that arose soon after the demise of the Master and were constantly branching off at and after the time of King Açoka. The probability is, that Buddha himself did not have any stereotyped conception of Nirvâna, and, as most great minds do, expressed his ideas outright as formed under various circumstances; though of course they could not be in contradiction with his central beliefs, which must have remained the same throughout the course of his religious life. Therefore, to understand a problem in all its apparently contradictory aspects, it is very necessary to grasp at the start the spirit of the author of the problem, and when this is done the rest will be understood comparatively much easier. Non-Buddhist critics lack in this most important qualification; therefore, it is no wonder that

Buddhists themselves are always reluctant to accede to their interpretations.

Enough for apology. Nirvâna, according to Buddhists, does not signify an annihilation of consciousness nor a temporal or permanent suppression of mentation, as imagined by some; but it is the annihilation of the notion of ego-substance and of all the desires that arise from this erroneous conception. But this represents the negative side of the doctrine, and its positive side consists in universal love or sympathy (*karunâ*) for all beings.

These two aspects of Nirvâna, i.e., negatively, the destruction of evil passions, and, positively, the practice of sympathy, are complementary to each other; and when we have one we have the other. Because, as soon as the heart is freed from the cangue of egoism, the same heart, hitherto so cold and hard, undergoes a complete change, shows animation, and, joyously escaping from self-imprisonment, finds its freedom in the bosom of Dharmakâya. In this latter sense, Nirvâna is the "humanisation" of Dharmakâya, that is to say, "God's will done in earth as it is in heaven." If we make use of the terms, subjective and objective, Nirvâna is the former, and the Dharmakâya is the latter, phase of one and the same principle. Again, psychologically, Nirvâna is enlightenment, the actualisation of the Bodhicitta (Heart of Intelligence).

The gospel of love and the doctrine of Nirvâna may appear to some to contradict each other, for they think that the former is the source of energy and activity, while the latter is a lifeless, inhuman, ascetic quietism. But the truth is, love is the emotional aspect and Nirvâna the intellectual aspect of the inmost religious consciousness which constitutes the essence of the Buddhist life.

That Nirvâna is the destruction of selfish desires is plainly shown in this stanza:

> "To the giver merit is increased;
> When the senses are controlled anger arises not,
> The wise forsake evil,
> By the destruction of desire, sin, and infatuation,
> A man attains to Nirvâna."

The following, which was breathed forth by Buddha against a certain class of monks, testifies that when Nirvâna is understood in the sense of quietism or pessimism, he vigorously repudiated it:

"Fearing an endless chain of birth and death,
And the misery of transmigration,
Their heart is filled with worry,
But they desire their safety only.

"Quietly sitting and reckoning the breaths,
They're bent on the Anâpânam.
They contemplate on the filthiness of the body,—
Thinking how impure it is!

"They shun the dust of the triple world,
And in ascetic practice their safety they seek:
Incapable of love and sympathy are they,
For on Nirvâna abides their thought."

Against this ascetic practice of some monks, the Buddha sets forth what might be called the ideal of the Buddhist life:

"Arouse thy will, supreme and great,
Practise love and sympathy, give joy and protection;
Thy love like unto space,
Be it without discrimination, without limitation.

"Merits establish, not for thy own sake,
But for charity universal;
Save and deliver all beings,
Let them attain the wisdom of the Great Way."

It is apparent that the ethical application of the doctrine of Nirvâna is naught else than the Golden Rule,[5] so called. The

---

[5] The sentiment of the Golden Rule is not the monopoly of Christianity; it has been expressed by most of the leaders of thought, thus, for instance: "Requite hatred with virtue" (Lao-tze). "Hate is only appeased by love" (Buddha). "Do not do to others what ye would not have done to you by others" (Confucius). "One must neither return evil, nor do any evil to any one among men, not even if one has to suffer from them" (Plato, *Crito*, 49).

Golden Rule, however, does not give any reason why we should so act, it is a mere command whose authority is ascribed to a certain superhuman being. This does not satisfy an intellectually disposed mind, which refuses to accept anything on mere authority, for it wants to go to the bottom of things and see on what ground they are standing. Buddhism has solved this problem by finding the oneness of things in Dharmakâya, from which flows the eternal stream of love and sympathy. As we have seen before, when the cursed barrier of egoism is broken down, there remains nothing that can prevent us from loving others as ourselves.

Those who wish to see nothing but an utter barrenness of heart after the annihilation of egoism, are much mistaken in their estimation of human nature. For they think its animation comes from selfishness, and that all forms of activity in our life are propelled simply by the desire to preserve self and the race. They, therefore, naturally shrink from the doctrine that teaches that all things worldly are empty, and that there is no such thing as ego-substance whose immortality is so much coveted by most people. But the truth is, the spring of love does not lie in the idea of self, but in its removal. For the human heart, being a reflection of the Dharmakâya which is love and intelligence, recovers its intrinsic power and goodness, only when the veil of ignorance and egoism is cast aside. The animation, energy, strenuousness, which were shown by a self-centered will, and which therefore were utterly despicable, will surely not die out with the removal of their odious atmosphere in which egoism had enveloped them. But they will gain an ever nobler interpretation, ever more elevating and satisfying significance; for they have gone through a baptism of fire, by which the last trace of egoism has been thoroughly consumed. The old evil master is eternally buried, but the willing servants are still here and ever ready to do their service, now more efficiently, for their new legitimate and more authoritative lord.

Destruction is in common parlance closely associated with nothingness, hence Nirvâna, the destruction of egoism, is ordinarily understood as a synonym of nihilism. But the removal of darkness does not bring desolation, but means enlightenment and order and peace. It is the same chamber, all the furniture is left there as it was before. In darkness chaos reigned, goblins walked wild; in enlightenment everything is in its proper place. And did we not state plainly that Nirvâna was enlightenment?

## THE INTELLECTUAL TENDENCY OF BUDDHISM

One thing which in this connection I wish to refer to, is what makes Buddhism appear somehow cold and impassive. By this I mean its intellectuality.

The fact is that anything coming from India greatly savors of philosophy. In ancient India everybody of the higher castes seems to have indulged in intellectual and speculative exercises. Being rich in natural resources and thus the struggle for existence being reduced to a minimum, the Brahmans and the Kṣatriyas gathered themselves under most luxuriously growing trees, or retired to the mountain-grottoes undisturbed by the hurly-burly of the world, and there they devoted all their leisure hours to metaphysical speculations and discussions. Buddhism, as a product of these people, is naturally deeply imbued with intellectualism.

Futher, in India there was no distinction between religion and philosophy. Every philosophical system was at the same time a religion, and *vice versa*. Philosophy with the Hindus was not an idle display of logical sublety which generally ends in entangling itself in the meshes of sophistry. Their aim of philosophising was to have an intellectual insight into the significance of existence and the destiny of humanity. They did not believe in anything blindly nor accept anything on mere tradition. Buddha most characteristically echoes this sentiment when he says, "Follow my teachings not as taught by a Buddha, but as being in accord with truth." This spirit of self-reliance and self-salvation later became singularly Buddhistic. Even when Buddha was still merely an enthusiastic aspirant for Nirvâna, he seems to have been strongly possessed of this spirit, for he most emphatically

declared the following famous passage, in response to the pa-
thetic persuasion of his father's ministers, who wanted him to
come home with them: "The doubt whether there exists anything
or not, is not to be settled for me by another's words. Arriving at
the truth either by mortification or by tranquilisation, I will grasp
myself whatever is ascertainable about it. It is not mine to receive
a view which is full of conflicts, uncertainties, and contradictions.
What enlightened men would go by others' faith? The multi-
tudes are like the blind led in the darkness by the blind."

To say simply, "Love your enemy," was not satisfactory to the
Hindu mind, it wanted to see the reason why. And as soon as
the people were convinced intellectually, they went even so far
as to defend the faith with their lives. It was not an uncommon
event that before a party of Hindu philosophers entered into a
discussion they made an agreement that the penalty of defeat
should be the sacrifice of one's life. They were, above all, a people
of intellect, though of course not lacking in religious sentiment.

It is no wonder, then, that Buddha did not make the first
proclamation of his message by "Repent, for the kingdom of
heaven is at hand," but by the establishment of the Four Noble
Truths. One appeals to the feeling, and the other to the intellect.
That which appeals to the intellect naturally seems to be less
passionate, but the truth is, feeling without the support of intellect leads to fanaticism and is always ready to yield itself to
bigotry and superstition.

The doctrine of Nirvâna is doubtless more intellectual than
the Christian gospel of love. It first recognises the wretchedness
of human life as is proved by our daily experiences; it then finds
its cause in our subjective ignorance as to the true meaning of
existence, and in our egocentric desires which, obscuring our
spiritual insight, make us tenaciously cling to things chimerical;
it then proposes the complete annihilation of egoism, the root of
all evil, by which, subjectively, tranquillity of heart is restored,
and, objectively, the realisation of universal love becomes possible. Buddhism, thus, proceeds most logically in the development
of its doctrine of Nirvâna and universal love.

Says Victor Hugo (*Les Misérables,* vol. II): "The reduction of the universe to a single being, the expansion of a single being even to God, this is love." When a man clings to the self and does not want to identify himself with other fellow-selves, he cannot expand his being to God. When he shuts himself in the narrow shell of ego and keeps all the world outside, he cannot reduce the universe to his innermost self. To love, therefore, one must first enter Nirvâna.

The truth is everywhere the same and is attained through the removal of ignorance. But as individual disposition differs according to the previous karma, some are more prone to intellectualism, while the others to sentimentality (in its psychological sense). Let us then follow our own inclination conscientiously and not speak evil of others. This is called the Doctrine of Middle Path.

CHAPTER V

# The Essence
# of Buddhism

### HEINRICH ZIMMER

The Buddha's doctrine is called *yāna*. The word means "a
vehicle," or, more to the point, "a ferryboat." The "ferryboat" is
the principal image employed in Buddhism to render the sense
and function of the doctrine. The idea persists through all the
differing and variously conflicting teachings of the numerous
Buddhist sects that have evolved in many lands, during the long
course of the magnificent history of the widely disseminated
doctrine. Each sect describes the vehicle in its own way, but no
matter how described, it remains always the ferry.

To appreciate the full force of this image, and to understand
the reason for its persistence, one must begin by realizing that
in everyday Hindu life the ferryboat plays an extremely prominent role. It is an indispensable means of transportation in a
continent traversed by many mighty rivers and where bridges
are practically nonexistent. To reach the goal of almost any
journey one will require a ferry, time and time again, the only
possible crossing of the broad and rapid streams being by boat
or by a ford. The Jainas called their way of salvation the ford
(*tīrtha*), and the supreme Jaina teachers were, as we have seen,
*Tīrthaṅkaras*, "those making, or providing, a ford." In the same
sense, Buddhism, by its doctrine, provides a ferryboat across the

rushing river of saṁsāra to the distant bank of liberation. Through enlightenment (*bodhi*) the individual is transported.

The gist of Buddhism can be grasped more readily and adequately by fathoming the main metaphors through which it appeals to our intuition than by a systematic study of the complicated superstructure, and the fine details of the developed teaching. For example, one need only think for a moment about the actual, everyday experience of the process of crossing a river in a ferryboat, to come to the simple idea that inspires and underlies all of the various rationalized systematizations of the doctrine. To enter the Buddhist vehicle—the boat of the discipline—means to begin to cross the river of life, from the shore of the common-sense experience of non-enlightenment, the shore of spiritual ignorance (*avidyā*), desire (*kāma*), and death (*māra*), to the yonder bank of transcendental wisdom (*vidyā*), which is liberation (*mokṣa*) from this general bondage. Let us consider, briefly, the actual stages involved in any crossing of a river by ferry, and see if we can experience the passage as a kind of initiation-by-analogy into the purport of the stages of the Buddhist pilgrim's progress to his goal.

Standing on the nearer bank, this side the stream, waiting for the boat to put in, one is a part of its life, sharing in its dangers and opportunities and in whatever may come to pass on it. One feels the warmth or coolness of its breezes, hears the rustle of its trees, experiences the character of its people, and knows that its earth is underfoot. Meanwhile the other bank, the far bank, is beyond reach—a mere optical image across the broad, flowing waters that divide us from its unknown world of forms. We have really no idea what it will be like to stand in that distant land. How this same scenery of the river and its two shorelines will appear from the other side we cannot imagine. How much of these houses will be visible among the trees? What prospects up and down the river will unfold? Everything over here, so tangible and real to us at present—these real, solid objects, these tangible forms—will be no more than remote, visual patches, inconsequential optical effects, without power to touch us, either to help or to harm. This solid earth itself will be a visual, horizontal line beheld from afar, one detail of an extensive scenic view, beyond our experience, and of no more force for us than a mirage.

The ferryboat arrives; and as it comes to the landing we regard it with a feeling of interest. It brings with it something of the air of that yonder land which will soon be our destination. Yet when we are entering it we still feel like members of the world from which we are departing, and there is still that feeling of unreality about our destination. When we lift our eyes from the boat and boatman, the far bank is still only a remote image, no more substantial than it was before.

Softly the ferryboat pushes off and begins to glide across the moving waters. Presently one realizes that an invisible line has been recently, imperceptibly passed, beyond which the bank left behind is assuming gradually the unsubstantiality of a mere visual impression, a kind of mirage, while the farther bank, drawing slowly nearer, is beginning to turn into something real. The former dim remoteness is becoming the new reality and soon is solid ground, creaking under keel—real earth—the sand and stone on which we tread in disembarking; whereas the world left behind, recently so tangible, has been transmuted into an optical reflex devoid of substance, out of reach and meaningless, and has forfeited the spell that it laid upon us formerly—with all its features, all its people and events—when we walked upon it and ourselves were a portion of its life. Moreover, the new reality, which now possesses us, provides an utterly new view of the river, the valley, and the two shores, a view very different from the other, and completely unanticipated.

Now while we were in the process of crossing the river in the boat, with the shore left behind becoming gradually vaguer and more meaningless—the streets and homes, the dangers and pleasures, drawing steadily away—there was a period when the shoreline ahead was still rather far off too; and during that time the only tangible reality around us was the boat, contending stoutly with the current and precariously floating on the rapid waters. The only details of life that then seemed quite substantial and that greatly concerned us were the various elements and implements of the ferryboat itself: the contours of the hull and gunwales, the rudder and the sail, the various ropes, and perhaps a smell of tar. The rest of existence, whether out ahead or left behind, signified no more than a hopeful prospect and a fading recollection—two poles of unrealistic sentimental association affiliated with certain clusters of optical effects far out-of-hand.

In the Buddhist texts this situation of the people in a ferryboat is compared to that of the good folk who have taken passage in the vehicle of the doctrine. The boat is the teaching of the Buddha, and the implements of the ferry are the various details of Buddhist discipline: meditation, yoga-exercises, the rules of ascetic life, and the practice of self-abnegation. These are the only things that disciples in the vehicle can regard with deep conviction; such people are engrossed in a fervent belief in the Buddha as the ferryman and the Order as their bounding gunwale (framing, protecting, and defining their perfect ascetic life) and in the guiding power of the doctrine. The shoreline of the world has been left behind but the distant one of release not yet attained. The people in the boat, meanwhile, are involved in a peculiar sort of middle prospect which is all their own.

Among the conversations of the Buddha known as the "Medium-length Dialogues," there appears a discourse on the value of the vehicle of the doctrine. First the Buddha describes a man who, like himself or any of his followers, becomes filled with a loathing of the perils and delights of secular existence. That man decides to quit the world and cross the stream of life to the far land of spiritual safety. Collecting wood and reeds, he builds a raft, and by this means succeeds in attaining the other shore. The Buddha confronts his monks, then, with the question.

"What would be your opinion of this man," asks the Buddha, "would he be a clever man, if, out of gratitude for the raft that has carried him across the stream to safety, he, having reached the other shore, should cling to it, take it on his back, and walk about with the weight of it?"

The monks reply. "No, certainly the man who would do that would not be a clever man."

The Buddha goes on. "Would not the clever man be the one who left the raft (of no use to him any longer) to the current of the stream, and walked ahead without turning back to look at it? Is is not simply a tool to be cast away and forsaken once it has served the purpose for which it was made?"

The disciples agree that this is the proper attitude to take toward the vehicle, once it has served its purpose.

The Buddha then concludes. "In the same way the vehicle of the doctrine is to be cast away and forsaken, once the other shore of Enlightenment (*nirvāṇa*) has been attained."

The rules of the doctrine are intended for beginners and advanced pupils, but become meaningless for the perfect. They can be of no service to the truly enlightened, unless to serve him, in his role of teacher, as a convenient medium by which to communicate some suggestion of the truth to which he has attained. It was by means of the doctrine that the Buddha sought to express what he had realized beneath the tree as inexpressible. He could communicate with the world through his doctrine and thus help his unprepared disciples when they were at the start, or somewhere in the middle, of the way. Talking down to the level of relative or total ignorance, the doctrine can move the still imperfect yet ardent mind; but it can say nothing any more, nothing ultimately real, to the mind that has cast away darkness. Like the raft, it must be left behind, therefore, once the goal has been attained; for it can thenceforth be no more than an inappropriate burden.

Moreover, not the raft only, but the stream too, becomes void of reality for the one who has attained the other shore. When such a one turns around to look again at the land left behind, what does he see? What *can* one see who has crossed the horizon beyond which there is no duality? He looks—and there *is* no "other shore"; there is no torrential separating river; there is no raft; there is no ferryman; there can have been no crossing of the nonexistent stream. The whole scene of the two banks and the river between is simply gone. There can be no such thing for the enlightened eye and mind, because to see or think of anything as something "other" (a distant reality, different from one's own being) would mean that full Enlightenment had not yet been attained. There can be an "other shore" only for people still in the spheres of dualistic perception; those this side the stream or still inside the boat and heading for the "other shore"; those who have not yet disembarked and thrown away the raft. Illumination means that the delusory distinction between the two shores of a worldly and a transcendental existence no longer holds. There *is* no stream of rebirths flowing between two separated shores: no saṁsāra and no nirvāṇa.

Thus the long pilgrimage to perfection through innumerable existences, motivated by the virtues of self-surrender and accomplished at the cost of tremendous sacrifices of ego, disappears like a landscape of dreams when one awakes. The long-continued story of the heroic career, the many lives of increasing self-purification, the picture-book legend of detachment won through the long passion, the saintly epic of the way to become a savior—enlightened and enlightening—vanishes like a rainbow. All becomes void; whereas once, when the dream was coming to pass step by step, with ever-recurrent crises and decisions, the unending series of dramatic sacrifices held the soul completely under its spell. The secret meaning of Enlightenment is that this titan-effort of pure soul-force, this ardent struggle to reach the goal by acts, ever-renewed, of beautiful self-surrender, this supreme, long strife through ages of incarnations to attain release from the universal law of moral causation (*karma*)—is without reality. At the threshold of its own realization it dissolves, together with its background of self-entangled life, like a nightmare at the dawn of day.

For the Buddha, therefore, even the notion of nirvāṇa is without meaning. It is bound to the pairs-of-opposites and can be employed only in opposition to saṁsāra—the vortex where the life-force is spellbound in ignorance by its own polarized passions of fear and desire.

The Buddhist way of ascetic training is designed to conduce
to the understanding that there is no substantial ego—nor any
object anywhere—that lasts, but only spiritual processes, welling
and subsiding: sensations, feelings, visions. These can be suppressed or set in motion and watched at will. The idea of the
extinction of the fire of lust, ill will, and ignorance becomes
devoid of meaning when this psychological power and point of
view has been attained; for the process of life is no longer experienced as a burning fire. To speak seriously, therefore, of
nirvāṇa as a goal to be attained is simply to betray the attitude
of one still remembering or experiencing the process at the burning of the fire. The Buddha himself adopts such an attitude only
for the teaching of those still suffering, who feel that they would
like to make the flames extinct. His famous Fire Sermon is an
accommodation, not by any means the final word of the sage
whose final word is silence. From the perspective of the Awake,
the Illumined One, such opposed verbalizations as nirvāṇa and
saṁsāra, enlightenment and ignorance, freedom and bondage,
are without reference, void of content. That is why the Buddha
refused to discuss nirvāṇa. The pointlessness of the connotations
that would inevitably seem to be intended by his words would
confuse those trying to follow his mysterious way. They being
still in the ferryboat framed of these conceptions and requiring
them as devices of transport to the shore of understanding, their
teacher would not deny before them the practical function of
such convenient terms; and yet would not give the terms weight,
either, by discussion. Words like "enlightenment," "ignorance,"
"freedom," and "entanglement" are preliminary helps, referring
to no ultimate reality, mere hints or signposts for the traveler,
which serve to point him to the goal of an attitude beyond their
own suggestions of a contrariety. The raft being finally left behind, and the vision lost of the two banks and the separating
river, then there is in truth neither the realm of life and death
nor that of release. Moreover, there is no Buddhism—no boat,
since there are neither shores nor waters between. There is no
boat, and there is no boatman—no Buddha.

The great paradox of Buddhism, therefore, is that no Buddha has ever come into existence to enlighten the world with Buddhist teachings. The life and mission of Gautama Śākyamuni is only a general misunderstanding by the unenlightened world, helpful and necessary to guide the mind toward illumination, but to be discarded when—and if—enlightenment is to be attained. Any monk failing to get rid of such ideas clings (by clinging to them) to the general mundane delusion which he imagines himself to be striving to leave behind. For, briefly, so long as nirvāṇa is looked upon as something different from saṁsāra, the most elementary error about existence still has to be overcome. These two ideas mirror contrary attitudes of the semiconscious individual toward himself and the outer sphere in which he lives; but beyond this subjective range they have no substantiation.

Buddhism—this popular creed which has won the reverence of all Eastern Asia—contains this boldest paradox at its very root; the most startling reading of reality ever whispered into human ear. All good Buddhists tend to avoid, therefore, statements about existence and non-existence. Their "Middle Path" goes between by simply pointing out that the validity of a conception is always relative to one's position along the road of progress from Ignorance to Buddhahood. Attitudes of assertion and negation belong to worldly beings on the hither bank of ignorance, and to pious people making headway in the crowded ferryboat of the doctrine. Such a conception as Voidness (*śūnyatā*) can have meaning only for an ego clinging to the reality of things; one who has lost the feeling that things are real can make no sense of such a word. And yet words of this kind remain in all the texts and teachings. Indeed, the great *practical* miracle of Buddhism is that terms of this kind, used successfully as steppingstones, do not become rocks on which to found and build a creed.

The greater portion of the Buddhist literature that has become available and familiar to us in translation is adjusted in this way, pedagogically, to the general human attitude of partial ignorance. It is intended for the teaching and guidance of disciples. It outlines and points the way along the path of the Buddhas (*buddha-mārga*), depicting the career of the hero "going to enlightenment" (*bodhicarya*). Its position, therefore, is comparable to that of the ferryman inviting people on our hither bank to enter his boat and cross the waters, or guiding his crew in their handling of the craft during the passage. The yonder bank is represented only in a preliminary, very sketchy way; only hinted at and attractively suggested, for the captivation and continued inspiration of those still spellbound by the notions of this dualistic shore—men and women trying to make up their minds to leave, or else in the toilsome stages of crossing to an absolutely contrary point of view, which they will perceive presently to be utterly inconsistent with their expectation.

This pedagogical interest of Buddhism entails, unavoidably, a screening of the ultimate essence of the doctrine. The introductory statements, graded as they are, lead right up to the goal —but then have to be put behind, or the goal itself will never be attained.

## CHAPTER VI

# Hinayana

## Hinayana Buddhism

*M. Hiriyanna*

The story of Buddha's life as familiarly known, is, for the most part, based on tradition long posterior to the time when he lived. According to this account, he was born at Kapilavastu, his father being the ruler of a principality. . . . The date of his birth is now generally taken as 563 B.C. He is represented as a greatly accomplished prince. He was married at the age of 16, and a son was born to him in course of time. It was about this time that he began to reflect upon the vanities of life and upon the tragedy of death, disease and old age which afflict mankind. This is picturesquely represented in the story as his meeting an old man, a sick man and a corpse in succession. Those sights were followed by that of a recluse who had completely renounced the world; and it led to his resolve that he would free himself from all worldly ties and strive his utmost to discover the way out of life's unending misery. In pursuance of this resolve, he left the palace the same night, looking upon it as "a place of dust," and went away to a distant forest. There, in the company of five others, he practised severe penance, mortifying his body as it was

Reprinted from M. Hiriyanna, *The Essentials of Indian Philosophy* (London: George Allen & Unwin, Ltd., 1949), pages 70-80. Used by permission of the publisher.

the common practice at the time for intensely religious-minded people to do. He led this kind of life for six years; but not succeeding in his object thereby, he began a fresh course of self-discipline characterized by less severity. Then his companions left him, dissenting from his view. In this second attempt, he was successful and he became fully enlightened (*buddha*) and reached, as it is expressed, "the end of cravings."

He did not, however, remain content with this personal illumination, but decided to teach the way to it to others also. His first disciples were the five ascetics who had earlier parted from him, and were at the time in a place near Benares known as Sārnāth or the "Deer Park." It is in the first sermon which he delivered to them, after converting them to his way of think-ing, that, as tradition has it, he dwelt upon the Four Noble Truths (*ārya-satya*) to which we shall refer later. He thereafter succeeded in converting many others, including his own family. His activities, however, were confined to a relatively limited region which comprised portions of modern Behar, the United Provinces and Nepal. He died in 483 B.C. at the age of 80 at Kuśīnara on the day, it is said, which was the anniversary of his birth, as also of the attainment by him of complete enlighten-ment. This event took place between two *sāla* trees, a circum-stance which is piously depicted in the sculptures and bas-reliefs relating to the closing scene of his life. Buddha is undoubtedly one of the great religious teachers of the world. In the third century B.C. the famous emperor, Aśoka, became a Buddhist; and it is commonly believed that through the impetus he gave to it, Buddhism began to spread not only in other parts of India but also beyond it.

## I

There is much difficulty in determining the original form of this creed for . . . we have no record of it come down to us from the period in which it was first promulgated. The earliest works relating to it, which constitute its "canonical literature," may contain much that was actually uttered by Buddha; but there is no means of knowing for certain what those portions are. Hence there has been a good deal of difference of opinion among modern scholars regarding the exact character of his teaching. It is obvious, however, that Buddhism began as a religion and that it was forced, not long after, to become a philosophy since it had to defend itself against metaphysical schools of Hindu and Jaina thought.

A similar difficulty is experienced in defining the relation of early Buddhism to Brahmanism. That it should have been greatly influenced by the latter, the dominant faith of the land at the time, goes without saying. The points to be considered are the extent of the influence, and the precise form of Brahmanism which influenced it. It is now generally believed that primitive Buddhism represents a new expansion, not against, but within Brahmanism. The canonical literature, no doubt, now and again criticizes Brahmanism, but mostly on its ritualistic side. The conclusion to be drawn from it is that Buddha's teaching was a protest against the over-elaborate ceremonialism that, in one sense, had given rise to the Upanishadic doctrine itself. An important consequence of this rejection of ritual was the emphasis placed on morality which, though by no means ignored in Brahmanism, was assigned a somewhat subordinate place in it. The references to the Upanishadic doctrine, the other aspect of Brahmanism, are far fewer, showing that Buddhism did not diverge from it very much. There are, however, some differences, to the more important among which we may now draw attention.

The Upanishadic doctrine was . . . intended for only a select few. The characteristic feature of Buddha's teaching, on the other hand, was that it admitted no esoteric truths, and was meant for all who were not satisfied with leading a life of natural inclinations. It was "a folk-gospel," as it has been described. Its message was for the plain man, and it accordingly gave rise to a general uplift of great significance. A second divergence was that, while Brahmanism relied overmuch on the instruction given by others, Buddhism laid particular stress on self-reliance and self-effort in knowing the ultimate truth. The disciple was asked to think for himself, and to accept others' opinions only after he had been fully convinced of their soundness. That is, it was not dogmatic even in the least. For the rest, early Buddhism was the same as Brahmanism of this type, and believed in the same cosmological and eschatological views, including the doctrine of karma. The main features of primitive Buddhism may be summarized as follows:

We have seen that in the early Vedic period, man was re-garded as distinct from the divine, and that this view had been gradually transformed by the time of the Upanishads into the view that he was himself essentially divine. It is this God-in-man that Buddha understood by ātman—neither body nor mind, but spirit. He also believed that, as spirit, it persists here as well as hereafter so that it is wrong to say, as is often done, that Buddha denied the self or identified it with the body and the mind. It, however, represented to him not man as he is, but as what he might or ought to be. In other words, it stood for the ideal self, to realize which there is an innate urge in man. His foremost task in life accordingly is to act in response to it; and the result of so acting, viz. the "waning out" of his lower nature, of the lust and hate in him, is all that is meant by liberation or nirvana, a word with which we have already become familiar in connection with Jainism. It is not the annihilation of the self, but only the extinguishing of selfhood in the ordinary acceptation of the term. Early Buddhism is thus a gospel of hope, and not a gospel of despair as it is commonly represented to be.

But what is the means to such liberation? The Upanishads, whose teaching is nearly the same, lay down a course of disci-pline for the self becoming Brahman. But, according to one of the two interpretations of them, the lapse of man from his true spiritual state is conceived not as real, taking place in time, but as only apparent. The goal is not therefore anything which is to be reached in fact; it has only to be realized in thought. It thus lays little stress on "becoming," in the sense of attaining what has not yet been attained. The other interpretation of the Upanishads, according to which spirit is self-evolving, is, no doubt, very different in this respect; but there, it is the goal that is represented as important, and not so much the way leading to it, as here. For original Buddhism, it is man as an aspirant after perfection that matters more than man as having achieved it. Further, in the Upanishadic view, the immediate means recommended for attaining the ultimate goal, even when it is conceived as *growing into* Brahman, is *yoga;* Buddha's emphasis, on the other hand, is throughout on *dharma* in its ethical sense. It is described as "the lamp of life," and signifies perfect conduct or godly living, not a mere code of dogmas as it came to do afterwards.

## II

The original form of the creed, thus reconstructed, must contain elements that are hypothetical. It also seems to do less than justice to certain aspects of the teaching of the Upanishads. For example, it ignores that a dynamic conception of Brahman finds a conspicuous place in them; and it also minimizes the importance attached therein to moral purity in the scheme of discipline for the realization of the ultimate truth. However that may be, the point for us to note now is that the teaching of Buddha was positive and constructive. But the negative and analytic view came in course of time to prevail; and, as a consequence of it, Buddhism gradually became thoroughly monastic in character. This transformation had already taken place by the time the systems proper took rise. It forms the chief teaching of the Pali Buddhistic literature whose main features we are now to sketch very briefly. We shall be able to do this best by explaining what is meant by the Four Noble Truths which, according to the Pali canon, formed the subject-matter of the very first sermon Buddha delivered at Benares. The account that has come down to us of these Truths is now taken to represent, on the whole, a later stage of the teaching—the result of "monkish misapprehension." Their implication is that life is an evil; and their chief aim, to point out how it can be overcome. In these Truths, we have what corresponds to a physician's treatment of a disease—ascertaining the nature of the disease, discovering its cause and setting about its cure by adopting appropriate means thereto. They are:

(1) *Life is evil.*—The whole teaching, as shown by its implied comparison of life to a disease, is based upon a pessimistic view, betokening monkish influence. But even in this later form of the doctrine, evil is not to be taken as the final fact in life. Its pessimism means that life is full of pain and suffering, not in itself, but only as it is ordinarily lived, for the doctrine holds out the hope that they can be completely overcome in the stage of nirvana which can be reached here and now, if one so wills.

(2) *Ignorance is the source of evil.*—The origin of evil is in ignorance (*avidyā*), or not knowing the true nature of the self. We commonly assume it to be an integral something which is other than the bodily organism; and we believe that this self not only persists as long as the organism does but also survives it. According to canonical Buddhism, this is an absolute error, and there is no self other than the complex of the body (*rūpa*) and the mind (*nāma*). It is sometimes spoken of as consisting not of these two, but of five factors (called *skandhas*), one of which is the physical body (*rūpa*), and the rest represent different phases of mind (*nāma*) like cognition and feeling—a view which shows how the spirit of analysis came to prevail more and more. Even in this sense of being a mere complex, whether of two or of five factors, the self is not permanent. It is undergoing change almost constantly; and in nirvana, it completely ceases to be. It is the clinging to this false self, as a result of our ignorance of its real nature, that explains all the misery of life as it is commonly lived. Thus Buddhism, which postulated a changing self as a protest against a static one as conceived by some at the time, came in course of time to virtually repudiate it. We should add that this principle of explanation was soon extended to other cases, with the result that all things, and not the self alone, were deemed to be mere aggregates (*saṁghāta*) of their respective component parts. A chariot, for example, is nothing more than an assemblage of the pole, wheels, etc. This is known as the doctrine of the non-substantiality (*nairātmya*) of things.

(3) *Evil can be overcome.*—It is possible to remove this evil, for it is caused, and whatever is caused is removable according to this teaching. Given the cause, the effect follows; and, if the one can be removed, the other will necessarily cease to be. The fact that life's evil is caused is exhibited in the form of twelve links, known as the "chain of causation." The first of them is ignorance of the true nature of the self, which implies that, as in the case of the Upanishadic doctrine, evil is radically of the metaphysical type. Of the remaining eleven, it will do to mention only three, viz. craving or thirst (*tṛṣṇā*), death and rebirth. That is, man's ignorance gives rise to a selfish craving for things; and unsatisfied cravings lead to rebirth after death. It is this recurring cycle of birth and death that should be ended; and the result is nirvana, which may accordingly be described as the cessation of ignorance, of craving or of birth and death. The goal of life is thus conceived here as purely negative while, in the original teaching, it meant the complete development of the higher self, through overcoming the tyranny of the lower. A person who succeeds in breaking through this circle of *saṁsāra* can, it was believed, attain the serene composure of nirvana in the present life; and he is, as in Jainism, called an *arhat* or "the worthy one." The principle underlying the chain of causation, which was originally formulated to account for the evil of life, was later extended to all things, whether psychical or physical; and they likewise came to be regarded as caused, and therefore as ultimately exterminable. This is known as the doctrine of the impermanence (*anityatva*) of things.

(4) *Right knowledge is the means of removing evil.*—As knowledge is the logical antithesis of ignorance, enlightenment about the true nature of one's self will remove evil. By this enlightenment, we should understand an inner conviction which, to be effectively secured, requires a long course of previous moral training. Here we find the emphasis which, as we stated earlier, Buddha had once laid on right conduct. But in consonance with the general trend of the development of the doctrine, the emphasis is now shifted on to knowledge or wisdom (*prajñā*) and meditative practice (*yoga*) chiefly on the Four Truths. Even so

far as it continues to emphasize conduct, an ascetic spirit comes
to prevail though, as compared with Jaina teaching, it is mild.
It certainly imposed on its advanced adherents strict rules of
discipline; but, at the same time, it discouraged them from
resorting to any form of self-torture in their enthusiasm for
reaching the goal. It was "a middle path" that it commended—
a path like that which Buddha himself is stated to have followed
before he attained illumination. These three, viz. right conduct
(*śīla*), right knowledge (*prajñā*) and right concentration
(*samādhi*) are the most important elements in the discipline. It
includes five more, and is therefore known as the Eightfold Path;
but it is not necessary to specify them here. This discipline, it
should be added, is in its entirety intended for those who enter
the order of ascetics. As in Jainism, it was less rigorous in the
case of lay disciples.


## III

We have now made a rapid survey of two stages in the history
of Buddhism, and seen how vastly they differ from each other.
One of the most noteworthy features of it in the next stage is
its spread far beyond the limits of India, to countries like China
and Japan. In those countries it has, with its emphasis on compassion, a feature which it shares with Jainism, greatly helped
the growth of beneficence. Referring to Japan in this connection,
a modern writer says that "it is still the greatest of the influences
which make for mercy among a Spartan people." The break-up
of the doctrine into numerous sects is another feature of the
same kind. We read of many sects in India itself, so that its dis-
ruption is not all to be ascribed to its coming into contact with
alien faiths in other lands. It will suffice for our purpose to draw
attention only to a broad distinction that arose in the doctrine,
viz. that between what are known as the Hīnayāna and Mahāyāna schools. Perhaps the distinction in some form is older than
the present stage. The significance of these terms is not exactly
known. They probably mean the "lower" and the "higher"

path respectively. Their chronological sequence and their precise relation to the teaching of Buddha again are undetermined. In presenting these doctrines, we shall follow mainly the account given in Indian works, particularly those by Hindu and Jaina writers. These are a few beliefs common to both the Hīnayāna and Mahāyāna forms of the creed, and we shall refer to the most striking among them before considering the two separately.

It is known as the doctrine of momentariness (*kṣaṇa-bhaṅga-vāda*), because it avers that nothing that is, lasts for longer than one instant. We have seen that, in canonical Buddhism, all things had come to be conceived as impermanent. This view is now pushed farther, and attempts are made to show that the only distinction in the history of a thing is the one between origin and destruction, and that it does not continue to be even for a single moment after birth. If a thing emerges at this instant (say), it is no more at the next. It is not possible to refer here to the elaborate arguments by which this doctrine is supported. We shall only remark that reality according to it, whether material or spiritual, is a flux or a flow (*saṁtāna*) since none in the succession of states constituting it is static. Hence all our notions of stability are illusory. "No man can step into the same stream twice," it is said, because the stream in the two moments is only similar and not identical. Objects are ever changing. Even when a thing is not changing into something *else,* it is not constant but is reproducing itself and is therefore to be regarded as a series of like forms succeeding one another perpetually as in the case of a lamp flame.

Our previous account has shown that, although Buddhism regarded reality as but an aggregate, it did not deny either external objects or the self (*sarvāsti-vāda*). It recognized both, and was therefore fully realistic in its view of knowledge. This feature survives in Hīnayāna Buddhism; but naturally it is modified in accordance with the new hypothesis of momentariness. Neither external reality, nor the self, consequently lasts longer than an instant. But everything, it is believed, may continue *as a series* for any length of time, the similarity of its several members, as already mentioned, giving rise in our mind to the illusion of sameness or identity. The flame of a lamp appears to be the same in any two moments; but really it signifies two separate states of it, which have no substantial identity. In other words, there are modifications but nothing that endures through them. Here we see the antithesis between Buddhism and Jainism which acknowledges identity as also similarity. Both doctrines accept change, but while it is partial in the one case, it is total in the other.

When we remember that Buddhism repudiates the idea of an enduring substance, we see that the self (ignoring for the moment the physical element entering into its make-up) should be conceived in it as a continuous stream of ideas. If so, it may be asked how the Buddhist can account for facts like memory, which involve reference to the past. The answer is that, when a particular idea constituting the self of a particular moment disappears, it does so after leaving its mark behind and that the self of the next moment is consequently informed by it through and through. That is, the self of a person at any instant, though not the same as it was at a previous instant, is not quite different from it. It is by this subtle, and not quite convincing, distinction that moral responsibility is maintained to belong to an individual for what he does. The criminal who is punished may not be the same person that committed the crime; but yet he merits punishment, it is argued, for, being a continuation of the criminal, he cannot be considered as another.

As regards external reality, which also is conceived as momentary, each member of the series constituting an object is called a sva-lakṣaṇa—a term which literally means "like itself" or "unique." It represents a bare particular. If it still appears as characterized in some manner, say as blue or sweet, that characteristic is purely an illusion. The predicates, which all represent universals or common features like qualities and actions, are called sāmānya-lakṣaṇas. They are really figments of the mind which appear transferred to the object—constitutives of our thought, and not of the external world on which it is directed. The contrast here again with Jainism, which regards such features as actually characterizing objects, is clear. The *sva-lakṣaṇas*, which are the ultimate basis of external reality, may be taken to stand for the data of sense like colour or taste; only we should remember that the momentary sensation is, to take particular instances, merely "blue" or "sweet" and not *something* that is qualified by "blueness" or "sweetness." The number of *sva-lakṣaṇas*, which are the ultimate facts of the outer world, is infinite. The conception of an external thing in this school accordingly is that it is a series of particulars or aggregates of them which are really devoid of all characteristics, although they appear to possess them.

## A. Pali Literature—Selections

*Translated by Henry Clarke Warren*

### SERMON NUMBER 2

*Translated from the Majjhima-Nikāya, and constituting Sutta 72:*
Thus have I heard.

On a certain occasion The Blessed One was dwelling at Sāvatthi in Jetavana monastery in Anāthapiṇḍika's Park. Then drew near Vaccha, the wandering ascetic, to where The Blessed One was; and having drawn near, he greeted The Blessed One; and having passed the compliments of friendship and civility, he sat down respectfully at one side. And seated respectfully at one side, Vaccha, the wandering ascetic, spoke to The Blessed One as follows:—

"How is it, Gotama? Does Gotama hold that the world is eternal, and that this view alone is true, and every other false?"

"Nay, Vaccha. I do not hold that the world is eternal, and that this view alone is true, and every other false."

Reprinted from Henry Clarke Warren, *Buddhism in Translations* (Harvard University Press, 1896).

"But how is it, Gotama? Does Gotama hold that the world is not eternal, and that this view alone is true, and every other false?"

"Nay, Vaccha. I do not hold that the world is not eternal, and that this view alone is true, and every other false."

"How is it, Gotama? Does Gotama hold that the world is finite, . . .

"How is it, Gotama? Does Gotama hold that the soul and the body are identical, . . .

"How is it, Gotama? Does Gotama hold that the saint exists after death, . . .

"How is it, Gotama? Does Gotama hold that the saint both exists and does not exist after death, and that this view alone is true, and every other false?"

"Nay, Vaccha. I do not hold that the saint both exists and does not exist after death, and that this view alone is true, and every other false."

"But how is it, Gotama? Does Gotama hold that the saint neither exists nor does not exist after death, and that this view alone is true, and every other false?"

"Nay, Vaccha. I do not hold that the saint neither exists nor does not exist after death, and that this view alone is true, and every other false."

"How is it, Gotama, that when you are asked, 'Does the monk Gotama hold that the world is eternal, and that this view alone is true, and every other false?' you reply, 'Nay, Vaccha. I do not hold that the world is eternal, and that this view alone is true, and every other false'?

"But how is it, Gotama, that when you are asked, 'Does the monk Gotama hold that the world is not eternal, and that this view alone is true, and every other false?' you reply, 'Nay, Vaccha. I do not hold that the world is not eternal, and that this view alone is true, and every other false'?

"How is it, Gotama, that when you are asked, 'Does Gotama hold that the world is finite, . . .'?

"How is it, Gotama, that when you are asked, 'Does Gotama hold that the soul and the body are identical, . . .'?

"How is it, Gotama, that when you are asked, 'Does Gotama hold that the saint exists after death, . . .'?

"How is it, Gotama, that when you are asked, 'Does the monk Gotama hold that the saint both exists and does not exist after death, and that this view alone is true, and every other false?' you reply, 'Nay, Vaccha. I do not hold that the saint both exists and does not exist after death, and that this view alone is true, and every other false'?

"But how is it, Gotama, that when you are asked, 'Does the monk Gotama hold that the saint neither exists nor does not exist after death, and that this view alone is true, and every other false?' you reply, 'Nay, Vaccha. I do not hold that the saint neither exists nor does not exist after death, and that this view alone is true, and every other false'? What objection does Gotama perceive to these theories that he has not adopted any one of them?"

"Vaccha, the theory that the world is eternal, is a jungle, a wilderness, a puppet-show, a writhing, and a fetter, and is coupled with misery, ruin, despair, and agony, and does not tend to aversion, absence of passion, cessation, quiescence, knowledge, supreme wisdom, and Nirvana.

. . . . . . . . . .

"Vaccha, the theory that the saint neither exists nor does not exist after death, is a jungle, a wilderness, a puppet-show, a writhing, and a fetter, and is coupled with misery, ruin, despair, and agony, and does not tend to aversion, absence of passion, cessation, quiescence, knowledge, supreme wisdom, and Nirvana.

"This is the objection I perceive to these theories, so that I have not adopted any one of them."

"But has Gotama any theory of his own?"

"The Tathāgata, O Vaccha, is free from all theories; but this, Vaccha, does The Tathāgata know,—the nature of form, and how form arises, and how form perishes; the nature of sensation, and how sensation arises, and how sensation perishes; the nature of perception, and how perception arises, and how perception perishes; the nature of the predispositions, and how the predispositions arise, and how the predispositions perish; the nature of consciousness, and how consciousness arises, and how consciousness perishes. Therefore say I that The Tathāgata has attained deliverance and is free from attachment, inasmuch as all imaginings, or agitations, or false notions concerning an Ego or anything pertaining to an Ego, have perished, have faded away, have ceased, have been given up and relinquished."

"But, Gotama, where is the priest reborn who has attained to this deliverance for his mind?"

"Vaccha, to say that he is reborn would not fit the case."

"Then, Gotama, he is not reborn."

"Vaccha, to say that he is not reborn would not fit the case."

"Then, Gotama, he is both reborn and is not reborn."

"Vaccha, to say that he is both reborn and not reborn would not fit the case."

"Then, Gotama, he is neither reborn nor not reborn."

"Vaccha, to say that he is neither reborn nor not reborn would not fit the case."

"When I say to you, 'But, Gotama, where is the priest reborn who has attained to this deliverance for his mind?' you reply, 'Vaccha, to say that he is reborn would not fit the case.' And when I say to you, 'Then, Gotama, he is not reborn,' you reply, 'Vaccha, to say that he is not reborn would not fit the case.' And when I say to you, 'Then, Gotama, he is both reborn and not reborn,' you reply, 'Vaccha, to say that he is both reborn and not reborn would not fit the case.' And when I say to you, 'Then, Gotama, he is neither reborn nor not reborn,' you reply, 'Vaccha, to say that he is neither reborn nor not reborn would not fit the case.' Gotama, I am at a loss what to think in this matter, and I have become greatly confused, and the faith in Gotama inspired by a former conversation has now disappeared."

"Enough, O Vaccha! Be not at a loss what to think in this matter, and be not greatly confused. Profound, O Vaccha, is this doctrine, recondite, and difficult of comprehension, good, excellent, and not to be reached by mere reasoning, subtile, and intelligible only to the wise; and it is a hard doctrine for you to learn, who belong to another sect, to another faith, to another persuasion, to another discipline, and sit at the feet of another teacher. Therefore, Vaccha, I will now question you, and do you make answer as may seem to you good. What think you, Vaccha? Suppose a fire were to burn in front of you, would you be aware that the fire was burning in front of you?"

"Gotama, if a fire were to burn in front of me, I should be aware that a fire was burning in front of me."

"But suppose, Vaccha, some one were to ask you, 'On what does this fire that is burning in front of you depend?' what would you answer, Vaccha?"

"Gotama, if some one were to ask me, 'On what does this fire that is burning in front of you depend?' I would answer, Gotama, 'It is on fuel of grass and wood that this fire that is burning in front of me depends.'"

"But, Vaccha, if the fire in front of you were to become extinct, would you be aware that the fire in front of you had become extinct?"

"Gotama, if the fire in front of me were to become extinct, I should be aware that the fire in front of me had become extinct."

"But, Vaccha, if some one were to ask you, 'In which direction has that fire gone,—east, or west, or north, or south?' what would you say, O Vaccha?"

"The question would not fit the case, Gotama. For the fire which depended on fuel of grass and wood, when that fuel has all gone, and it can get no other, being thus without nutriment, is said to be extinct."

"In exactly the same way, Vaccha, all form by which one could predicate the existence of the saint, all that form has been abandoned, uprooted, pulled out of the ground like a palmyra-tree, and become non-existent and not liable to spring up again in the future. The saint, O Vaccha, who has been released from what is styled form, is deep, immeasurable, unfathomable, like the mighty ocean. To say that he is reborn would not fit the case. To say that he is not reborn would not fit the case. To say that he is both reborn and not reborn would not fit the case. To say that he is neither reborn nor not reborn would not fit the case.

"All sensation . . .

"All perception . . .

"All the predispositions . . .

"All consciousness by which one could predicate the existence of the saint, all that consciousness has been abandoned, uprooted, pulled out of the ground like a palmyra-tree, and become non-existent and not liable to spring up again in the future. The saint, O Vaccha, who has been released from what is styled conscious-ness, is deep, immeasurable, unfathomable, like the mighty ocean. To say that he is reborn would not fit the case. To say that he is not reborn would not fit the case. To say that he is both reborn and not reborn would not fit the case. To say that he is neither reborn nor not reborn would not fit the case."

When The Blessed One had thus spoken, Vaccha, the wander-ing ascetic, spoke to him as follows:

"It is as if, O Gotama, there were a mighty sal-tree near to some village or town, and it were to lose its dead branches and twigs, and its loose shreds of bark, and its unsound wood, so that afterwards, free from those branches and twigs, and the loose shreds of bark, and the unsound wood, it were to stand neat and clean in its strength. In exactly the same way doth the word of Gotama, free from branches and twigs, and from loose shreds of bark, and from unsound wood, stand neat and clean in its strength. O wonderful is it, Gotama! O wonderful is it, Gotama! It is as if, O Gotama, one were to set up that which was over-turned; or were to disclose that which was hidden; or were to point out the way to a lost traveller; or were to carry a lamp into a dark place, that they who had eyes might see forms. Even so has Gotama expounded the Doctrine in many different ways. I betake myself to Gotama for refuge, to the Doctrine, and to the Congregation of the priests. Let Gotama receive me who have betaken myself to him for refuge, and accept me as a disciple from this day forth as long as life shall last."

## § 15. There Is No Ego

*Translated from the Milindapañha (25):*

Then drew near Milinda the king to where the venerable Nāgasena was; and having drawn near, he greeted the venerable
Nāgasena; and having passed the compliments of friendship and
civility, he sat down respectfully at one side. And the venerable
Nāgasena returned the greeting; by which, verily, he won the
heart of king Milinda.

And Milinda the king spoke to the venerable Nāgasena as
follows:—

"How is your reverence called? Bhante, what is your name?"

"Your majesty, I am called Nāgasena; my fellow-priests, your
majesty, address me as Nāgasena: but whether parents give one
the name Nāgasena, or Sūrasena, or Vīrasena, or Sīhasena, it is,
nevertheless, your majesty, but a way of counting, a term, an
appellation, a convenient designation, a mere name, this Nāgasena; for there is no Ego here to be found."

Then said Milinda the king,—

"Listen to me, my lords, ye five hundred Yonakas, and ye eighty
thousand priests! Nāgasena here says thus: 'There is no Ego here
to be found.' Is it possible, pray, for me to assent to what he says?"

And Milinda the king spoke to the venerable Nāgasena as
follows:—

"Bhante Nāgasena, if there is no Ego to be found, who is it
then furnishes you priests with the priestly requisites,—robes,
food, bedding, and medicine, the reliance of the sick? who is it
makes use of the same? who is it keeps the precepts? who is it
applies himself to meditation? who is it realizes the Paths, the
Fruits, and Nirvana? who is it destroys life? who is it takes what
is not given him? who is it commits immorality? who is it tells
lies? who is it drinks intoxicating liquor? who is it commits the
five crimes that constitute 'proximate karma'? In that case, there
is no merit; there is no demerit; there is no one who does or
causes to be done meritorious or demeritorious deeds; neither
good nor evil deeds can have any fruit or result. Bhante Nāga-

sena, neither is he a murderer who kills a priest, nor can you priests, bhante Nāgasena, have any teacher, preceptor, or ordination. When you say, 'My fellow-priests, your majesty, address me as Nāgasena,' what then is this Nāgasena? Pray, bhante, is the hair of the head Nāgasena?"

"Nay, verily, your majesty."

"Is the hair of the body Nāgasena?"

"Nay, verily, your majesty."

"Are nails . . . teeth . . . skin . . . flesh . . . sinews . . . bones . . . marrow of the bones . . . kidneys . . . heart . . . liver . . . pleura . . . spleen . . . lungs . . . intestines . . . mesentery . . . stomach . . . faeces . . . bile . . . phlegm . . . pus . . . blood . . . sweat . . . fat . . . tears . . . lymph . . . saliva . . . snot . . . synovial fluid . . . urine . . . brain of the head Nāgasena?"

"Nay, verily, your majesty."

"Is now, bhante, form Nāgasena?"

"Nay, verily, your majesty."

"Is sensation Nāgasena?"

"Nay, verily, your majesty."

"Is perception Nāgasena?"

"Nay, verily, your majesty."

"Are the predispositions Nāgasena?"

"Nay, verily, your majesty."

"Is consciousness Nāgasena?"

"Nay, verily, your majesty."

"Are, then, bhante, form, sensation, perception, the predispositions, and consciousness unitedly Nāgasena?"

"Nay, verily, your majesty."

"Is it, then, bhante, something besides form, sensation, perception, the predispositions, and consciousness, which is Nāgasena?"

"Nay, verily, your majesty."

"Bhante, although I question you very closely, I fail to discover any Nāgasena. Verily, now, bhante, Nāgasena is a mere empty sound. What Nāgasena is there here? Bhante, you speak a falsehood, a lie: there is no Nāgasena."

Then the venerable Nāgasena spoke to Milinda the king as follows:—

"Your majesty, you are a delicate prince, an exceedingly delicate prince; and if, your majesty, you walk in the middle of the day on hot sandy ground, and you tread on rough grit, gravel, and sand, your feet become sore, your body tired, the mind is oppressed, and the body-consciousness suffers. Pray, did you come afoot, or riding?"

"Bhante, I do not go afoot: I came in a chariot."

"Your majesty, if you came in a chariot, declare to me the chariot. Pray, your majesty, is the pole the chariot?"

"Nay, verily, bhante."

"Is the axle the chariot?"

"Nay, verily, bhante."

"Are the wheels the chariot?"

"Nay, verily, bhante."

"Is the chariot-body the chariot?"

"Nay, verily, bhante."

"Is the banner-staff the chariot?"

"Nay, verily, bhante."

"Is the yoke the chariot?"

"Nay, verily, bhante."

"Are the reins the chariot?"

"Nay, verily, bhante."

"Is the goading-stick the chariot?"

"Nay, verily, bhante."

"Pray, your majesty, are pole, axle, wheels, chariot-body, banner-staff, yoke, reins, and goad unitedly the chariot?"

"Nay, verily, bhante."

"Is it, then, your majesty, something else besides pole, axle, wheels, chariot-body, banner-staff, yoke, reins, and goad which is the chariot?"

"Nay, verily, bhante."

"Your majesty, although I question you very closely, I fail to discover any chariot. Verily now, your majesty, the word 'chariot' is a mere empty sound. What chariot is there here? Your majesty, you speak a falsehood, a lie: there is no chariot. Your majesty, you are the chief king in all the continent of India; of whom are you afraid that you speak a lie? Listen to me, my lords, ye five

hundred Yonakas, and ye eighty thousand priests! Milinda the
king here says thus: 'I came in a chariot'; and being requested,
'Your majesty, if you came in a chariot, declare to me the chariot,'
he fails to produce any chariot. Is it possible, pray, for me to
assent to what he says?"

When he had thus spoken, the five hundred Yonakas applauded the venerable Nāgasena and spoke to Milinda the king
as follows:—

"Now, your majesty, answer, if you can."

Then Milinda the king spoke to the venerable Nāgasena as
follows:—

"Bhante Nāgasena, I speak no lie: the word 'chariot' is but a
way of counting, term, appellation, convenient designation, and
name for pole, axle, wheels, chariot-body, and banner-staff."

"Thoroughly well, your majesty, do you understand a chariot.
In exactly the same way, your majesty, in respect of me, Nāgasena is but a way of counting, term, appellation, convenient designation, mere name for the hair of my head, hair of my body . . .
brain of the head, form, sensation, perception, the predispositions,
and consciousness. But in the absolute sense there is no Ego here
to be found. And the priestess Vajirā, your majesty, said as follows in the presence of The Blessed One:—

> " 'Even as the word of "chariot" means
> That members join to frame a whole;
> So when the Groups appear to view,
> We use the phrase, "A living being." ' "

"It is wonderful, bhante Nāgasena! It is marvellous, bhante
Nāgasena! Brilliant and prompt is the wit of your replies. If The
Buddha were alive, he would applaud. Well done, well done,
Nāgasena! Brilliant and prompt is the wit of your replies."

*Translated from the Visuddhi-Magga (chap. xviii):*

Just as the word "chariot" is but a mode of expression for axle,
wheels, chariot-body, pole, and other constituent members, placed
in a certain relation to each other, but when we come to examine
the members one by one, we discover that in the absolute sense

there is no chariot; and just as the word "house" is but a mode of expression for wood and other constituents of a house, surrounding space in a certain relation, but in the absolute sense there is no house; and just as the word "fist" is but a mode of expression for the fingers, the thumb, etc., in a certain relation; and the word "lute" for the body of the lute, strings, etc.; "army" for elephants, horses, etc.; "city" for fortifications, houses, gates, etc.; "tree" for trunk, branches, foliage, etc., in a certain relation, but when we come to examine the parts one by one, we discover that in the absolute sense there is no tree; in exactly the same way the words "living entity" and "Ego" are but a mode of expression for the presence of the five attachment groups, but when we come to examine the elements of being one by one, we discover that in the absolute sense there is no living entity there to form a basis for such figments as "I am," or "I"; in other words, that in the absolute sense there is only name and form. The insight of him who perceives this is called knowledge of the truth.

He, however, who abandons this knowledge of the truth and believes in a living entity must assume either that this living entity will perish or that it will not perish. If he assume that it will not perish, he falls into the heresy of the persistence of existences; or if he assume that it will perish, he falls into that of the annihilation of existences. And why do I say so? Because, just as sour cream has milk as its antecedent, so nothing here exists but what has its own antecedents. To say, "The living entity persists," is to fall short of the truth; to say, "It is annihilated," is to outrun the truth. Therefore has The Blessed One said:—

"There are two heresies, O priests, which possess both gods and men, by which some fall short of the truth, and some outrun the truth; but the intelligent know the truth.

"And how, O priests, do some fall short of the truth?

"O priests, gods and men delight in existence, take pleasure in existence, rejoice in existence, so that when the Doctrine for the cessation of existence is preached to them, their minds do not leap toward it, are not favorably disposed toward it, do not rest in it, do not adopt it.

"Thus, O priests, do some fall short of the truth.

"And how, O priests, do some outrun the truth?

"Some are distressed at, ashamed of, and loathe existence, and welcome the thought of non-existence, saying, 'See here! When they say that on the dissolution of the body this Ego is annihilated, perishes, and does not exist after death, that is good, that is excellent, that is as it should be.'

"Thus, O priests, do some outrun the truth.

"And how, O priests, do the intelligent know the truth?

"We may have, O priests, a priest who knows things as they really are, and knowing things as they really are, he is on the road to aversion for things, to absence of passion for them, and to cessation from them.

"Thus, O priests, do the intelligent know the truth."

*Translated from the Samyutta-Nikāya (xxii. 85):*

Thus have I heard.

On a certain occasion the venerable Sāriputta was dwelling at Sāvatthi in Jetavana monastery in Anāthapiṇḍika's Park.

Now at that time the following wicked heresy had sprung up in the mind of a priest named Yamaka: "Thus do I understand the doctrine taught by The Blessed One, that on the dissolution of the body the priest who has lost all depravity is annihilated, perishes, and does not exist after death."

And a number of priests heard the report: "The following wicked heresy has sprung up in the mind of a priest named Yamaka: 'Thus do I understand the doctrine taught by The Blessed One, that on the dissolution of the body the priest who has lost all depravity is annihilated, perishes, and does not exist after death.'"

Then drew near these priests to where the venerable Yamaka was; and having drawn near, they greeted the venerable Yamaka; and having passed the compliments of friendship and civility, they sat down respectfully at one side. And seated respectfully at one side, these priests spoke to the venerable Yamaka as follows: "Is the report true, brother Yamaka, that the following wicked heresy has sprung up in your mind: 'Thus do I understand the doctrine taught by The Blessed One, that on the dissolution of the body the priest who has lost all depravity is annihilated, perishes, and does not exist after death'?"

"Even so, brethren, do I understand the doctrine taught by The Blessed One, that on the dissolution of the body the saint who has lost all depravity is annihilated, perishes, and does not exist after death."

"Say not so, brother Yamaka. Do not traduce The Blessed One; for it is not well to traduce The Blessed One. The Blessed One would never say that on the dissolution of the body the saint who has lost all depravity is annihilated, perishes, and does not exist after death."

Nevertheless, in spite of all these priests could say, the venerable Yamaka persisted obstinately to adhere to his pestiferous delusion: "Thus do I understand the doctrine taught by The Blessed One, that on the dissolution of the body the priest who has lost all depravity is annihilated, perishes, and does not exist after death."

And when these priests found themselves unable to detach the venerable Yamaka from this wicked heresy, then these priests arose from their seats and drew near to where the venerable Sāriputta was. And having drawn near they spoke to the venerable Sāriputta as follows:—

"Brother Sāriputta, the following wicked heresy has sprung up in the mind of a priest named Yamaka: 'Thus do I understand the doctrine taught by The Blessed One, that on the dissolution of the body the priest who has lost all depravity is annihilated, perishes, and does not exist after death.' Pray, let the venerable Sāriputta be so kind as to draw near to where the priest Yamaka is."

And the venerable Sāriputta consented by his silence.

Then the venerable Sāriputta in the evening of the day arose from meditation, and drew near to where the venerable Yamaka was; and having drawn near, he greeted the venerable Yamaka; and having passed the compliments of friendship and civility, he sat down respectfully at one side. And seated respectfully at one side, the venerable Sāriputta spoke to the venerable Yamaka as follows: "Is the report true, brother Yamaka, that the following wicked heresy has sprung up in your mind: 'Thus do I understand the doctrine taught by The Blessed One, that on the dissolution of the body the priest who has lost all depravity is annihilated, perishes, and does not exist after death'?"

"Even so, brother, do I understand the doctrine taught by The Blessed One, that on the dissolution of the body the priest who has lost all depravity is annihilated, perishes, and does not exist after death."

"What think you, brother Yamaka? Is form permanent, or transitory?"

"It is transitory, brother."

"And that which is transitory—is it evil, or is it good?"

"It is evil, brother."

"And that which is transitory, evil, and liable to change—is it possible to say of it: 'This is mine; this am I; this is my Ego'?"

"Nay, verily, brother."

"Is sensation . . . perception . . . the predispositions . . . consciousness, permanent or transitory?"

"It is transitory, brother."

"And that which is transitory—is it evil, or is it good?"

"It is evil, brother."

"And that which is transitory, evil, and liable to change—is it possible to say of it: 'This is mine; this am I; this is my Ego'?"

"Nay, verily, brother."

"Accordingly, brother Yamaka, as respects all form whatsoever, past, future, or present, be it subjective or existing outside, gross or subtile, mean or exalted, far or near, the correct view in the light of the highest knowledge is as follows: 'This is not mine; this am I not; this is not my Ego.'

"As respects all sensation whatsoever, . . . as respects all perception whatsoever, . . . as respects all predispositions whatsoever, . . . as respects all consciousness whatsoever, past, future, or present, be it subjective or existing outside, gross or subtile, mean or exalted, far or near, the correct view in the light of the highest knowledge is as follows: 'This is not mine; this am I not; this is not my Ego.'

"Perceiving this, brother Yamaka, the learned and noble disciple conceives an aversion for form, conceives an aversion for sensation, conceives an aversion for perception, conceives an aversion for the predispositions, conceives an aversion for consciousness. And in conceiving this aversion he becomes divested of passion, and by the absence of passion he becomes free, and when he is free he becomes aware that he is free; and he knows that rebirth is exhausted, that he has lived the holy life, that he has done what it behooved him to do, and that he is no more for this world.

"What think you, brother Yamaka? Do you consider form as the saint?"

"Nay, verily, brother."

"Do you consider sensation . . . perception . . . the predispositions . . . consciousness as the saint?"

"Nay, verily, brother."

"What think you, brother Yamaka? Do you consider the saint as comprised in form?"

"Nay, verily, brother."

"Do you consider the saint as distinct from form?"

"Nay, verily, brother."

"Do you consider the saint as comprised in sensation? . . . as distinct from sensation? . . . as comprised in perception? . . . as distinct from perception? . . . as comprised in the predispositions? . . . as distinct from the predispositions? . . . as comprised in consciousness?"

"Nay, verily, brother."

"Do you consider the saint as distinct from consciousness?"

"Nay, verily, brother."

"What think you, brother Yamaka? Are form, sensation, perception, the predispositions, and consciousness unitedly the saint?"

"Nay, verily, brother."

"What think you, brother Yamaka? Do you consider the saint as a something having no form, sensation, perception, predispositions, or consciousness?"

"Nay, verily, brother."

"Considering now, brother Yamaka, that you fail to make out and establish the existence of the saint in the present life, is it reasonable for you to say: 'Thus do I understand the doctrine taught by The Blessed One, that on the dissolution of the body the priest who has lost all depravity is annihilated, perishes, and does not exist after death'?"

"Brother Sāriputta, it was because of my ignorance that I held this wicked heresy; but now that I have listened to the doctrinal instruction of the venerable Sāriputta, I have abandoned that wicked heresy and acquired the true doctrine."

"But if others were to ask you, brother Yamaka, as follows: 'Brother Yamaka, the priest who is a saint and has lost all depravity, what becomes of him on the dissolution of the body, after death?' what would you reply, brother Yamaka, if you were asked that question?"

"Brother, if others were to ask me as follows: 'Brother Yamaka, the priest who is a saint and has lost all depravity, what becomes of him on the dissolution of the body, after death?' I would reply, brother, as follows, if I were asked that question: 'Brethren, the form was transitory, and that which was transitory was evil, and that which was evil has ceased and disappeared. The sensation ... perception ... predispositions ... consciousness was transitory, and that which was transitory was evil, and that which was evil has ceased and disappeared.' Thus would I reply, brother, if I were asked that question."

"Well said! well said! brother Yamaka. Come now, brother Yamaka, I will give you an illustration that you may still better comprehend this matter.

"Suppose, brother Yamaka, there were a householder, or a son of a householder, rich, wealthy, and affluent, and thoroughly well guarded, and some man were to become unfriendly, inimical, and hostile to him, and were to wish to kill him. And suppose it were to occur to this man as follows: 'This householder, or son of a householder, is rich, wealthy, and affluent, and thoroughly well-guarded. It would not be easy to kill him by violence. What if now I were to ingratiate myself with him and then kill him.'

And suppose he were to draw near to that householder, or son of a householder, and say as follows: 'Lord, I would fain enter your service.' And suppose the householder, or son of a householder, were to admit him into his service; and the man were to be his servant, rising before him and retiring after him, willing and obliging and pleasant-spoken. And suppose the householder, or son of a householder, were to treat him as a friend, were to treat him as a comrade, and repose confidence in him. And suppose then, brother, that when that man judged that the householder, or son of a householder, had acquired thorough confidence in him, he were to get him into some secluded spot and kill him with a sharp weapon.

"What think you, brother Yamaka? When that man drew near to that householder, or son of a householder, and said as follows: 'Lord, I would fain enter your service,' was he not a murderer, though not recognized as such?

"And also when he was his servant, rising before him and retiring after him, willing and obliging and pleasant-spoken, was he not a murderer, though not recognized as such?

"And also when he got him into a secluded spot and killed him with a sharp weapon, was he not a murderer, though not recognized as such?"

"Even so, brother."

"In exactly the same way, brother, the ignorant, unconverted man, who is not a follower of noble disciples, not conversant with the Noble Doctrine, not disciplined in the Noble Doctrine, not a follower of good people, not conversant with the Doctrine held by good people, not trained in the Doctrine held by good people, not disciplined in the Doctrine held by good people, considers form in the light of an Ego—either the Ego as possessing form, or form as comprised in the Ego, or the Ego as comprised in form. Considers sensation . . . perception . . . the predispositions . . . consciousness in the light of an Ego—either the Ego as possessing consciousness, or consciousness as comprised in the Ego, or the Ego as comprised in consciousness.

"He does not recognize the fact that form is transitory. He

does not recognize the fact that sensation . . . perception . . . the predispositions . . . consciousness is transitory.

"He does not recognize the fact that form . . . sensation . . . perception . . . the predispositions . . . consciousness is evil.

"He does not recognize the fact that form . . . sensation . . . perception . . . the predispositions . . . consciousness is not an Ego.

"He does not recognize the fact that form . . . sensation . . . perception . . . the predispositions . . . consciousness is due to causes.

"He does not recognize the fact that form . . . sensation . . . perception . . . the predispositions . . . consciousness is a murderer.

"And he seeks after form, attaches himself to it, and makes the affirmation that it is his Ego. And he seeks after sensation, . . . perception, . . . the predispositions, . . . consciousness, attaches himself to it, and makes the affirmation that it is his Ego. And these five attachment-groups, sought after and become attached, long inure to his detriment and misery.

"But the learned and noble disciple, brother, who is a follower of noble disciples, conversant with the Noble Doctrine, disciplined in the Noble Doctrine, a follower of good people, conversant with the Doctrine held by good people, disciplined in the Doctrine held by good people, does not consider form in the light of an Ego—neither the Ego as possessing form, nor form as comprised in the Ego, nor the Ego as comprised in form. Does not consider sensation . . . perception . . . the predispositions . . . consciousness in the light of an Ego—neither the Ego as possessing consciousness, nor consciousness as comprised in the Ego, nor the Ego as comprised in consciousness.

"He recognizes the fact that form . . . sensation . . . perception . . . the predispositions . . . consciousness is transitory.

"He recognizes the fact that form . . . sensation . . . perception . . . the predispositions . . . consciousness is evil.

"He recognizes the fact that form . . . sensation . . . perception . . . the predispositions . . . consciousness is not an Ego.

"He recognizes the fact that form . . . sensation . . . perception . . . the predispositions . . . consciousness is due to causes.

"He recognizes the fact that form . . . sensation . . . perception . . . the predispositions . . . consciousness is a murderer.

"And he does not seek after form, . . . sensation, . . . perception, . . . the predispositions, . . . consciousness, nor attach himself to it, nor make the affirmation that it is his Ego. And these five attachment-groups, not sought after and not become attached, long inure to his welfare and happiness."

"Even so, brother Sāriputta, is it with those venerable persons who have for co-religionists such compassionate and benevolent exhorters and instructors as you. And now that I have listened to the doctrinal instruction of the venerable Sāriputta my mind has lost all attachment and become released from the depravities."

Thus spake the venerable Sāriputta, and, delighted, the venerable Yamaka applauded the speech of the venerable Sāriputta.

## THE ORIGIN AND CESSATION OF THE HUMAN BEING

*Translated from the Saṁyutta-Nikāya (xxii. 22):*

Thus have I heard.

On a certain occasion The Blessed One was dwelling at Sāvatthi in Jetavana monastery in Anāthapiṇḍika's Park. And there The Blessed One addressed the priests.

"Priests," said he.

"Lord," said the priests to The Blessed One in reply.

And The Blessed One spoke as follows:—

"I will teach you, O priests, the burden, the bearer of the burden, the taking up of the burden, and the laying down of the burden.

"And what, O priests, is the burden?

"Reply should be made that it is the five attachment-groups. And what are the five? They are: the form-attachment-group, the sensation-attachment-group, the perception-attachment-group, the predisposition-attachment-group, the consciousness-attachment-group. These, O priests, are called the burden.

"And who, O priests, is the bearer of the burden?

"Reply should be made that it is the individual; the venerable

So-and-so of such-and-such a family. He, O priests, is called the
bearer of the burden.

"And what, O priests, is the taking up of the burden?"

"It is desire leading to rebirth, joining itself to pleasure and
passion, and finding delight in every existence,—desire, namely,
for sensual pleasure, desire for permanent existence, desire for
transitory existence. This, O priests, is called the taking up of
the burden.

"And what, O priests, is the laying down of the burden?"

"It is the complete absence of passion, the cessation, giving up,
relinquishment, forsaking, and non-adoption of desire. This, O
priests, is called the laying down of the burden."

Thus spake The Blessed One; and when The Happy One had
so spoken, The Teacher afterwards spoke as follows:—

> "The five groups form the heavy load,
> And man this heavy load doth bear;
> This load 't is misery to take up,
> The laying down thereof is bliss.

> "He who this heavy load lays down,
> Nor any other taketh up,
> By extirpating all desire
> Shall hunger lose, Nirvana gain."

*Translated from the Saṁyutta-Nikāya (xxii. 53):*
Thus have I heard.

On a certain occasion The Blessed One was dwelling at Sāvatthi in Jetavana monastery in Anāthapiṇḍika's Park. And there
The Blessed One addressed the priests.

"Priests," said he.

"Lord," said the priests to The Blessed One in reply.

And The Blessed One spoke as follows:—

"Not to seek for anything, O priests, is to be free; to seek for
anything is not to be free.

"If consciousness abide, O priests, it is because of a seeking for
form that it abides, and supported by form, and resting in form,

and taking delight therein, it attains to growth, increase, and development. When consciousness abides, O priests, it is because of a seeking for sensation, . . . perception, . . . the predispositions, that it abides, and supported by the predispositions, and resting in the predispositions, and taking delight therein, it attains to growth, increase, and development.

"It is impossible, O priests, for any one to say that he can declare either the coming, or the going, or the passing out of an existence, or the springing up into an existence, or the growth, or the increase, or the development of consciousness apart from form, apart from sensation, apart from perception, apart from the predispositions.

"If passion for form, O priests, is abandoned, then through the abandonment of passion the support is cut off, and there is no resting-place for consciousness. If passion for sensation, . . . for perception, . . . for the predispositions is abandoned, then through the abandonment of passion the support is cut off, and there is no resting-place for consciousness.

"When that consciousness has no resting-place, does not increase, and no longer accumulates karma, it becomes free; and when it is free, it becomes quiet; and when it is quiet, it is blissful; and when it is blissful, it is not agitated; and when it is not agitated, it attains Nirvana in its own person; and it knows that rebirth is exhausted, that it has lived the holy life, that it has done what it behooved it to do, and that it is no more for this world."

*Translated from the Samyutta-Nikāya (xxii. 112):*
Thus have I heard.

On a certain occasion The Blessed One was dwelling at Sāvatthi in Jetavana monastery in Anāthapiṇḍika's Park. And there The Blessed One addressed the priests.

"Priests," said he.

"Lord," said the priests to The Blessed One in reply.

And The Blessed One spoke as follows:—

"O priests, abandon all wish, passion, delight, desire, seeking, attachment, mental affirmation, proclivity, and prejudice in re-

spect of form. Thus will form be abandoned, uprooted, pulled
out of the ground like a palmyra-tree, and become non-existent
and not liable to spring up again in the future.

"Abandon all wish, passion, delight, desire, seeking, attachment, mental affirmation, proclivity, and prejudice in respect of
sensation, . . . perception, . . . the predispositions, . . . consciousness. Thus will consciousness be abandoned, uprooted, pulled out
of the ground like a palmyra-tree, and become non-existent and
not liable to spring up again in the future."

*Translated from the Saṁyutta-Nikāya (i.6):*

> What is it causeth man to be?
> What has he, will not be controlled?
> Who are they that rebirth endure?
> From what can respite ne'er be found?
>
> Desire causeth man to be.
> Man's thoughts refuse to be controlled.
> All sentient life rebirth endures.
> From misery no release is found.

## THE MIDDLE DOCTRINE

*Translated from the Saṁyutta-Nikāya (xxii. 90):*

The world, for the most part, O Kaccāna, holds either to a
belief in being or to a belief in non-being. But for one who in the
light of the highest knowledge, O Kaccāna, considers how the
world arises, belief in the non-being of the world passes away.
And for one who in the light of the highest knowledge, O Kaccāna, considers how the world ceases, belief in the being of the
world passes away. The world, O Kaccāna, is for the most part
bound up in a seeking, attachment, and proclivity [for the
groups], but a priest does not sympathize with this seeking and
attachment, nor with the mental affirmation, proclivity, and prejudice which affirms an Ego. He does not doubt or question that
it is only evil that springs into existence, and only evil that ceases
from existence, and his conviction of this fact is dependent on no

one besides himself. This, O Kaccāna, is what constitutes Right Belief.

That things have being, O Kaccāna, constitutes one extreme of doctrine; that things have no being is the other extreme. These extremes, O Kaccāna, have been avoided by The Tathāgata, and it is a middle doctrine he teaches:—

On ignorance depends karma;
On karma depends consciousness;
On consciousness depend name and form;
On name and form depend the six organs of sense;
On the six organs of sense depends contact;
On contact depends sensation;
On sensation depends desire;
On desire depends attachment;
On attachment depends existence;
On existence depends birth;
On birth depend old age and death, sorrow, lamentation, misery, grief, and despair. Thus does this entire aggregation of misery arise.

But on the complete fading out and cessation of ignorance ceases karma;
On the cessation of karma ceases consciousness;
On the cessation of consciousness cease name and form;
On the cessation of name and form cease the six organs of sense;
On the cessation of the six organs of sense ceases contact;
On the cessation of contact ceases sensation;
On the cessation of sensation ceases desire;
On the cessation of desire ceases attachment;
On the cessation of attachment ceases existence;
On the cessation of existence ceases birth;
On the cessation of birth cease old age and death, sorrow, lamentation, misery, grief, and despair. Thus does this entire aggregation of misery cease.

### IGNORANCE

*Translated from the Visuddhi-Magga (chap. xvii.):*

According to the Sutta-Piṭaka, ignorance is want of knowledge concerning four matters, namely, misery etc.; according to the

Abhidhamma-Piṭaka, concerning eight, namely, in addition to the above, anteriority etc.

For it has been said as follows:

"What is ignorance? Want of knowledge concerning misery, want of knowledge concerning the origin of misery, want of knowledge concerning the cessation of misery, want of knowledge concerning the path leading to the cessation of misery, want of knowledge concerning anteriority, want of knowledge concerning posteriority, want of knowledge concerning anteriority and posteriority, want of knowledge concerning definite dependence and of the elements of being sprung from dependence."

In the above quotation ignorance is only considered in its aspect as a concealer of the verities cited, although, except in the case of the two transcendent truths [*i.e.* the truth concerning the cessation of misery and the truth concerning the path leading to the cessation of misery], it also comes into being with reference to objects of sense. Having come into being, it conceals the truth concerning misery, and does not allow of the comprehension of its essential elements and characteristics, as also it conceals the origin of misery, the cessation of misery, the path, the five groups of the past, otherwise called anteriority, the five groups of the future otherwise called posteriority, both sets of groups otherwise called anteriority and posteriority, and both definite dependence and the elements of being sprung from dependence, and does not allow of the comprehension of their essential elements and characteristics, so that one can discriminate and say, "This is ignorance; this is karma," and so on. Thus is it said to be "want of knowledge concerning misery, . . . want of knowledge concerning both definite dependence and the elements of being sprung from dependence."

*Translated from the Visuddhi-Magga (chap. xvii.):*

But why is ignorance put at the beginning? Is it because ignorance, like the *natura naturans* of the Sankhya philosophers, is the causeless primary cause of the world? It is not causeless. For in the quotation, "On the arising of the depravities depends the arising of ignorance," the cause of ignorance is declared. But there is an occasion when ignorance may be said to be a primary cause. What is that occasion? When it is made the starting-point of a discourse concerning the round of rebirth.

For The Blessed One in his discourses on the round of rebirth was accustomed to choose from Dependent Origination two of the factors of being as his starting-points: either, on the one hand, ignorance, as when he says, "As I have told you, O priests, the first beginning of ignorance cannot be discerned, nor can one say, 'Before a given point of time there was no ignorance, it came into being afterwards.' Nevertheless, O priests, it can be discerned that ignorance possesses a definite dependence"; or, on the other hand, desire for existence, as when he says, "As I have told you, O priests, the first beginning of desire for existence cannot be discerned, nor can one say, 'Before a given point of time there was no desire for existence, it came into being afterwards.' Nevertheless, O priests, it can be discerned that desire for existence possesses a definite dependence."

But why was The Blessed One in his discourses on the round of rebirth accustomed to choose these two factors of being as his starting-points? Because they constitute the difference between the karma which conducts to blissful states of existence and the karma which conducts to unhappy states of existence. For the cause of the karma which conducts to unhappy states of existence is ignorance. And why do I say so? Because, just as a cow about to be slaughtered, overcome by weariness due to fiery heat and to blows of the stick, will, as the result of that exhaustion, drink water that is hot, although it is unpleasant and does her harm; so the unconverted man, overcome by ignorance, will take life and perform many other kinds of karma which conduct to unhappy states of existence, although such karma is unpleasant on account of the fiery heat of the corruptions, and does him harm by casting him into unhappy states of existence.

But the cause of the karma which conducts to blissful states of existence is desire for existence. And why do I say so? Because, just as the cow described above will thirstily drink cold water, and the drink will be pleasant to her and remove her weariness; so the unconverted man, overcome by desire for existence, ridding himself of the fiery heat of the corruptions, will cease from taking life and perform many other kinds of karma which conduct to blissful states of existence, and such karma will be pleasant, as it conducts to blissful states of existence and removes the weariness of the misery of unhappy states of existence.

Now in his discourses on the round of rebirth The Blessed One sometimes sets out from only one of these factors, as when he says, "Thus, O priests, ignorance causes karma; karma causes consciousness," etc.; or, "When a man lives, O priests, absorbed in the fascinations of objects of attachment, then does desire increase, and on desire depends attachment," etc.; sometimes from both, as when he says, "O priests, it is because the fool is blinded by ignorance and joined to desire that thus his body has come to be. Such is the origin not merely of one's own body, but also of name and form existing outside. Verily it is in dependence on these two, ignorance and desire, that arise contact and the six organs of sense, and that the fool experiences happiness and misery," etc.

*Translated from the Visuddhi-Magga (chap. xvii.):*

Whereas, however, sorrow etc. are mentioned last, they constitute the fruition of the ignorance mentioned in the Wheel of Existence's opening phrase, "On ignorance depends karma." And it is to be understood that this Wheel of Existence constantly and continuously rolls onward, without known beginning, without a personal cause or passive recipient and empty with a twelvefold emptiness.

If it be asked: How do sorrow etc. constitute the fruition of ignorance? How is the Wheel of Existence without known beginning? How is it without a personal cause or passive recipient? How is it empty with a twelvefold emptiness?—we reply:—

Of him who is not free from ignorance there is sorrow, grief, and despair, and of him who is infatuated there is lamentation. Thus it is when sorrow etc. have ripened that ignorance attains to fruition.

Moreover, it has been said, "Ignorance springs from the depravities." Sorrow etc. also spring from the depravities. And how? Sorrow springs from the depravity of sensual pleasures as soon as the object of sensual desire is removed. As it is said:

> "The man who lives for sensual joys,
> And findeth his delight therein,
> When joys of sense have taken flight,
> Doth smart as if with arrows pierced."

And as it is said:

> "From sensual pleasure sorrow springs."

Also sorrow etc. all spring from the depravity of heresy. As it is said:
"When he has become possessed with the notion, 'I am form; form belongs to the I,' then through the changing and alteration of form arise sorrow, misery, grief, and despair."

And just as they spring from the depravity of heresy, so also do they spring from the depravity of desire for existence, as occurs in the case of the gods when frightened by the fear of death on perceiving the five omens. As it is said:
"Also the gods long-lived, handsome, and dwelling long ages in lofty palaces in a plentitude of bliss, they also on hearing the doctrinal instruction of The Tathāgata become afraid, alarmed, and agitated."

And just as they spring from the depravity of desire for existence, so also do they spring from the depravity of ignorance. As it is said:
"The foolish man, O priests, experiences even in the present life a threefold misery and grief."

Thus, inasmuch as sorrow etc. spring from the depravities, therefore in ripening they accomplish the fruition of the depravities, which are the causes of ignorance. Thus it is when the depravities have ripened that ignorance attains to fruition, as it is one of them.

After this manner, therefore, is to be understood the clause: *Ignorance attains to fruition in sorrow etc.*

Inasmuch, however, as when ignorance has thus attained to fruition in sorrow etc., as being one of their causes, there is then no end to the succession of cause and effect, "On ignorance depends karma; on karma depends consciousness," etc.; therefore we have a twelve-membered Wheel of Existence without known beginning, continuing to exist by virtue of a concatenation of cause and effect.

If it be objected—"In that case it is contradictory to say, 'On ignorance depends karma,' and to call this the beginning,"—we reply—"This is not the beginning; this merely enunciates the chief of the elements of being." For ignorance is chief in the three rounds. For when the fool seizes hold of it, then the rounds of corruption, of karma, and of the fruition of karma, coil themselves about him; just as when a man seizes the head of a serpent all the rest of the body coils itself about his arm. But when the annihilation of ignorance has been effected, deliverance is thereby gained; just as when the serpent's head has been cut off the arm becomes delivered of the coils. As it is said:

"On the complete fading out and cessation of ignorance ceases karma"; and so forth.

Thus, inasmuch as ignorance is the imprisonment of him who seizes it, and the deliverance of him who lets it go, it is the chief but not the beginning.

Thus is to be understood the clause: *The Wheel of Existence is without known beginning.*

Now inasmuch as the factors of being, karma etc., exist by reason of their own causes, ignorance etc., therefore is this same Wheel of Existence wanting in any other cause for the round of rebirth, such as Brahma etc., conceived of under the names of Brahma, Great Brahma, The Chief, The Victorious One, and is also wanting in any Ego passively recipient of happiness and misery, conceived of as "This I that talks and feels." Thus is to be understood the phrase: *Without a personal cause or passive recipient.*

Inasmuch, however, as ignorance is empty of stability from being subject to a coming into existence and a disappearing from existence, and is empty of loveliness from being corrupted and one of the corruptions, and is empty of happiness from being harassed by coming into existence and disappearing from existence, and is empty of a self-determining Ego from being subject to dependence,—and similarly with reference to karma and the remaining terms; or, in other words, inasmuch as ignorance is not an Ego, belongs to no Ego, is comprised in no Ego, possesses no Ego, and similarly with reference to karma and the rest,—therefore is it to be understood of the Wheel of Existence that it is *empty with a twelvefold emptiness.*

When he has learned this, he next perceives that ignorance and desire are its root; that the past etc. are its three times; and that these contain two, eight, and two members respectively.

Respecting this Wheel of Existence it is to be understood that the two factors *ignorance and desire are its root;* and that this root is twofold: the root ignorance, deriving from the past and ending with sensation; and the root desire, continuing into the future and ending with old age and death. Here the first of these two roots is specified with reference to him who is inclined to heresy, the latter with reference to him who is inclined to desire. For the ignorance of those who are inclined to heresy, and the desire of those who are inclined to desire, conduct to the round of rebirth. Or again, the first is designed to destroy the heresy of the annihilation of existences, by showing that the causes for the springing up of fruit are never annihilated; the second to destroy the heresy of the persistence of existences, by showing that those causes which have sprung up are subject to old age and death. Or again, the first is to show the gradual coming into existence of such beings as are born from the womb, the latter the instantaneous coming into complete existence of apparitional existences.

The past, the present, and the future *are its three times.* As touching the question which those members are which are stated by the text to occur in each of these *respectively,*—ignorance and karma are the *two* which belong to past time; those which belong to present time are the *eight* which begin with consciousness and end with existence; while birth and old-age-and-death are the *two* which belong to future time.

Again it is to be understood that this Wheel of Existence has three connections of cause and effect and of cause and a predecessor: that it has four divisions, twenty component spokes, three rounds, and incessantly revolves.

Here between karma and rebirth-consciousness is one connection of cause and effect; between sensation and desire is a connection of effect and cause; and between existence and birth a connection of cause and effect. Thus is to be understood the phrase *this Wheel of Existence has three connections of cause and effect and of cause and a predecessor.*

Its four divisions begin and end at these connections, namely: ignorance and karma form one division; consciousness, name-and-form, the six organs of sense, contact, and sensation, the second; desire, attachment, and existence, the third; birth and old age, the fourth. Thus is to be understood the statement that this Wheel of Existence *has four divisions.*

> Five causes are there in the past
> And five fruitions now at hand.
> Five causes are there now at hand
> And five fruitions yet to come.

With these twenty spokes called component is to be understood that it has twenty component spokes. Of the causes mentioned in the phrase *five causes are there in the past,* two, ignorance and karma, have been mentioned above; but inasmuch as the ignorant man has strong desires and having strong desires attaches himself, and on attachment depends existence, therefore desire, attachment, and existence are also included. Therefore has it been said,

"In a former-karma-existence, infatuation-ignorance, initiatory karma, longing desire, approximating attachment, and thought-existence, these five factors were the dependence for conception into this existence."

Here by the phrase *in a former-karma-existence* is meant a former karma-existence; the sense is a karma-existence taking place in a previous birth.

*Infatuation-ignorance* means the ignorance belonging to that previous birth which consists of infatuation in respect of the truths concerning misery etc., under the influence of which the infatuated man produces karma.

*Initiatory karma* consists of the antecedent thoughts of the one who performs that karma, as for instance the antecedent thoughts of him who gets ready objects to give away in alms, in order that he may give them away a month or a year later. The thoughts, however, of him who places a gift in the hands of a recipient is thought-existence. Or again, thought in the six swiftnesses containing one contemplation is initiatory karma. The seventh thought is existence. Or again, any thought is existence; the conjoined thought is initiatory karma.

*Longing desire* is that desire on the part of him who performs karma which consists in a longing or aspiration for its fruition in a rebirth-existence.

*Approximating attachment:*—This attachment is any approximating, seizing hold of, or affectation that has become the dependence of karma-existence, as, for instance, "This action will yield sensual pleasure in such and such a grade of being"; or again, "I shall be annihilated."

*Thought-existence* is thought-existence as explained at the end of Initiatory Karma. Thus are these expressions to be understood.

Now as to the phrase, *and five fruitions now at hand,* these are the five beginning with consciousness and ending with sensation. As it has been said,

"Rebirth-consciousness, the descent of name and form, the sensitiveness of the organs of sense, the contact experienced, the sensation felt, these five factors belonging to the originating-existence of the present time depend on the karma of a previous existence."

Here by *rebirth-consciousness* is meant the consciousness called rebirth, inasmuch as it springs into being by a process of rebirth into another existence.

*The descent of name and form* consists in the descent of the elements of being into the womb not only of those with form but also of those without, as it were, their coming and entering.

*The sensitiveness of the senses:*—By this are meant the five organs of sense, eye etc.

*The contact experienced:*—The contact which arises from contact experienced when in contact with an object of sense.

*The sensation felt* consists in the fruition-sensation that springs into being in company with either the rebirth-consciousness or the contact which depends on the six organs of sense. Thus are these expressions to be understood.

*Five causes are there now at hand:*—These are desire, attachment, and existence as mentioned in the text above; but when existence has been obtained, then karma, either that which is antecedent to existence or conjoined with it, is included; and that ignorance which, in the taking up of desire and attachment, is conjoined with these two factors, or that whereby the infatuated man performs karma, that also is included. Thus there are five.

Therefore has it been said,

"When the senses have matured, then infatuation-ignorance, initiatory karma, longing desire, approximating attachment, and thought-existence, these five factors of a present karma-existence are the dependence of rebirth in the future."

Here by the phrase *when the senses have matured* is shown the infatuation which occurs at the time of the performance of karma in the case of one who has his senses matured. The meaning of the rest is plain.

By *five fruitions yet to come* are meant the five, consciousness etc. These are all included in speaking of birth; and old age and death are the old age and death of them alone. Therefore has it been said,

"The rebirth-consciousness, the descent of name and form, the sensitiveness of the organs of sense, the contact experienced, the sensation felt, these five factors belonging to the originating-existence of a future life depend on the karma performed in this one."

After this manner, therefore, has this Wheel of Existence *twenty component spokes.*

*And incessantly revolves:*—Here it is to be understood that karma and existence form the round of karma; ignorance, desire, and attachment form the round of the corruptions; and consciousness, name and form, the six organs of sense, contact, and sensation form the round of fruition. And it is through these three that this Wheel of Existence is said to have three rounds; and as long as the round of corruptions is uninterrupted, because its dependence has not been cut off, the Wheel of Existence is *incessant;* and inasmuch as it turns over and over again, it *revolves.*

## ATTACHMENT

*Translated from the Visuddhi-Magga (chap. xvii.):*
In the proposition, *On desire depends attachment,*

> Attachments are in number four:
> Whose definition various,
> Their short description, and their long,
> And sequence must one seek to show.

The following is the *showing:*—

The following are the *four attachments;* the attachment of sensual pleasure, the attachment of heresy, the attachment of fanatical conduct, the attachment of the assertion of an Ego.

The following is the *definition various.*

The attachment of sensual pleasure is attachment with some form of sensual pleasure as its object. Or, again, it is the attachment of sensual pleasure because it is at the same time attachment and sensual pleasure. The word attachment means a tenacious grasp. The syllables *u-pa* strengthen the word, just as in *upāyāsa, upakkuṭṭha,* etc.

In like manner the attachment of heresy is heresy and attachment; or it is attachment to some form of heresy, whether concerning the past or the future, as when one says, "The Ego and the world are persistent," etc.

In like manner the attachment of fanatical conduct is attach-

ment to some mode of fanatical conduct; or it is attachment and
fanatical conduct. Cattle-conduct, cattle-behavior, and the like
are attachments because they involve the belief that thus purity
can be obtained.

In like manner assertion is what people assert; attachment is
that by which they attach themselves. What do they assert? and
to what do they attach themselves? The Ego. The attachment of
the assertion of an Ego is the attachment to the assertion of an
Ego, or it is the simple assertion of an Ego. The attachment of
the assertion of an Ego is when people attach themselves by the
assertion of an Ego.

The above, then, is the *definition various.*
*Their short description, and their long.*
First in regard to the attachment of sensual pleasure.

"What is the attachment of sensual pleasure? Sensual craving,
sensual passion, sensual delight, sensual desire, sensual affection,
sensual torment, sensual infatuation, sensual cleaving, this is
called the attachment of sensual pleasure." In short, in this quotation, attachment is described as tenacity of desire. Tenacious
desire is when an earlier desire has become tenacious by the
proximate dependence. Some, however, say, "Desire is the quest
of an object before it is obtained, as when a robber gropes about
in the dark; attachment is the seizing hold of an object within
reach, as when the robber gets hold of his booty. And both are
inimical to moderation and contentment and are the roots out of
which grow seeking and guarding.

The short description of the other three attachments is that
they are heresy.

In their long description, however, the attachment of sensual
pleasure is tenacity of the aforesaid one-hundred-and-eight-fold
desire for forms and other objects of sense.

The attachment of heresy consists of heretical views regarding
ten different subjects.

"What is the attachment of heresy? 'There is no such thing as
a gift, a sacrifice, an offering, a fruition or result of good or evil
deeds, a present life, a future life, a mother, a father, apparitional

existence, or any monk or Brahman having found the right road and correct line of conduct who can proclaim of his own knowledge and perception either this world or the next!' any such heresy, heretical belief, heretical jungle, heretical wilderness, heretical puppet-show, heretical writhing, heretical fetter, figment, notion, persuasion, affectation, byway, false way, falsity, schismatic doctrine, or error is called the attachment of heresy."

The heresy of fanatical conduct is the affectation of the belief that purity is by fanatical conduct. As it is said:

"What is the attachment of fanatical conduct? Purity is by conduct; purity is by fanaticism; purity is by fanatical conduct, —any such heresy, heretical belief, heretical jungle, heretical wilderness, heretical puppet-show, heretical writhing, heretical fetter, figment, notion, persuasion, affectation, byway, false way, falsity, schismatic doctrine, or error is called the attachment of fanatical conduct."

The attachment of the assertion of an Ego is the twentyfold heresy of individuality. As it is said:

"What is the heresy of the assertion of an Ego? Here an ignorant, unconverted man, who is not a follower of noble disciples, not conversant with the Noble Doctrine, not disciplined in the Noble Doctrine, not a follower of good people, not conversant with the doctrine held by good people, not disciplined in the doctrine of good people, considers form in the light of an Ego—either the Ego as possessing form, or form as comprised in the Ego, or the Ego as comprised in form; considers sensation . . . perception . . . the predispositions . . . consciousness as the Ego, or the Ego as possessing consciousness, or consciousness as comprised in the Ego, or the Ego as comprised in consciousness,—any such heresy, heretical belief, heretical jungle, heretical wilderness, heretical puppet-show, heretical writhing, heretical fetter, figment, notion, persuasion, affectation, byway, false way, falsity, schismatic doctrine, or error is called the attachment of the assertion of the Ego."

The above is *their short description, and their long.*

*And sequence:*—That sequence is threefold; sequence in originating, sequence in abandoning, sequence in teaching.

Now, as the round of rebirth is without known beginning and it is impossible to say which corruption first arises, no absolute order of sequence can be laid down; but in any particular existence the order most commonly followed is for the heresy of the assertion of an Ego to come first and be followed by a heretical belief either in the persistence of existences or in their annihilation. Then he who believes that the Ego is persistent adopts the attachment of the heresy of fanatical conduct to purify his Ego, and he who believes that the Ego is annihilated, being reckless of a future life, adopts the attachment of sensual pleasure. Thus the sequence of originating in any particular existence is for the attachment of the heresy of the assertion of an Ego to come first, and after it the attachments of heresy, fanatical conduct, and sensual pleasure.

The attachment of heresy, the attachment of fanatical conduct, and the attachment of the assertion of an Ego are first abandoned, as they are destroyed by the Path of Conversion; the attachment of sensual pleasure afterwards by the Path of Arhatship. This is the sequence in abandonment.

The attachment of sensual pleasure is first taught both on account of its extent and of its conspicuousness. For as it occurs in conjunction with eight of the consciousnesses it has a large extent; the others have but little, being conjoined with only four. And as mankind is for the most part given over to its lusts, the attachment of sensual pleasure is conspicuous; not so the others. Or, the attachment of sensual pleasure is for the purpose of obtaining objects of lust, and the attachment of heresy in the form of belief in the persistence of the Ego comes next as being more a question of speculative curiosity and the like. This has two divisions, the attachment of fanatical conduct, and the attachment of the assertion of an Ego. Of these two, the attachment of fanatical conduct is first taught from its grossness as one can see cattle-practices and dog-practices with one's own eyes; the attachment of the assertion of an Ego comes last on account of its subtileness. This is the sequence in teaching.

## EXISTENCE

*Translated from the Visuddhi-Magga (chap. xvii.):*
In the proposition, *On attachment depends existence,*

> The sense, the different elements,
> The use, divisions, summings up,
> And which the dependence makes of which,
> Must now be understood in full.

"Existence" is so called because it is an existing. It is twofold; karma-existence, and originating-existence. As it has been said: "Existence is twofold: there is a karma-existence, and there is an originating-existence." Here *karma-existence* is equivalent to karma; and in like manner *originating-existence* is equivalent to originating. Originating is called existence because it is an existing; but karma is called existence because it causes existence, just as the birth of a Buddha is called happy because it results in happiness.

This, then, is the full understanding of *the sense.*

*The different elements:*—Karma-existence is in brief thought and the elements covetousness etc., which go under the name of karma and exist conjoined with thought. As it has been said,

"What is karma-existence? Meritorious karma, demeritorious karma, and karma leading to immovability, all these are called karma-existence, whether they be of little or great extent. Moreover all karma conducive to existence is karma-existence."

In the above, the term meritorious karma includes thirteen thoughts, demeritorious karma includes twelve, and the term, karma leading to immovability, includes four thoughts. Also, by the phrase, "Whether of little or great extent," is meant the slight or large amount of fruition of these same thoughts, and, by the phrase, "And all karma conducive to existence," are meant covetousness and so on conjoined with thought.

Originating-existence, however, is in brief the groups which have come into existence through karma, and it has a ninefold division. As it is said,

"What is originating-existence? Existence in the realm of sensual pleasure, existence in the realm of form, existence in the realm of formlessness, existence in the realm of perception, existence in the realm of non-perception, existence in the realm of neither perception nor yet non-perception, existence once infected, existence four times infected, existence five times infected, all these are originating-existence."

In the above, existence in the realm of sensual pleasure is the existence called sensual pleasure, and similarly in respect of existence in the realm of form, and of existence in the realm of formlessness. Existence in the realm of perception is so called either because perception constitutes that existence, or because there is perception in that existence. The converse is the case with existence in the realm of non-perception. Existence in the realm of neither perception nor yet non-perception is so called because, as there is no gross perception there, but only a subtle one, there is neither perception nor yet non-perception in that existence. Existence once infected is existence infected with the form-group alone, or it is called existence once infected because there is but one infection to that existence, and similarly in regard to existences four times and five times infected.

Existence in the realm of sensual pleasure is the five attachment-groups, and existence in the realm of form is the same. Existence in the realm of formlessness is four attachment-groups. Existence in the realm of perception is five attachment-groups, and existence in the realm of non-perception is one attachment-group. Existence in the realm of neither perception nor yet non-perception is four attachment-groups, and existence once infected etc., is one, four, or five attachment-groups.

This, then, is the full understanding of *the different elements*.

*The use:*—It is true that the meritorious and the other karmas have been already spoken of in the exposition of karma. However, this karma was the karma of a previous existence and hence given as constituting the dependence for conception into this one, —while in the present case they are present karma and given as constituting the dependence for conception into a future existence. Thus the repetition is of use. Or again, when it was said,

"What is meritorious karma? It is meritorious thoughts in the realm of sensual pleasure," and so on, only thoughts were included in the term karma, while in the present instance where it is said, "And all karma conducive to existence," there are also included the elements of being which are conjoined with thoughts. Or again, only that karma which is the dependence of consciousness was in the first instance intended by the term karma, but now that also which gives rise to an existence in the realm of non-perception. But why make a long story of it? By the meritorious karma etc. intended in the proposition, "On ignorance depends karma," meritorious and demeritorious factors of being only are meant; but in the present case, in the proposition, "On attachment depends existence," inasmuch as originating-existence is included, all elements of being, whether meritorious or demeritorious or indeterminate are intended. Accordingly the repetition is useful from every point of view.

This, then, is the full understanding of *the use*.

*Divisions, summings up:*—The divisions and summings up of an existence dependent on attachment. For, whatever karma depends on the attachment of sensual pleasure and produces existence in the realm of sensual pleasure, this is karma-existence, and the groups that spring from it are originating-existence. Similarly in regard to existence in the realm of form and existence in the realm of formlessness. This makes two existences in the realm of sensual pleasure besides the therewith included existence in the realm of perception and existence five times infected; two existences in the realm of form besides the therewith included existence in the realm of perception, existence in the realm of non-perception, existence once infected, and existence five times infected; and two existences in the realm of formlessness besides the therewith included existence in the realm of perception, existence in the realm of neither perception nor yet non-perception, and existence four times infected, all of which depend on the attachment of sensual pleasure—six existences besides the therewith included existences. And just as six existences and the therewith included existences depend on the attachment of sensual pleasure, so also do six existences depend on each of the other three attachments. Thus in respect of their divisions there are twenty-four existences besides the therewith included existences, all of which depend on attachment.

In regard to their summings up, however, by putting karma-existence and originating-existence together we have existence in the realm of sensual pleasure and the therewith included existences, existence in the realm of form, and existence in the realm of formlessness, making three existences which depend on the attachment of sensual pleasure; and similarly in regard to the remaining attachments. Thus there sum up twelve existences besides the therewith included existences, all of which depend on attachment. Moreover, to speak absolutely, karma-existence is karma which leads to existence in the realm of sensual pleasure and is dependent on attachment, and the groups which spring from it are originating-existence. And it is the same in regard to existence in the realm of form and existence in the realm of formlessness. This makes two existences in the realm of sensual pleasure, two existences in the realm of form, and two existences in the realm of formlessness besides the therewith included existences, all of which depend on attachment. By another method of computation, the six existences, by not dividing into karma-existence and originating-existence, sum up as three existences, namely, existence in the realm of sensual pleasure etc., besides the existences therewith included. Also by not dividing into existence in the realm of sensual pleasure etc., karma-existence and originating-existence become two existences; and again, by not dividing into karma-existence and originating-existence, there remains in the proposition, "On attachment depends existence," only existence.

This, then, is the full understanding *of the divisions* and *summings up* of existence dependent on attachment.

*And which the dependence makes of which:*—The sense is, it must be fully understood which attachment is the dependence of which? But which is the dependence of which? Every one is the dependence of every one else. For the unconverted are like madmen, and fail to reflect on what is suitable and what is unsuitable.

As the result of any and every attachment, they long for any and every existence and perform any and every karma. Therefore the view of those who say that existence in the realm of form and existence in the realm of formlessness do not come about by the attachment of fanatical conduct is not to be accepted. But on the contrary, any and every existence comes about by any and every attachment. As follows:—

We may have one who, because of what he hears reported or by inference from what he sees, reflects as follows: "Sensual pleasures obtain in the world of men in wealthy families of the warrior caste and so forth and so on, and also in the six heavens of sensual pleasures." Then he becomes deceived by listening to false doctrine and takes a wrong way to attain them, and thinking, "By this kind of karma I shall obtain sensual pleasures," he adopts the attachment of sensual pleasure and does evil with his body, evil with his voice, and evil with his mind, and when he has fulfilled his wickedness he is reborn in a lower state of existence. Or again, he adopts the attachment of sensual pleasure through being desirous of sensual pleasure and of protecting that which he has already obtained, and does evil with his body, evil with his voice, and evil with his mind, and when he has fulfilled his wickedness he is reborn in a lower state of existence. Here the karma that was the cause of his rebirth is karma-existence. The groups which sprang from that karma were originating-existence. Existence in the realm of perception and existence five times infected are therewith included.

Another, however, strengthens his knowledge by listening to the Good Doctrine, and thinking, "By this kind of karma I shall obtain sensual pleasures," adopts the attachment of sensual pleasure and does good with his body, good with his voice, and good with his mind; and when he has fulfilled his righteousness he is reborn either among the gods or among men. Here the karma that was the cause of his rebirth is karma-existence. The groups which sprang from that karma were originating-existence. Existence in the realm of form and existence five times infected are therewith included. Accordingly the attachment of sensual plea-

sure is the dependence of existence in the realm of sensual pleasure together with its divisions and whatever existences are therewith included.

Another, having heard or come to the conclusion that there
are superior sensual pleasures in the realm of form and in the
realm of formlessness, adopts the attachment of sensual pleasure
and achieves the trances of the realm of form and of the realm
of formlessness, and by the might of these trances is reborn in a
Brahma-heaven. Here the karma that was the cause of his rebirth
was karma-existence. The groups which sprang from that karma
were originating-existence. Existence in the realm of perception,
existence in the realm of non-perception, existence in the realm
of neither perception nor yet non-perception, existence once infected, and existence five times infected, are therewith included.
Accordingly the attachment of sensual pleasure is the dependence of existence in the realm of form and existence in the
realm of formlessness, together with their divisions and the existences therewith included.

Another adopts the heresy of the annihilation of existences
and thinking either that it would be a good plan to have his Ego
undergo annihilation while in the realm of sensual pleasure or
else while in the realm of form or else while in the realm of
formlessness, performs karma leading to those existences. This
karma of his is karma-existence and the groups that spring from
it are originating-existence. Existence in the realm of perception
etc. are therewith included. Accordingly the attachment of heresy
is the dependence of all three modes of existence, viz., of existence in the realm of sensual pleasure, existence in the realm of
form, and existence in the realm of formlessness, together with
their divisions and the existences therewith included.

Another, thinking either that his Ego is happy when in the
realm of sensual pleasure, or else when in the realm of form, or
else when in the realm of formlessness, by the attachment of the
assertion of an Ego performs karma leading to those existences.
This karma of his is karma-existence and the groups that spring
from it are originating-existence. Existence in the realm of perception etc. are therewith included. Accordingly the attachment

of the assertion of an Ego is the dependence for the three modes of existence together with their divisions and the existences therewith included.

Another, thinking that fanatical conduct attains to a happy fulfillment either in the realm of sensual pleasure, or else in the realm of form, or else in the realm of formlessness, adopts the attachment of fanatical conduct and performs the karma leading to those existences. This karma of his is karma-existence and the groups that spring from it are originating-existence. Existence in the realm of perception etc. are therewith included. Accordingly the attachment of fanatical conduct is the dependence for the three modes of existence together with their divisions and the existences therewith included.

This, then, is the full understanding of *and which the dependence makes of which.*

Now, if it be asked, "But how is which the dependence of which existence?" we answer that attachment is to be understood as the proximate dependence of existence in the realm of form and in the realm of formlessness, and the connate etc. dependence of existence in the realm of sensual pleasure.

For when a being is in the realm of sensual pleasure, then the four attachments are the dependence of meritorious karma and of originating-existence in the realm of form and in the realm of formlessness by the proximate dependence alone. When conjoined with demeritorious karma they are the dependence by the connate dependence etc., that is, by the connate, the mutual, the basal, the conjoined, the actual, the abiding, and the causal dependence; but when not so conjoined, by the proximate dependence alone.

This is the full discussion of the proposition "On attachment depends existence."

### THE ROUND OF EXISTENCE

*Translated from the Milindapañha (77):*

"Bhante Nāgasena," said the king, "when you say 'round of existence,' what is that?"

"Your majesty, to be born here and die here, to die here and be born elsewhere, to be born there and die there, to die there and be born elsewhere,—this, your majesty, is the round of existence."

"Give an illustration."

"It is as if, your majesty, a man were to eat a ripe mango, and plant the seed; and from that a large mango-tree were to spring and bear fruit; and then the man were to eat a ripe mango from that tree also and plant the seed; and from that seed also a large mango-tree were to spring and bear fruit; thus of these trees there is no end discernible. In exactly the same way, your majesty, to be born here and die here, to die here and be born elsewhere, to be born there and die there, to die there and be born elsewhere, this, your majesty, is the round of existence."

"You are an able man, bhante Nāgasena."

## Cause of Rebirth

*Translated from the Milindapañha (32):*

"Bhante Nāgasena," said the king, "are there any who die without being born into another existence?"

"Some are born into another existence," said the elder, "and some are not born into another existence."

"Who is born into another existence, and who is not born into another existence?"

"Your majesty, he that still has the corruptions is born into another existence; he that no longer has the corruptions is not born into another existence."

"But will you, bhante, be born into another existence?"

"Your majesty, if there shall be in me any attachment, I shall be born into another existence; if there shall be in me no attachment, I shall not be born into another existence."

"You are an able man, bhante Nāgasena."

## Is This to Be My Last Existence?

*Translated from the Milindapañha (41):*

"Bhante Nāgasena," said the king, "does a man know when he is not to be born into another existence?"

"Assuredly, your majesty, a man knows when he is not to be born into another existence."

"Bhante, how does he know it?"

"He knows it from the cessation of all cause or reason for being born into another existence."

"Give an illustration."

"It is as if, your majesty, a house-holding farmer were to plow and sow and fill his granary; and then were neither to plow nor sow, and were to use the grain previously stored up, or give it away, or do with it however else might suit him: your majesty, would this house-holding farmer know that his granary would not become filled up again?"

"Assuredly, bhante, would he know it."

"How would he know it?"

"He would know it from the cessation of all cause or reason for the filling up of the granary."

"In exactly the same way, your majesty, a man knows when he is not to be born into another existence, from the cessation of all cause or reason for being born into another existence."

"You are an able man, bhante Nāgasena."

## CONCENTRATION

*Translated from the Visuddhi-Magga (chap. iii.):*

What is concentration? Concentration is manifold and various, and an answer which attempted to be exhaustive would both fail of its purpose and tend to still greater confusion. Therefore we will confine ourselves to the meaning here intended, and say— Concentration is an intentness of meritorious thoughts.

*Translated from the Anguttara-Nikāya (iii. 88):*

And what, O priests, is the discipline in elevated concentration?

Whenever, O priests, a priest, having isolated himself from sensual pleasures, having isolated himself from demeritorious traits, and still exercising reasoning, still exercising reflection, enters upon the first trance, which is produced by isolation and characterized by joy and happiness; when, through the subsidence of reasoning and reflection, and still retaining joy and happiness, he enters upon the second trance, which is an interior tranquilization and intentness of thoughts, and is produced by concentration; when, through the paling of joy, indifferent, contemplative, conscious, and in the experience of bodily happiness —that state which eminent men describe when they say, "Indifferent, contemplative, and living happily"—he enters upon the third trance; when, through the abandonment of happiness, through the abandonment of misery, through the disappearance of all antecedent gladness and grief, he enters upon the fourth trance, which has neither misery nor happiness, but is contemplation as refined by indifference, this, O priests, is called the discipline in elevated concentration.

*Translated from the Aṅguttara-Nikāya (ii. 3):*

What advantage, O priests, is gained by training in quiescence? The thoughts are trained. And what advantage is gained by the training of the thoughts? Passion is abandoned.

## THE EIGHTFOLD PATH

And what, O priests, is the noble truth of the path leading to the cessation of misery?

It is this noble eightfold path, to wit, right belief, right resolve, right speech, right behavior, right occupation, right effort, right contemplation, right concentration.

And what, O priests, is right belief?

The knowledge of misery, O priests, the knowledge of the origin of misery, the knowledge of the cessation of misery, and the knowledge of the path leading to the cessation of misery, this, O priests, is called "right belief."

And what, O priests, is right resolve?

The resolve to renounce sensual pleasures, the resolve to have malice towards none, and the resolve to harm no living creature, this, O priests, is called "right resolve."

And what, O priests, is right speech?

To abstain from falsehood, to abstain from backbiting, to abstain from harsh language, and to abstain from frivolous talk, this, O priests, is called "right speech."

And what, O priests, is right behavior?

To abstain from destroying life, to abstain from taking that which is not given one, and to abstain from immorality, this, O priests, is called "right behavior."

And what, O priests, is right occupation?

Whenever, O priests, a noble disciple, quitting a wrong occupation, gets his livelihood by a right occupation, this, O priests, is called "right occupation."

And what, O priests, is right effort?

Whenever, O priests, a priest purposes, makes an effort, heroically endeavors, applies his mind, and exerts himself that evil and demeritorious qualities not yet arisen may not arise; purposes, makes an effort, heroically endeavors, applies his mind, and exerts himself that evil and demeritorious qualities already arisen may be abandoned; purposes, makes an effort, heroically endeavors, applies his mind, and exerts himself that meritorious qualities not yet arisen may arise; purposes, makes an effort, heroically endeavors, applies his mind, and exerts himself for the preservation, retention, growth, increase, development, and perfection of meritorious qualities already arisen, this, O priests, is called "right effort."

And what, O priests, is right contemplation?

Whenever, O priests, a priest lives, as respects the body, observant of the body, strenuous, conscious, contemplative, and has rid himself of lust and grief; as respects sensations, observant of sensations, strenuous, conscious, contemplative, and has rid himself of lust and grief; as respects the mind, observant of the mind, strenuous, conscious, contemplative, and has rid himself of lust and grief; as respects the elements of being, observant of the elements of being, strenuous, conscious, contemplative, and has rid himself of lust and grief, this, O priests, is called "right contemplation."

And what, O priests, is right concentration?

Whenever, O priests, a priest, having isolated himself from sensual pleasures, having isolated himself from demeritorious traits, and still exercising reasoning, still exercising reflection, enters upon the first trance which is produced by isolation and characterized by joy and happiness; when, through the subsidence of reasoning and reflection, and still retaining joy and happiness, he enters upon the second trance, which is an interior tranquilization and intentness of the thoughts, and is produced by concentration; when, through the paling of joy, indifferent, contemplative, conscious, and in the experience of bodily happiness—that state which eminent men describe when they say, "Indifferent, contemplative, and living happily"—he enters upon the third trance; when, through the abandonment of happiness, through the abandonment of misery, through the disappearance of all antecedent gladness and grief, he enters upon the fourth trance, which has neither misery nor happiness, but is contemplation as refined by indifference, this, O priests, is called "right concentration."

This, O priests, is called the noble truth of the path leading to the cessation of misery.

*End of the Exposition of the Path Leading*
*to the Cessation of Misery*


Thus he lives, either in his own person, as respects the elements of being, observant of the elements of being, or in other persons, as respects the elements of being, observant of the elements of being, or both in his own person and in other persons, as respects the elements of being, observant of the elements of being; either observant of origination in the elements of being, or observant of destruction in the elements of being, or observant of both origination and destruction in the elements of being; and the recognition of the elements of being by his intent contemplation is merely to the extent of this knowledge, merely to the extent of this contemplation, and he lives unattached, nor clings to anything in the world.

Thus, O priests, does a priest live, as respects the elements of being, observant of the elements of being.

*End of the Intent Contemplation of the Elements of Being*

Any one, O priests, who for seven years shall thus practise these Four Intent Contemplations, may expect one or the other of two rewards—either he will attain to perfect knowledge in his present life, or, if at death the groups still remain, to never returning.

But setting aside, O priests, all question of seven years, any one, O priests, who for six years shall thus practise the above Four Intent Contemplations, may expect one or the other of two rewards—either he will attain to perfect knowledge in his present life, or, if at death the groups still remain, to never returning.

But setting aside, O priests, all question of six years, . . . five years, . . . four years, . . . three years, . . . two years, . . . one year, . . . seven months, . . . six months, . . . five months, . . . four months, . . . three months, . . . two months, . . . one month, . . . a half month, any one, O priests, who for seven days shall thus practise the above Four Intent Contemplations, may expect one or the other of two rewards—either he will attain to perfect knowledge in his present life, or, if at death the groups still remain, to never returning.

This, therefore, is the meaning of my opening words: "Priests, there is but one way open to mortals for the attainment of purity, for the overcoming of sorrow and lamentation, for the abolition of misery and grief, for the acquisition of the correct rule of conduct, for the realization of Nirvana, and that is the Four Intent Contemplations."

Thus spake The Blessed One, and the delighted priests applauded the speech of The Blessed One.

*End of the Sermon on the Four Intent Contemplations*

## THE ATTAINMENT OF THE PATHS

*Translated from the Visuddhi-Magga (chap. xxi.):*

"Behold how empty is the world,
Mogharāja! In thoughtfulness

Let one remove belief in self
And pass beyond the realm of death.
The king of death can never find
The man who thus the world beholds."

When in the course of his application of the Three Characteristics the ascetic has thus considered the constituents of being in
the light of their emptiness, he abandons all fear and joy in regard to them, and becomes indifferent and neutral, and does not
deem them as "I" or "mine," like a man who has given up his
wife.

Just as a man might have a wife beloved, delightful, and charming, from whom he could not bear to be separated for a moment,
and on whom he excessively doted. If he then were to see that
woman standing or sitting in company with another man, and
talking and joking with him, he would be angry and displeased,
and experience bitter grief. But if subsequently he were to discover that she had been guilty of a fault, he would lose all desire
for her and let her go, and no longer look on her as "mine."
From that time on, whenever he might see her engaged with
any one else, he would not be angry or grieved, but simply indifferent and neutral. In exactly the same way the ascetic by grasping the constituents of being with the reflective insight becomes
desirous of being released from them, and perceiving none of
them worthy of being deemed "I" or "mine," he abandons all
fear and joy in regard to them, and becomes indifferent and
neutral. When he has learnt and perceived this, his mind draws
in, contracts, and shrinks away from the three modes of existence,
the four species of being, the five destinies in rebirth, the seven
stages of consciousness, the nine grades of being, and does not
spread out, and only indifference or disgust abides.

Just as drops of water on a gently inclined lotus-leaf draw in,
contract, and shrink away, and do not spread out; in exactly the
same way his mind draws in, contracts, and shrinks away from
the three modes of existence, the four species of being, the five
destinies in rebirth, the seven stages of consciousness, the nine

grades of being, and does not spread out, and only indifference or disgust abides. Just as a cock's feather, . . . if thrown into the fire, draws in, contracts, and shrinks away, and does not spread out; in exactly the same way his mind draws in, contracts, and shrinks away from the three modes of existence, the four species of being, the five destinies in rebirth, the seven stages of consciousness, the nine grades of being, and does not spread out, but only indifference or disgust abides. Thus has he attained to the knowledge consisting in indifference to the constituents of being.

If this knowledge be such that it sees Nirvana, the abode of peace, to be the good, then it gives up everything made of the constituents of being, and leaps towards it; but if it be not such that it sees Nirvana to be the good, it will again and again take the constituents of being as its object, resembling in this the crow of the sailors.

They say that sea-faring traders take what is called a land-sighting crow when they go aboard ship. And when the ship is tossed about by the winds, and out of its course, and land no longer to be seen, then they let go that land-sighting crow. Such a bird springs into the air from the mast-head, and going to all the quarters and intermediate quarters flies to the shore if he sees it; but if he does not see it, he returns again and again and alights on the mast. In exactly the same way, if the knowledge consisting in indifference to the constituents of being be such that it sees Nirvana, the abode of peace, to be the good, then it gives up everything made of the constituents of being, and leaps towards it; but if it be not such that it sees Nirvana to be the good, it will again and again take the constituents of being as its object. It grasps the constituents of being in many different ways, as if they were so much meal being sorted in the kitchen, or so much cotton unrolled and being shredded, and having abandoned all fear and joy in regard to them and become neutral by its sifting of the constituents of being, it abides as the threefold insight. And abiding thus, it becomes the threefold starting-point of deliverance, and the dependence for the distinction of the seven noble individuals.

Now this knowledge, existing as the threefold insight, becomes by the predominance of three qualities the threefold starting-point of deliverance. For the three insights are called the three starting-points of deliverance. As it is said:

"Moreover, deliverance has three starting-points for escape from the world: the consideration of the beginnings and endings of the constituents of being for the thoughts to spring to the unconditioned; the agitating of the mind concerning the constituents of being for the thoughts to spring to the desireless; the consideration of all the elements of being as not an Ego for the thoughts to spring to the empty. These are the three starting-points of deliverance for escape from the world."

Here *the beginnings and endings*—the beginnings and endings in the springing up and disappearance of things. For the insight into transitoriness, by coming to the conclusion, "The constituents of being did not exist before they sprang up," determines beginnings; and by observing their destiny, and coming to the conclusion, "They continue no more after they have disappeared, but vanish right then," determines endings.

The *agitating of the mind*—the agitating of the thoughts. For by insight into the misery of the constituents of being the thoughts are agitated.

The *consideration of all the elements of being as not an Ego*—considering them as not an "I" or "mine."

Accordingly these three propositions are to be understood as spoken concerning the insight into transitoriness etc. Therefore was it thereafter said in answer to a question,

"To one who considers them in the light of their transitoriness the constituents of being seem perishable. To one who considers them in the light of their misery they seem frightful. To one who considers them in the light of their want of an Ego they seem empty.

But how many are the deliverances of which these insights are the starting-points? There are three: the unconditioned, the desireless, and the empty. For it has been said as follows:

"He who considers them [the constituents of being] in the

light of their transitoriness abounds in faith and obtains the
unconditioned deliverance; he who considers them in the light of
their misery abounds in tranquillity and obtains the desireless
deliverance; he who considers them in the light of their want
of an Ego abounds in knowledge and obtains the empty deliverance."

Here *the unconditioned deliverance* is the Noble Path realized
by meditation on Nirvana in its unconditioned aspect. For the
Noble Path is unconditioned from having sprung out of the
unconditioned, and it is a deliverance from being free from the
corruptions. In the same way the Noble Path when realized by
meditation on Nirvana in its desireless aspect is to be understood
as *desireless;* when realized by meditation on Nirvana in its
empty aspect as *empty*.


## Nirvana to Be Attained at Death

*Translated from the Visuddhi-Magga (chap. xxii.):*
Just as, however, a man displeased with the flowers, fruit, etc.
of a tree, will pierce it on each of its four sides with the poisonous
thorn called the maṇḍu-thorn, and then that tree, when its earth-
extracted juices and its sap have become exhausted by the application of that poison, will arrive at a state of inability to bear
fruit and not be able to reproduce itself; in exactly the same way
a youth of good family, displeased with the existence of the
groups, will, like the man who applied poison to the tree on each
of its four sides, begin to apply the meditation of the Four Paths
to the series of his groups. And then the series of his groups,
when the rebirth-causing corruptions have become exhausted by
the application of the poison of the Four Paths, resolves itself into
such bodily and other kinds of karma as constitute barren action;
and arriving at a state of not being liable to be reborn in the
future, and unable to reproduce itself in the next existence, by
the cessation of the last consciousness becomes like a fire without
fuel, and passes into Nirvana without attachment.

## The Summum Bonum

*Translated from the Majjhima-Nikāya, and constituting Sutta 26:*

Thus have I heard.

On a certain occasion The Blessed One was dwelling at Sāvatthi in Jetavana monastery in Anāthapiṇḍika's Park. Then The Blessed One, having put on his tunic in the morning, and taken his bowl and his robes, entered Sāvatthi for alms.

Then a great number of priests drew near to where the venerable Ānanda was; and having drawn near, they spoke to the venerable Ānanda as follows:

"It is a long time, brother Ānanda, since we listened to a doctrinal discourse from the mouth of The Blessed One. Come, brother Ānanda, let us obtain an opportunity to listen to a doctrinal discourse from the mouth of The Blessed One."

"Well, then, venerable sirs, draw near to the monastery of Rammaka the Brahman. Perchance you may obtain an opportunity to listen to a doctrinal discourse from the mouth of The Blessed One."

"Yes, brother," said the priests to the venerable Ānanda in assent.

Then The Blessed One, when he had gone the rounds for alms in Sāvatthi, returned from his begging, and after breakfast, addressed the venerable Ānanda:

"Let us go hence, Ānanda, and to Eastern Monastery, and to the storied mansion of Migāra's mother will we draw near for our noon-day rest."

"Yes, Reverend Sir," said the venerable Ānanda to The Blessed One in assent.

Then The Blessed One, in company with the venerable Ānanda, drew near to Eastern Monastery, and to the storied mansion of Migāra's mother, for his noon-day rest. Then The Blessed One, in the afternoon, rose from meditation, and addressed the venerable Ānanda:

"Let us go hence, Ānanda, and to Eastern Tank will we draw near to bathe our limbs."

"Yes, Reverend Sir," said the venerable Ānanda to The Blessed One in assent.

Then The Blessed One, in company with the venerable Ānanda, drew near to Eastern Tank to bathe his limbs; and having bathed his limbs in Eastern Tank and come up out of the water, he stood with but a single garment on, drying his limbs.

Then the venerable Ānanda spoke to The Blessed One as follows:

"Reverend Sir, here is the monastery of Rammaka the Brahman, but a short way off. Delightful, Reverend Sir, is the monastery of Rammaka the Brahman; enchanting, Reverend Sir, is the monastery of Rammaka the Brahman. Reverend Sir, pray let The Blessed One be so kind as to draw near to where the monastery of Rammaka the Brahman is." And The Blessed One consented by his silence.

Then The Blessed One drew near to where the monastery of Rammaka the Brahman was. Now at that time a great number of priests were seated in the monastery of Rammaka the Brahman, engaged in doctrinal discourse. Then The Blessed One stood outside in the entrance porch, and awaited the end of the discourse. Then The Blessed One, when he perceived that the discourse had come to an end, coughed, and rattled the bolt of the door. And the priests opened the door for The Blessed One. Then The Blessed One entered the monastery of Rammaka the Brahman, and sat on the seat that was spread for him. And when The Blessed One had sat down, he addressed the priests:

"What, O priests, was the subject of the present meeting? and what the discourse you were holding?"

"Reverend Sir, our doctrinal discourse was concerning The Blessed One, and then The Blessed One arrived."

"Well said, O priests! This, O priests, is worthy of you as youths of good family, who have through faith retired from the household life to the houseless one, that ye sit together in doctrinal discourse. O priests, one of two things should you do when you meet together: either hold a doctrinal discourse, or maintain a noble silence.

"There are two cravings, O priests; the noble one, and the ignoble one. And what, O priests, is the ignoble craving?

"We may have, O priests, the case of one who, himself subject to birth, craves what is subject to birth; himself subject to old age, craves what is subject to old age; himself subject to disease, . . . death, . . . sorrow, . . . corruption, craves what is subject to corruption.

"And what, O priests, should one consider as subject to birth?

"Wife and child, O priests, are subject to birth; slaves, male and female, . . . goats and sheep . . . fowls and pigs . . . elephants, cattle, horses and mares . . . gold and silver are subject to birth. All the substrata of being, O priests, are subject to birth; and enveloped, besotted, and immersed in them, this person, himself subject to birth, craves what is subject to birth.

"And what, O priests, should one consider as subject to old age . . . disease . . . death . . . sorrow . . . corruption?

"Wife and child, O priests, are subject to corruption; slaves, male and female, . . . goats and sheep . . . fowls and pigs . . . elephants, cattle, horses and mares . . . gold and silver are subject to corruption. All the substrata of being, O priests, are subject to corruption; and enveloped, besotted, and immersed in them, this person, himself subject to corruption, craves what is subject to corruption.

"This, O priests, is the ignoble craving.

"And what, O priests, is the noble craving?

"We may have, O priests, the case of one who, himself subject to birth, perceives the wretchedness of what is subject to birth, and craves the incomparable security of a Nirvana free from birth; himself subject to old age, . . . disease, . . . death, . . . sorrow, . . . corruption, perceives the wretchedness of what is subject to corruption, and craves the incomparable security of a Nirvana free from corruption.

"This, O priests, is the noble craving.

"Now I, O priests, before my Buddhaship, being not yet a

Buddha, but a Future Buddha, myself subject to birth, craved what was subject to birth; myself subject to old age, . . . disease, . . . death, . . . sorrow, . . . corruption, craved what was subject to corruption. And it occurred to me, O priests, as follows:

" 'Why, myself subject to birth, do I crave what is subject to birth? myself subject to old age, . . . disease, . . . death, . . . sorrow, . . . corruption, do I crave what is subject to corruption? What if now, myself subject to birth, and perceiving the wretchedness of what is subject to birth, I were to crave the incomparable security of a Nirvina free from birth; myself subject to old age, . . . disease, . . . death, . . . sorrow, . . . corruption, I were to crave the incomparable security of a Nirvana free from corruption?'

"Subsequently, O priests, although of tender age, with the black hair of a lad, and in the hey-day of my youth, and just entering on my prime, and although my mother and my father were unwilling, and tears streamed from their eyes, I had my hair and my beard shaved off, and put on yellow garments, and retired from the household life to the houseless one. And having thus retired from the world, and craving the summum bonum, the incomparable peaceful state, I drew near to where Ālāra Kālāma was; and having drawn near, I spoke to Ālāra Kālāma as follows:

" 'Brother Kālāma, I would like to lead the religious life under your doctrine and discipline.'

"When I had thus spoken, O priests, Ālāra Kālāma spoke to me as follows:

" 'Let your venerable worship do so. Such is this doctrine that in no long time an intelligent man can learn for himself, realize, and live in the possession of all that his master has to teach.'

"Then I, O priests, in no long time, quickly acquired that doctrine. And I, O priests, and others with me, by a mere lip-profession, and a mere verbal assertion, claimed that we knew and had perceived the true knowledge and the orthodox doctrine. And it occurred to me, O priests, as follows:

" 'It is not through mere faith in this doctrine that Ālāra Kā-

lāma announces that he has learnt it for himself, realized it, and
lives in the possession of it. Āḷāra Kālāma surely knows and
perceives this doctrine.'

"Then, O priests, I drew near to where Āḷāra Kālāma was;
and having drawn near; I spoke to Āḷāra Kālāma as follows:

" 'Brother Kālāma, how far does this doctrine conduct, concerning which you announce that you have learnt it for yourself,
realized it, and entered upon it?'

"When I had thus spoken, O priests, Āḷāra Kālāma announced
that it conducted to the realm of nothingness. And it occurred to
me, O priests, as follows:

" 'Faith is not peculiar to Āḷāra Kālāma: I also have faith.
Heroism . . . contemplation . . . concentration . . . wisdom is not
peculiar to Āḷāra Kālāma: I also have wisdom. What if now I
were to strive for the realization of that doctrine, concerning
which Āḷāra Kālāma: I also have wisdom. What if now I were
to strive for the realization of that doctrine, concerning which
Āḷāra Kālāma announces that he has learnt it for himself, realized
it, and lives in the possession of it.' Then I, O priests, in no long
time, quickly learnt that doctrine for myself, realized it, and lived
in the possession of it. Then, O priests, I drew near to where
Āḷāra Kālāma was; and having drawn near, I spoke to Āḷāra
Kālāma as follows:

" 'Brother Kālāma, is this as far as the doctrine conducts, concerning which you announce that you have learnt it for yourself,
realized it, and entered upon it?'

" 'This, brother, is as far as the doctrine conducts, concerning
which I announce that I have learnt it for myself, realized it,
and entered upon it.'

" 'I also, brother, have learnt this doctrine for myself, realized
it, and live in the possession of it.'

" 'How fortunate, brother, are we! What supreme good fortune, brother, is ours that we should light on such a coreligionist
as is your venerable worship. Thus the doctrine concerning which
I announce that I have learnt it for myself, realized it, and entered upon it, that doctrine you have learnt for yourself, realized,

and live in the possession of; the doctrine which you have learnt
for yourself, realized, and live in the possession of, concerning
that doctrine I announce that I have learnt it for myself, realized
it, and entered upon it. Thus you know this doctrine, and I know
this doctrine. You are the same as I am, and I am the same as
you are. Come, brother, let us lead this following in common.'

"Thus, O priests, did Āḷāra Kālāma, my teacher, take me, his
pupil, and make me every whit the equal of himself, and honor
me with very great honor. And it occurred to me, O priests, as
follows:

" 'This doctrine does not lead to aversion, absence of passion,
cessation, quiescence, knowledge, supreme wisdom, and Nirvana,
but only as far as the realm of nothingness.'

"And I, O priests, did not honor that doctrine with my adhesion, and being averse to that doctrine, I departed on my
journey.

"And craving, O priests, the summum bonum, the incomparable peaceful state, I drew near to where Uddaka, the disciple of
Rāma, was; and having drawn near, I spoke to Uddaka, the
disciple of Rāma, as follows:

" 'Brother, I would like to lead the religious life under your
doctrine and discipline.'

"When I had thus spoken, O priests, Uddaka, the disciple of
Rāma, spoke to me as follows:

" 'Let your venerable worship do so. Such is this doctrine that
in no long time an intelligent man can learn for himself, realize,
and live in the possession of all that his master has to teach.'

"Then I, O priests, in no long time, quickly acquired that
doctrine. And I, O priests, and others with me, by a mere lip-
profession, and a mere verbal assertion, claimed that we knew
and had perceived the true knowledge and the orthodox doctrine.
And it occurred to me, O priests, as follows:

" 'It was not through mere faith in this doctrine that Rāma
announced that he had learnt it for himself, realized it, and lived
in the possession of it. Rāma surely knew and perceived this
doctrine.'

"Then, O priests, I drew near to where Uddaka, the disciple of Rāma, was; and having drawn near, I spoke to Uddaka, the disciple of Rāma, as follows:

"'Brother, how far does this doctrine conduct, concerning which Rāma made known that he had learnt it for himself, realized it, and entered upon it?'

"When I had thus spoken, O priests, Uddaka, the disciple of Rāma, announced that it conducted to the realm of neither perception nor yet non-perception. And it occurred to me, O priests, as follows:

"'Faith is not peculiar to Rāma: I also have faith. Heroism . . . contemplation . . . concentration . . . wisdom is not peculiar to Rāma: I also have wisdom. What if now I were to strive for that doctrine, concerning which Rāma announced that he had learnt it for himself, realized it, and lived in the possession of it.' Then I, O priests, in no long time, quickly learnt that doctrine for myself, realized it, and lived in the possession of it. Then, O priests, I drew near to where Uddaka, the disciple of Rāma, was; and having drawn near. I spoke to Uddaka, the disciple of Rāma, as follows:

"'Brother, is this as far as the doctrine conducts, concerning which Rāma announced that he had learnt it for himself, realized it, and entered upon it?'

"'This, brother, is as far as the doctrine conducts, concerning which Rāma announced that he had learnt it for himself, realized, and entered upon it.'

"'I also, brother, have learnt this doctrine for myself, realized it, and live in the possession of it.'

"'How fortunate, brother, are we! What supreme good fortune, brother, is ours that we should light on such a coreligionist as is your venerable worship. Thus the doctrine concerning which Rāma announced that he had learnt it for himself, realized it, and entered upon it, that doctrine you have learnt for yourself, realized, and live in the possession of; the doctrine which you have learnt for yourself, realized, and live in the possession of, concerning that doctrine Rāma announced that he had learnt it for himself, realized it, and entered upon it. Thus you know this doctrine, and Rāma knew this doctrine. You are the same as Rāma was, and Rāma was the same as you are. Come, brother, lead this following.'

"Thus, O priests, did Uddaka, the disciple of Rāma, my co-religionist, make me his teacher, and honor me with very great honor. And it occurred to me, O priests, as follows:

" 'This doctrine does not lead to aversion, absence of passion, cessation, quiescence, knowledge, supreme wisdom, and Nirvana, but only as far as the realm of neither perception nor yet non-perception.'

"And I, O priests, did not honor that doctrine with my adhesion; and being averse to that doctrine, I departed on my journey.

"And craving, O priests, the summum bonum, the incomparable peaceful state, I came in the course of my journeyings among the Magadhans to Uruvelā, the General's Town. There I perceived a delightful spot with an enchanting grove of trees, and a silvery flowing river, easy of approach and delightful, and a village nearby in which to beg. And it occurred to me, O priests, as follows:

" 'Truly, delightful is this spot, enchanting this grove of trees, and this silvery river flows by, easy of approach and delightful, and there is a village nearby in which to beg. Truly, there is here everything necessary for a youth of good family who is desirous of struggling.'

"And there I settled down, O priests, as everything was suitable for struggling.

"And being, O priests, myself subject to birth, I perceived the wretchedness of what is subject to birth, and craving the incomparable security of a Nirvana free from birth, I attained the incomparable security of a Nirvana free from birth; myself subject to old age, . . . disease, . . . death, . . . sorrow, . . . corruption, I perceived the wretchedness of what is subject to corruption, and craving the incomparable security of a Nirvana free from corruption, I attained the incomparable security of a Nirvana free from corruption. And the knowledge and the insight sprang up within me, 'My deliverance is unshakable; this is my last existence; no more shall I be born again.' And it occurred to me, O priests, as follows:

" 'This doctrine to which I have attained is profound, recondite, and difficult of comprehension, good, excellent, and not to be reached by mere reasoning, subtile, and intelligible only to the wise. Mankind, on the other hand, is captivated, entranced, held spell-bound by its lusts; and forasmuch as mankind is captivated, entranced, and held spell-bound by its lusts, it is hard for them to understand the law of dependence on assignable reasons, the doctrine of Dependent Origination, and it is also hard for them to understand how all the constituents of being may be made to subside, all the substrata of being be relinquished, and desire be made to vanish, and absence of passion, cessation, and Nirvana be attained. If I were to teach the Doctrine, others would fail to understand me, and my vexation and trouble would be great.'

"Then, O priests, the following stanzas occurred to me, not heard of before from any one else:

> " 'This Doctrine out of toil begot
> I see 't is useless to proclaim:
> Mankind's by lusts and hates enthralled,
> 'T is hopeless they should master it.

> " 'Repugnant, abstruse would it prove,
> Deep, subtile, and beyond their ken;
> Th' infatuates live in clouds of lusts,
> And cannot for the darkness see.'

"Thus, O priests, did I ponder, and my mind was disinclined to action, and to any proclaiming of the Doctrine.

"Then, O priests, Brahma Sahampati perceived what was in my mind, and it occurred to him as follows:

" 'Lo, the world is lost, is ruined! For the mind of The Tathā-gata, The Saint, The Supreme Buddha, is disinclined to action, and to any proclaiming of the Doctrine.'

"Then, O priests, Brahma Sahampati, as quickly as a strong man might stretch out his bent arm, or might draw in his outstretched arm, even so, having vanished from the Brahma-world, appeared in my presence.

"Then, O priests, Brahma Sahampati threw his upper garment over his shoulder and, stretching out to me his joined palms, spoke as follows:

" 'Reverend Sir, let The Blessed One teach the Doctrine, let The Happy One teach the Doctrine. There are some beings having but little moral defilement, and through not hearing the Doctrine they perish. Some will be found to understand the Doctrine.'

"Thus, O priests, spoke Brahma Sahampati, and having thus spoken, he continued as follows:

> " 'The Magadhans hold hitherto a doctrine
> Impure, thought out by men themselves not spotless.
> Ope thou the door that to the deathless leadeth:
> Him let them hear who is himself unspotted.
>
> " 'As one who standeth on a rocky pinnacle,
> Might thence with wide-extended view behold mankind,
> Climb thou, Wise One, the top of Doctrine's palace,
> And thence gaze down serene on all the peoples,
> Behold how all mankind is plunged in sorrow,
> And how old age and death have overwhelmed them.
>
> " 'Rise thou, O Hero, Victor in the Battle!
> O Leader, Guiltless One, go 'mongst the nations!
> The Doctrine let The Buddha teach,
> Some will be found to master it.'

"Then I, O priests, perceiving the desire of Brahma, and having compassion on living beings, gazed over the world with the eye of a Buddha. And as I gazed over the world with the eye of a Buddha, I saw people of every variety: some having but little moral defilement, and some having great moral defilement; some of keen faculties, and some of dull faculties; some of good dis-

position, and some of bad disposition; some that were docile, and
some that were not docile; and also some who saw the terrors of
the hereafter and of blameworthy actions. Just as in a pond of
blue lotuses, of water-roses, or of white lotuses, some of the
blossoms which have sprung up and grown in the water, do not
reach the surface of the water but grow under water; some of
the blossoms which have sprung up and grown in the water, are
even with the surface of the water; and some of the blossoms
which have sprung up and grown in the water, shoot up above
the water and are not touched by the water; in exactly the same
way, O priests, as I gazed over the world with the eye of a
Buddha, I saw people of every variety: some having but little
moral defilement, and some having great moral defilement; some
of keen faculties, and some of dull faculties; some of good disposition, and some of bad disposition; some that were docile, and
some that were not docile; and also some who saw the terrors of
the hereafter and of blameworthy actions. And when I had seen
this, O priests, I addressed Brahma Sahampati in the following
stanza:

> " 'Let those with ears to hear come give me credence,
> For lo! the door stands open to the deathless.
> O Brahma, 't was because I feared annoyance
> That I was loath to tell mankind the Doctrine.'

"Then, O priests, thought Brahma Sahampati, 'The Blessed
One has granted my request that he should teach the Doctrine,'
and saluting me, he turned his right side towards me, and straightway disappeared.

"Then, O priests, it occurred to me as follows:

" 'To whom had I best teach the Doctrine first? Who would
quickly comprehend this Doctrine?'

"Then, O priests, it occurred to me as follows:

" 'Here is this Āḷāra Kālāma, who is learned, skilled, intelligent, and has long been a person having but little defilement.
What if I teach the Doctrine to Āḷāra Kālāma first? He would
quickly comprehend this Doctrine.'

"Then, O priests, a deity announced to me,

" 'Reverend Sir, Āḷāra Kālāma is dead these seven days.'

"Also in me the knowledge sprang up, 'Āḷāra Kālāma is dead these seven days.'

"Then, O priests, it occurred to me as follows:

" 'A noble man was Āḷāra Kālāma. Surely, if he could have heard this Doctrine, he would quickly have comprehended it.'

"Then, O priests, it occurred to me as follows:

" 'To whom had I best teach the Doctrine first? Who would quickly comprehend this Doctrine?'

"Then, O priests, it occurred to me as follows:

" 'Here is this Uddaka, the disciple of Rāma, who is learned, skilled, intelligent, and has long been a person having but little defilement. What if I teach the Doctrine to Uddaka, the disciple of Rāma, first? He would quickly comprehend this Doctrine.'

"Then, O priests, a deity announced to me,

" 'Reverend Sir, Uddaka, the disciple of Rāma, died yesterday at night-fall.'

"Also in me, O priests, the knowledge sprang up, 'Uddaka, the disciple of Rāma, died yesterday at night-fall.'

"Then, O priests, it occurred to me as follows:

" 'A noble man was Uddaka, the disciple of Rāma. Surely, if he could have heard this Doctrine, he would quickly have comprehended it.'

"Then, O priests, it occurred to me as follows:

" 'To whom had I best teach the Doctrine first? Who would quickly comprehend this Doctrine?'

"Then, O priests, it occurred to me as follows:

" 'Of great service has this band of five priests been, who waited upon me while I devoted myself to the struggle. What if I teach the Doctrine to the band of five priests first?'

"Then, O priests, it occurred to me as follows:

" 'Where does the band of five priests dwell at present?'

"And I, O priests, with my divinely clear vision surpassing that of men, saw the band of five priests dwelling at Benares, in the deer-park Isipatana.

"Then, O priests, having dwelt at Uruvelā as long as I wished, I proceeded on my wanderings in the direction of Benares. And Upaka, a naked ascetic, beheld me proceeding along the highway between the Bo-tree and Gayā. And having seen me, he spoke to me as follows:

" 'Placid, brother, are all your organs of sense; clear and bright is the color of your skin. To follow whom, brother, did you retire from the world? Who is your teacher? and whose doctrine do you approve?'

"When, O priests, Upaka, the naked ascetic, had thus spoken, I addressed him in the following stanzas:

> " 'All-conquering have I now become, all-knowing;
> Untainted by the elements of being.
> I've left all things, am freed through thirst's destruction,
> All wisdom's mine: what teacher should I follow?
>
> " 'I have no teacher anywhere;
> My equal nowhere can be found;
> In all the world with all its gods,
> No one to rival me exists.
>
> " 'The saintship, verily, I've gained,
> I am The Teacher, unsurpassed;
> I am The Buddha, sole, supreme;
> Lust's fire is quenched, Nirvana gained.
>
> " 'To found the Doctrine's reign I seek
> Benares, chief of Kāsi's towns;
> And for this blinded world I'll cause
> The drum of deathlessness to beat.'

" 'Which is as much as to say, brother, that you profess to be a saint, an immeasurable Conqueror.'

> " 'Yea, were The Conquerors like to me,
> Well rid of all depravity.
> I've conquered every evil trait;
> Thus, Upaka, a Conqueror I.'

" 'You may be right, brother,' replied Upaka, the naked ascetic; and shaking his head, he took another road and departed.

"Then, O priests, I proceeded on my wanderings from place to place, and drew near to Benares, to the deer-park Isipatana, and to where the band of five priests was. And, O priests, the band of five priests saw me approaching from afar, and, when they had seen me, they made an agreement among themselves, saying:

" 'Here, brethren, is the monk Gotama approaching, that luxurious fellow who gave up the struggle and devoted himself to a life of luxury. Yet us not salute him, nor rise and go to meet him, nor relieve him of his bowl and his robe. We will merely spread a seat for him: he can then sit down, if he is so inclined.'

"But, O priests, as I gradually approached, the band of five priests found themselves unable to hold to their agreement, and rising to meet me, one of them relieved me of my bowl and my robe, another spread a seat for me, and another brought water for washing my feet. But, O priests, they addressed me by my name, and by the title of 'Brother.' When, O priests, I noticed this, I spoke to the band of five priests as follows:

" 'O priests, address not The Tathāgata by his name, nor by the title of "Brother." A saint, O priests, is The Tathāgata, a Supreme Buddha. Give ear, O priests! The deathless has been gained, and I will instruct you, and teach you the Doctrine. If ye will do according to my instructions, in no long time, and in the present life, ye shall learn for yourselves, and shall realize and live in the possession of that highest good to which the holy life conducts, and for the sake of which youths of good family so nobly retire from the household life to the houseless one.'

"When I had thus spoken, O priests, the band of five priests said to me as follows:

" 'Brother Gotama, those practices of yours, that method of procedure, those stern austerities did not enable you to transcend human limitations and attain to pre-eminence in full and sublime knowledge and insight. How, then, now that you are luxurious, and have given up the struggle and devoted yourself to a life of luxury, can you have transcended human limitations and attained to pre-eminence in full and sublime knowledge and insight?'

"When they had thus spoken, O priests, I said to the band of
five priests as follows:

" 'O priests, The Tathāgata is not luxurious, and has not given
up the struggle and devoted himself to a life of luxury. A saint,
O priests, is The Tathāgata, a Supreme Buddha. Give ear, O
priests! The deathless has been gained, and I will instruct you,
and teach you the Doctrine. If ye will do according to my instructions, in no long time, and in the present life, ye shall learn for
yourselves, and shall realize and live in the possession of that
highest good to which the holy life conducts, and for the sake
of which youths of good family so nobly retire from the household life to the houseless one.'

"And a second time, O priests, the band of five priests spoke to
me as follows:

.     .     .     .     .     .     .     .     .

"And a second time, O priests, I replied to the band of five
priests as follows:

.     .     .     .     .     .     .     .     .

"And a third time, O priests, the band of five priests spoke to
me as follows:

.     .     .     .     .     .     .     .     .

"When they had thus spoken, O priests, I replied to the band
of five priests as follows:

" 'Confess, O priests, have I ever before spoken to you as I have
done this day?'

" 'Nay, verily, Reverend Sir.'

" 'A saint, O priests, is The Tathāgata, a Supreme Buddha.
Give ear, O priests! The deathless has been gained, and I will
instruct you, and teach you the Doctrine. If ye will do according
to my instructions, in no long time, and in the present life, ye
shall learn for yourselves, and shall realize and live in the possession of that highest good to which the holy life conducts, and
for the sake of which youths of good family so nobly retire from
the household life to the houseless one.'

"And I, O priests, succeeded in winning over the band of five
priests.

"And I, O priests, exhorted two priests, while three priests went for alms; and the food which the three priests brought back from their begging-rounds furnished subsistence for all us six. And I, O priests, exhorted three priests, while two priests went for alms; and the food which the two priests brought back from their begging-rounds furnished subsistence for all us six.

"Then, O priests, the band of five priests, thus exhorted and instructed by me, themselves subject to birth, perceived the wretchedness of what is subject to birth, and craving the incomparable security of a Nirvana free from birth, attained the incomparable security of a Nirvana free from birth; themselves subject to old age, . . . disease, . . . death, . . . sorrow, . . . corruption, . . . perceived the wretchedness of what is subject to corruption, and craving the incomparable security of a Nirvana free from corruption, attained the incomparable security of a Nirvana free from corruption. And the knowledge and the insight sprang up within them, 'Our deliverance is unshakable; this is our last existence; no more shall we be born again.'

"There are five sensual pleasures, O priests. And what are the five? Forms perceivable by the eye, delightful, pleasant, charming, lovely, accompanied with sensual pleasure, and exciting passion; sounds perceivable by the ear, . . . odors perceivable by the nose, . . . tastes perceivable by the tongue, . . . things tangible perceivable by the body, delightful, pleasant, charming, lovely, accompanied with sensual pleasure, and exciting passion. These, O priests, are the five sensual pleasures.

"All monks and Brahmans, O priests, who partake of these sensual pleasures, and are enveloped, besotted, immersed in them, and perceive not their wretchedness, and know not the way of escape, of them is it to be understood as follows: 'They have lighted on misfortune, have lighted on destruction, and are in the power of the Wicked One.'

"Just as if, O priests, a deer of the forest were to step into a snare, and were to be caught by it. Concerning this deer it is to be understood as follows: 'It has lighted on misfortune, has lighted on destruction, and is in the power of the hunter. When the hunter shall come, it will not be able to make its escape.' In exactly the same way, O priests, all monks and Brahmans who partake of these sensual pleasures, and enveloped, besotted, and immersed in them, perceive not their wretchedness, and know not the way of escape, of them is it to be understood as follows: 'They have lighted on misfortune, have lighted on destruction, and are in the power of the Wicked One.'

"On the other hand, O priests, all monks and Brahmans who partake of these sensual pleasures, and are not enveloped, besotted, and immersed in them, but perceive their wretchedness, and know the way of escape, of them is it to be understood as follows: 'They have not lighted on misfortune, have not lighted on destruction, and are not in the power of the Wicked One.'

"Just as if, O priests, a deer of the forest were to step into a snare, and were not to be caught by it. Concerning this deer it is to be understood as follows: 'It has not lighted on misfortune, has not lighted on destruction, and is not in the power of the hunter. When the hunter shall come, it will be able to make its escape.' In exactly the same way, O priests, all monks and Brahmans who do not partake of these sensual pleasures, and are not enveloped, nor besotted, nor immersed in them, perceive their wretchedness, and know the way of escape, of them is it to be understood as follows: 'They have not lighted on misfortune, have not lighted on destruction, and are not in the power of the Wicked One.'

"Just as if, O priests, a deer of the forest were to roam the woods and mountain slopes; he can walk, stand, squat, and lie down in confident security. And why? Because, O priests, he is out of the reach of the hunter. In exactly the same way, O priests, a priest, having isolated himself from sensual pleasures, having isolated himself from demeritorious traits, and still exercising reasoning, still exercising reflection, enters upon the first trance which is produced by isolation, and characterized by joy and happiness. Of such a priest, O priests, is it said, 'He has blinded Māra, made useless the eye of Māra, gone out of sight of the Wicked One.'

"But again, O priests, a priest, through the subsidence of reasoning and reflection, and still retaining joy and happiness, enters upon the second trance, which is an interior tranquilization and intentness of the thoughts, and is produced by concentration. Of such a priest, O priests, is it said, 'He has blinded Māra, made useless the eye of Māra, gone out of sight of the Wicked One.'

"But again, O priests, a priest through the paling of joy, indifferent, contemplative, conscious, and in the experience of bodily happiness—that state which eminent men describe when they say, 'Indifferent, contemplative, and living happily'—enters upon the third trance. Of such a priest, O priests, is it said, 'He has blinded Māra, made useless the eye of Māra, gone out of sight of the Wicked One.'

"But again, O priests, a priest through the abandonment of happiness, through the abandonment of misery, through the disappearance of all antecedent gladness or grief, enters upon the fourth trance, which has neither misery nor happiness, but is contemplation as refined by indifference. Of such a priest, O priests, is it said, 'He has blinded Māra, made useless the eye of Māra, gone out of sight of the Wicked One.'

"But again, O priests, a priest through having completely overpassed all perceptions of form, through the perishing of perceptions of inertia, and through ceasing to dwell on perceptions of diversity, says to himself, 'Space is infinite,' and dwells in the realm of the infinity of space. Of such a priest, O priests, is it said, 'He has blinded Māra, made useless the eye of Māra, gone out of sight of the Wicked One.'

"But again, O priests, a priest through having completely overpassed the realm of the infinity of space, says to himself, 'Consciousness is infinite,' and dwells in the realm of the infinity of consciousness. Of such a priest, O priests, is it said, 'He has blinded Māra, made useless the eye of Māra, gone out of sight of the Wicked One.'

"But again, O priests, a priest through having completely overpassed the realm of the infinity of consciousness, says to himself, 'Nothing exists,' and dwells in the realm of nothingness. Of such a priest, O priests, is it said, 'He has blinded Māra, made useless the eye of Māra, gone out of sight of the Wicked One.'

"But again, O priests, a priest through having completely overpassed the realm of nothingness, dwells in the realm of neither perception nor yet non-perception. Of such a priest, O priests, is it said, 'He has blinded Māra, made useless the eye of Māra, gone out of sight of the Wicked One.'

"But again, O priests, a priest through having completely over-passed the realm of neither perception nor yet non-perception, arrives at the cessation of perception and sensation, and before the clear vision of wisdom all his depravity wastes away. Of such a priest, O priests, is it said, 'He has blinded Māra, made useless the eye of Māra, gone out of sight of the Wicked One, and passed beyond all adhesion to the world.' He walks, stands, squats, and lies down in confident security. And why? Because, O priests, he is out of the reach of Māra."

Thus spake The Blessed One; and the delighted priests applauded the speech of The Blessed One.

*The Noble-craving Sermon*

## B. Selections from *Dhammapada*

*Translated by F. Max Müller*

### CHAPTER I

#### THE TWIN-VERSES

1. All that we are is the result of what we have thought: it is founded on our thoughts, it is made up of our thoughts. If a man speaks or acts with an evil thought, pain follows him, as the wheel follows the foot of the ox that draws the carriage.

2. All that we are is the result of what we have thought: it is founded on our thoughts, it is made up of our thoughts. If a man

Reprinted from F. Max Müller, tr., *The Sacred Books of the East*, Vol. X (1881).

speaks or acts with a pure thought, happiness follows him, like a shadow that never leaves him.

3. 'He abused me, he beat me, he defeated me, he robbed me,' —in those who harbour such thoughts hatred will never cease.

4. 'He abused me, he beat me, he defeated me, he robbed me,' —in those who do not harbour such thoughts hatred will cease.

5. For hatred does not cease by hatred at any time: hatred ceases by love, this is an old rule.

6. The world does not know that we must all come to an end here;—but those who know it, their quarrels cease at once.

7. He who lives looking for pleasures only, his senses uncontrolled, immoderate in his food, idle, and weak, Mâra (the tempter) will certainly overthrow him, as the wind throws down a weak tree.

8. He who lives without looking for pleasures, his senses well controlled, moderate in his food, faithful and strong, him Mâra will certainly not overthrow, any more than the wind throws down a rocky mountain.

9. He who wishes to put on the yellow dress without having cleansed himself from sin, who disregards also temperance and truth, is unworthy of the yellow dress.

10. But he who has cleansed himself from sin, is well grounded in all virtues, and regards also temperance and truth, he is indeed worthy of the yellow dress.

11. They who imagine truth in untruth, and see untruth in truth, never arrive at truth, but follow vain desires.

12. They who know truth in truth, and untruth in untruth, arrive at truth, and follow true desires.

13. As rain breaks through an ill-thatched house, passion will break through an unreflecting mind.

14. As rain does not break through a well-thatched house, passion will not break through a well-reflecting mind.

15. The evil-doer mourns in this world, and he mourns in the next; he mourns in both. He mourns and suffers when he sees the evil of his own work.

16. The virtuous man delights in this world, and he delights

in the next; he delights in both. He delights and rejoices, when he sees the purity of his own work.

17. The evil-doer suffers in this world, and he suffers in the next; he suffers in both. He suffers when he thinks of the evil he has done; he suffers more when going on the evil path.

18. The virtuous man is happy in this world, and he is happy in the next; he is happy in both. He is happy when he thinks of the good he has done; he is still more happy when going on the good path.

19. The thoughtless man, even if he can recite a large portion (of the law), but is not a doer of it, has no share in the priesthood, but is like a cowherd counting the cows of others.

20. The follower of the law, even if he can recite only a small portion (of the law), but, having forsaken passion and hatred and foolishness, possesses true knowledge and serenity of mind, he, caring for nothing in this world or that to come, has indeed a share in the priesthood.

## CHAPTER XII

### SELF

157. If a man hold himself dear, let him watch himself carefully; during one at least out of the three watches a wise man should be watchful.

158. Let each man direct himself first to what is proper, then let him teach others; thus a wise man will not suffer.

159. If a man make himself as he teaches others to be, then, being himself well subdued, he may subdue (others); one's own self is indeed difficult to subdue.

160. Self is the lord of self, who else could be the lord? With self well subdued, a man finds a lord such as few can find.

161. The evil done by oneself, self-begotten, self-bred, crushes the foolish, as a diamond breaks a precious stone.

162. He whose wickedness is very great brings himself down

to that state where his enemy wishes him to be, as a creeper does with the tree which it surrounds.

163. Bad deeds, and deeds hurtful to ourselves, are easy to do; what is beneficial and good, that is very difficult to do.

164. The foolish man who scorns the rule of the venerable (Arahat), of the elect (Ariya), of the virtuous, and follows false doctrine, he bears fruit to his own destruction, like the fruits of the Katthaka reed.

165. By oneself the evil is done, by oneself one suffers; by oneself evil is left undone, by oneself one is purified. Purity and impurity belong to oneself, no one can purify another.

166. Let no one forget his own duty for the sake of another's, however great; let a man, after he has discerned his own duty, be always attentive to his duty.


## CHAPTER XIV

### The Buddha (The Awakened)

179. He whose conquest is not conquered again, into whose conquest no one in this world enters, by what track can you lead him, the Awakened, the Omniscient, the trackless?

180. He whom no desire with its snares and poisons can lead astray, by what track can you lead him, the Awakened, the Omniscient, the trackless?

181. Even the gods envy those who are awakened and not forgetful, who are given to meditation, who are wise, and who delight in the repose of retirement (from the world).

182. Difficult (to obtain) is the conception of men, difficult is the life of mortals, difficult is the hearing of the True Law, difficult is the birth of the Awakened (the attainment of Buddhahood).

183. Not to commit any sin, to do good, and to purify one's mind, that is the teaching of (all) the Awakened.

184. The Awakened call patience the highest penance, long-suffering the highest Nirvâna; for he is not an anchorite (prav-

ragita) who strikes others, he is not an ascetic (sramana) who insults others.

185. Not to blame, not to strike, to live restrained under the law, to be moderate in eating, to sleep and sit alone, and to dwell on the highest thoughts,—this is the teaching of the Awakened.

186. There is no satisfying lusts, even by a shower of gold pieces; he who knows that lusts have a short taste and cause pain, he is wise;

187. Even in heavenly pleasures he finds no satisfaction, the disciple who is fully awakened delights only in the destruction of all desires.

188. Men, driven by fear, go to many a refuge, to mountains and forests, to groves and sacred trees.

189. But that is not a safe refuge, that is not the best refuge; a man is not delivered from all pains after having gone to that refuge.

190. He who takes refuge with Buddha, the Law, and the Church; he who, with clear understanding, sees the four holy truths:—

191. Viz. pain, the origin of pain, the destruction of pain, and the eightfold holy way that leads to the quieting of pain;—

192. That is the safe refuge, that is the best refuge; having gone to that refuge, a man is delivered from all pain.

193. A supernatural person (a Buddha) is not easily found, he is not born everywhere. Wherever such a sage is born, that race prospers.

194. Happy is the arising of the awakened, happy is the teaching of the True Law, happy is peace in the church, happy is the devotion of those who are at peace.

195, 196. He who pays homage to those who deserve homage, whether the awakened (Buddha) or their disciples, those who have overcome the host (of evils), and crossed the flood of sorrow, he who pays homage to such as have found deliverance and know no fear, his merit can never be measured by anybody.

# CHAPTER XX

## The Way

273. The best of ways is the eightfold; the best of truths the four words; the best of virtues passionlessness; the best of men he who has eyes to see.

274. This is the way, there is no other that leads to the purifying of intelligence. Go on this way! Everything else is the deceit of Mâra (the tempter).

275. If you go on this way, you will make an end of pain! The way was preached by me, when I had understood the removal of the thorns (in the flesh).

276. You yourself must make an effort. The Tathâgatas (Buddhas) are only preachers. The thoughtful who enter the way are freed from the bondage of Mâra.

277. 'All created things perish,' he who knows and sees this becomes passive in pain; this is the way to purity.

278. 'All created things are grief and pain,' he who knows and sees this becomes passive in pain; this is the way that leads to purity.

279. 'All forms are unreal,' he who knows and sees this becomes passive in pain; this is the way that leads to purity.

280. He who does not rouse himself when it is time to rise, who, though young and strong, is full of sloth, whose will and thought are weak, that lazy and idle man will never find the way to knowledge.

281. Watching his speech, well restrained in mind, let a man never commit any wrong with his body! Let a man but keep these three roads of action clear, and he will achieve the way which is taught by the wise.

282. Through zeal knowledge is gotten, through lack of zeal knowledge is lost; let a man who knows this double path of gain and loss thus place himself that knowledge may grow.

283. Cut down the whole forest (of lust), not a tree only! Danger comes out of the forest (of lust). When you have cut

down both the forest (of lust) and its undergrowth, then, Bhik-shus, you will be rid of the forest and free!

284. So long as the love of man towards women, even the smallest, is not destroyed, so long is his mind in bondage, as the calf that drinks milk is to its mother.

285. Cut out the love of self, like an autumn lotus, with thy hand! Cherish the road of peace. Nirvâna has been shown by Sugata (Buddha).

286. 'Here I shall dwell in the rain, here in winter and summer,' thus the fool meditates, and does not think of his death.

287. Death comes and carries off that man, praised for his children and flocks, his mind distracted, as a flood carries off a sleeping village.

288. Sons are no help, nor a father, nor relations; there is no help from kinsfolk for one whom death has seized.

289. A wise and good man who knows the meaning of this, should quickly clear the way that leads to Nirvâna.


# CHAPTER XXIV

## Thirst

334. The thirst of a thoughtless man grows like a creeper; he runs from life to life, like a monkey seeking fruit in the forest.

335. Whomsoever this fierce thirst overcomes, full of poison, in this world, his sufferings increase like the abounding Bîrana grass.

336. He who overcomes this fierce thirst, difficult to be conquered in this world, sufferings fall off from him, like waterdrops from a lotus leaf.

337. This salutary word I tell you, 'Do ye, as many as are here assembled, dig up the root of thirst, as he who wants the sweet-scented Usîra root must dig up the Bîrana grass, that Mâra (the tempter) may not crush you again and again, as the stream crushes the reeds.'

338. As a tree, even though it has been cut down, is firm so

long as its root is safe, and grows again, thus, unless the feeders
of thirst are destroyed, this pain (of life) will return again and
again.

339. He whose thirst running towards pleasure is exceeding
strong in the thirty-six channels, the waves will carry away that
misguided man, viz. his desires which are set on passion.

340. The channels run everywhere, the creeper (of passion)
stands sprouting; if you see the creeper springing up, cut its root
by means of knowledge.

341. A creature's pleasures are extravagant and luxurious;
sunk in lust and looking for pleasure, men undergo (again and
again) birth and decay.

342. Men, driven on by thirst, run about like a snared hare;
held in fetters and bonds, they undergo pain for a long time,
again and again.

343. Men, driven on by thirst, run about like a snared hare;
let therefore the mendicant drive out thirst, by striving after
passionlessness for himself.

344. He who having got rid of the forest (of lust) (i.e. after
having reached Nirvâna) gives himself over to forest-life (i.e.
to lust), and who, when removed from the forest (i.e. from lust),
runs to the forest (i.e. to lust), look at that man! though free,
he runs into bondage.

345. Wise people do not call that a strong fetter which is made
of iron, wood, or hemp; far stronger is the care for precious stones
and rings for sons and a wife.

346. That fetter wise people call strong which drags down,
yields, but is difficult to undo; after having cut this at last, people
leave the world, free from cares, and leaving desires and pleasures behind.

347. Those who are slaves to passions, run down with the
stream (of desires), as a spider runs down the web which he has
made himself; when they have cut this, at last, wise people leave
the world, free from cares, leaving all affection behind.

348. Give up what is before, give up what is behind, give up
what is in the middle, when thou goest to the other shore of

existence; if thy mind is altogether free, thou wilt not again enter
into birth and decay.

349. If a man is tossed about by doubts, full of strong passions,
and yearning only for what is delightful, his thirst will grow
more and more, and he will indeed make his fetters strong.

350. If a man delights in quieting doubts, and, always reflecting, dwells on what is not delightful (the impurity of the body,
&c.), he certainly will remove, nay, he will cut the fetter of
Mâra.

351. He who has reached the consummation, who does not
tremble, who is without thirst and without sin, he has broken
all the thorns of life: this will be his last body.

352. He who is without thirst and without affection, who understands the words and their interpretation, who knows the
order of letters (those which are before and which are after), he
has received his last body, he is called the great sage, the great
man.

353. 'I have conquered all, I know all, in all conditions of life
I am free from taint; I have left all, and through the destruction
of thirst I am free; having learnt myself, whom shall I teach?'

354. The gift of the law exceeds all gifts; the sweetness of the
law exceeds all sweetness; the delight in the law exceeds all
delights; the extinction of thirst overcomes all pain.

355. Pleasures destroy the foolish, if they look not for the
other shore; the foolish by his thirst for pleasures destroys himself, as if he were his own enemy.

356. The fields are damaged by weeds, mankind is damaged
by passion: therefore a gift bestowed on the passionless brings
great reward.

357. The fields are damaged by weeds, mankind is damaged
by hatred: therefore a gift bestowed on those who do not hate
brings great reward.

358. The fields are damaged by weeds, mankind is damaged
by vanity: therefore a gift bestowed on those who are free from
vanity brings great reward.

359. The fields are damaged by weeds, mankind is damaged

by lust: therefore a gift bestowed on those who are free from lust brings great reward.

## CHAPTER XXV

### THE BHIKSHU (MENDICANT)

360. Restraint in the eye is good, good is restraint in the ear, in the nose restraint is good, good is restraint in the tongue.

361. In the body restraint is good, good is restraint in speech, in thought restraint is good, good is restraint in all things. A Bhikshu, restrained in all things, is freed from all pain.

362. He who controls his hand, he who controls his feet, he who controls his speech, he who is well controlled, he who delights inwardly, who is collected, who is solitary and content, him they call Bhikshu.

363. The Bhikshu who controls his mouth, who speaks wisely and calmly, who teaches the meaning and the law, his word is sweet.

364. He who dwells in the law, delights in the law, meditates on the law, follows the law, that Bhikshu will never fall away from the true law.

365. Let him not despise what he has received, nor ever envy others: a mendicant who envies others does not obtain peace of mind.

366. A Bhikshu who, though he receives little, does not despise what he has received, even the gods will praise him, if his life is pure, and if he is not slothful.

367. He who never identifies himself with name and form, and does not grieve over what is no more, he indeed is called a Bhikshu.

368. The Bhikshu who acts with kindness, who is calm in the doctrine of Buddha, will reach the quiet place (Nirvâna), cessation of natural desires, and happiness.

369. O Bhikshu, empty this boat! if emptied, it will go quickly; having cut off passion and hatred, thou wilt go to Nirvâna.

370. Cut off the five (senses), leave the five, rise above the five. A Bhikshu, who has escaped from the five fetters, he is called Oghatinna, 'saved from the flood.'

371. Meditate, O Bhikshu, and be not heedless! Do not direct thy thought to what gives pleasure, that thou mayest not for thy heedlessness have to swallow the iron ball (in hell), and that thou mayest not cry out when burning, 'This is pain.'

372. Without knowledge there is no meditation, without meditation there is no knowledge: he who has knowledge and meditation is near unto Nirvâna.

373. A Bhikshu who has entered his empty house, and whose mind is tranquil, feels a more than human delight when he sees the law clearly.

374. As soon as he has considered the origin and destruction of the elements (khandha) of the body, he finds happiness and joy which belong to those who know the immortal (Nirvâna).

375. And this is the beginning here for a wise Bhikshu: watchfulness over the senses, contentedness, restraint under the law; keep noble friends whose life is pure, and who are not slothful.

376. Let him live in charity, let him be perfect in his duties; then in the fulness of delight he will make an end of suffering.

377. As the Vassikâ plant sheds its withered flowers, men should shed passion and hatred, O ye Bhikshus!

378. The Bhikshu whose body and tongue and mind are quieted, who is collected, and has rejected the baits of the world, he is called quiet.

379. Rouse thyself by thyself, examine thyself by thyself, thus self-protected and attentive wilt thou live happily, O Bhikshu!

380. For self is the lord of self, self is the refuge of self; therefore curb thyself as the merchant curbs a good horse.

381. The Bhikshu, full of delight, who is calm in the doctrine of Buddha will reach the quiet place (Nirvâna), cessation of natural desires, and happiness.

382. He who, even as a young Bhikshu, applies himself to the doctrine of Buddha, brightens up this world, like the moon when free from clouds.

## CHAPTER XXVI
### THE BRÂHMA*N*A (ARHAT)

383. Stop the stream valiantly, drive away the desires, O Brâhma*n*a! When you have understood the destruction of all that was made, you will understand that which was not made.

384. If the Brâhma*n*a has reached the other shore in both laws (in restraint and contemplation), all bonds vanish from him who has obtained knowledge.

385. He for whom there is neither this nor that shore, nor both, him, the fearless and unshackled, I call indeed a Brâhma*n*a.

386. He who is thoughtful, blameless, settled, dutiful, without passions, and who has attained the highest end, him I call indeed a Brâhma*n*a.

387. The sun is bright by day, the moon shines by night, the warrior is bright in his armour, the Brâhma*n*a is bright in his meditation; but Buddha, the Awakened, is bright with splendour day and night.

388. Because a man is rid of evil, therefore he is called Brâhma*n*a; because he walks quietly, therefore he is called Sama*n*a; because he has sent away his own impurities, therefore he is called Pravragita (Pabbagita, a pilgrim).

389. No one should attack a Brâhma*n*a, but no Brâhma*n*a (if attacked) should let himself fly at his aggressor! Woe to him whc strikes a Brâhma*n*a, more woe to him who flies at his aggressor!

390. It advantages a Brâhma*n*a not a little if he holds his mind back from the pleasures of life; when all wish to injure has vanished, pain will cease.

391. Him I call indeed a Brâhma*n*a who does not offend by body, word, or thought, and is controlled on these three points.

392. After a man has once understood the law as taught by the Well-awakened (Buddha), let him worship it carefully, as the Brâhma*n*a worships the sacrificial fire.

393. A man does not become a Brâhma*n*a by his platted hair, by his family, or by birth; in whom there is truth and righteousness, he is blessed, he is a Brâhma*n*a.

394. What is the use of platted hair, O fool! what of the raiment of goat-skins? Within thee there is ravening, but the outside thou makest clean.

395. The man who wears dirty raiments, who is emaciated and covered with veins, who lives alone in the forest, and meditates, him I call indeed a Brâhmana.

396. I do not call a man a Brâhmana because of his origin or of his mother. He is indeed arrogant, and he is wealthy: but the poor, who is free from all attachments, him I call indeed a Brâhmana.

397. Him I call indeed a Brâhmana who has cut all fetters, who never trembles, is independent and unshackled.

398. Him I call indeed a Brâhmana who has cut the strap and the thong, the chain with all that pertains to it, who has burst the bar, and is awakened.

399. Him I call indeed a Brâhmana who, though he has committed no offence, endures reproach, bonds, and stripes, who has endurance for his force, and strength for his army.

400. Him I call indeed a Brâhmana who is free from anger, dutiful, virtuous, without appetite, who is subdued, and has received his last body.

401. Him I call indeed a Brâhmana who does not cling to pleasures, like water on a lotus leaf, like a mustard seed on the point of a needle.

402. Him I call indeed a Brâhmana who, even here, knows the end of his suffering, has put down his burden, and is unshackled.

403. Him I call indeed a Brâhmana whose knowledge is deep, who possesses wisdom, who knows the right way and the wrong, and has attained the highest end.

404. Him I call indeed a Brâhmana who keeps aloof both from laymen and from mendicants, who frequents no houses, and has but few desires.

405. Him I call indeed a Brâhmana who finds no fault with other beings, whether feeble or strong, and does not kill nor cause slaughter.

406. Him I call indeed a Brâhmana who is tolerant with the

intolerant, mild with fault-finders, and free from passion among the passionate.

407. Him I call indeed a Brâhmana from whom anger and hatred, pride and envy have dropt like a mustard seed from the point of a needle.

408. Him I call indeed a Brâhmana who utters true speech, instructive and free from harshness, so that he offend no one.

409. Him I call indeed a Brâhmana who takes nothing in the world that is not given him, be it long or short, small or large, good or bad.

410. Him I call indeed a Brâhmana who fosters no desires for this world or for the next, has no inclinations, and is un-shackled.

411. Him I call indeed a Brâhmana who has no interests, and when he has understood (the truth), does not say How, how? and who has reached the depth of the Immortal.

412. Him I call indeed a Brâhmana who in this world is above good and evil, above the bondage of both, free from grief, from sin, and from impurity.

413. Him I call indeed a Brâhmana who is bright like the moon, pure, serene, undisturbed, and in whom all gaiety is extinct.

414. Him I call indeed a Brâhmana who has traversed this miry road; the impassable world and its vanity, who has gone through, and reached the other shore, is thoughtful, guileless, free from doubts, free from attachment, and content.

415. Him I call indeed a Brâhmana who in this world, leaving all desires, travels about without a home, and in whom all con-cupiscence is extinct.

416. Him I call indeed a Brâhmana who, leaving all longings, travels about without a home, and in whom all covetousness is extinct.

417. Him I call indeed a Brâhmana who, after leaving all bondage to men, has risen above all bondage to the gods, and is free from all and every bondage.

418. Him I call indeed a Brâhmana who has left what gives pleasure and what gives pain, who is cold, and free from all

germs (of renewed life), the hero who has conquered all the worlds.

419. Him I call indeed a Brâhmana who knows the destruction and the return of beings everywhere, who is free from bondage, welfaring (Sugata), and awakened (Buddha).

420. Him I call indeed a Brâhmana whose path the gods do not know, nor spirits (Gandharvas), nor men, whose passions are extinct, and who is an Arhat (venerable).

421. Him I call indeed a Brâhmana who calls nothing his own, whether it be before, behind, or between, who is poor, and free from the love of the world.

422. Him I call indeed a Brâhmana, the manly, the noble, the hero, the great sage, the conqueror, the impassible, the accomplished, the awakened.

423. Him I call indeed a Brâhmana who knows his former abodes, who sees heaven and hell, has reached the end of births, is perfect in knowledge, a sage, and whose perfections are all perfect.

## CHAPTER VII

# Mahayana

## Mahayana Buddhism

*Ananda Coomaraswamy*

### SYSTEM OF THE MAHĀYĀNA

The Mahāyāna or Great Vessel is so-called by its adherents, in contradistinction to the Hīnayāna or Little Vessel of primitive Buddhism, because the former offers to all beings in all worlds salvation by faith and love as well as by knowledge, while the latter only avails to convey over the rough sea of Becoming to the farther shore of Nibbāna those few strong souls who require no external spiritual aid nor the consolation of Worship. The Hīnayāna, like the 'unshown way' of those who seek the *'nirguna Brahman,'* is exceeding hard; whereas the burden of the Mahāyāna is light, and does not require that a man should immediately renounce the world and all the affections of humanity. The manifestation of the Body of the Law, says the Mahāyāna, is adapted to the various needs of the children of the Buddha; whereas the Hīnayāna is only of avail to those who have left their spiritual childhood far behind them. The Hīnayāna emphasizes the necessity of saving knowledge, and aims at the salvation of

Reprinted from Ananda Coomaraswamy, *Buddha and the Gospel of Buddhism* (London: George G. Harrap & Company Limited, 1916; New York: Harper & Row, Publishers, Inc., 1964), pages 226-252. Used by permission of George G. Harrap & Company Limited and Harper & Row, Publishers, Inc.

the individual, and refuses to develop the mystery of Nibbāna in a positive sense; the Mahāyāna lays as much or greater stress on love, and aims at the salvation of every sentient being, and finds in Nirvāna the One Reality, which is 'Void' only in the sense that it is free from the limitations of every phase of the limited or contingent experience of which we have empirical knowledge. The Buddhists of the primitive school, on the other hand, naturally do not accept the name of the 'Lesser Vessel,' and as true Protestants they raise objection to the theological and æsthetic accommodation of the true doctrine to the necessities of human nature.

Opinions thus differ as to whether we may regard the Mahā-yāna as a development or a degeneration. Even the professed exponents of the Hīnayāna have their doubts. Thus in one place Professor Rhys Davids speaks of the Bodhisattva doctrine as the *bīrana*-weed which "drove out the doctrine of the Ariyan path," and the weed "is not attractive": while in another, Mrs Rhys Davids writes of the cool detachment of the Arahat, that perhaps "a yet more saintly Sāriputta would have aspired yet further, even to an infinite series of rebirths, wherein he might, with ever-growing power and self-devotion, work for the furtherance of the religious evolution of his fellows," adding that "social and religious ideals evolve out of, yea, and even beyond the finished work and time-straitened vision of the Arahants of old." Perhaps we need not determine the relative value of either school: the way of knowledge will ever appeal to some, and the way of love and action to others, and the latter the majority. Those who are saved by knowledge stand apart from the world and its hopes and fears, offering to the world only that knowledge which shall enable others to stand aside in the same way: those others who are moved by their love and wisdom to perpetual activity—in whom the will to life is dead, but the will to power yet survives in its noblest and most impersonal forms—attain at last the same goal, and in the meanwhile effect a reconciliation of religion with the world, and the union of renunciation with action.

The development of the Mahāyāna is in fact the overflowing of Buddhism from the limits of the Order into the life of the

world; into whatever devious channels Buddhism may have ultimately descended, are we to say that that identification with the
life of the world, with all its consequences in ethic and æsthetic,
was a misfortune? Few who are acquainted with the history of
Asiatic culture would maintain any such thesis.

Mahāyānists do not hesitate to describe the Hīnayāna ideal as
selfish; and we have indicated in several places to what extent it
must in any case be called narrow. But the Mahāyānists—not to
speak of Christian critics of the Hīnayāna—do not sufficiently
realize that a selfish being could not possibly become an Arahat,
who must be free from even the conception of an ego, and still
more from every form of ego-assertion. The selfishness of the
would-be Arahat is more apparent than real. The ideal of self-
culture is not opposed to that of self-sacrifice: in any perfectly
harmonious development these seemingly opposite tendencies
are reconciled. To achieve this reconciliation, to combine renunciation with growth, knowledge with love, stillness with
activity, is the problem of all ethics. Curiously enough, though
its solution has often been attempted by oriental religions, it has
never been so clearly enunciated in the west as by the 'irreligious'
Nietzsche—the latest of the mystics—whose ideal of the Superman combines the Will to Power (*cf. pranidhāna*) with the
Bestowing Virtue (*cf. karunā*).

If the ideal of the Private Buddha seems to be a selfish one,
we may reply that the Great Man can render to his fellows no
higher service than to realize the highest possible state of his
being. From the Unity of life we cannot but deduce the identity
of (true) self-interest with the (true) interest of others. While
therefore the Mahāyānists may justly claim that their system is
indeed a greater vessel of salvation in the sense of greater con-
venience, or better adaptation to the needs of a majority of
voyagers, they cannot on the other hand justly accuse the captain
and the crew of the smaller ship of selfishness. Those who seek
the farther shore may select the means best suited to their own
needs: the final goal is one and the same.

The most essential part of the Mahāyāna is its emphasis on
the Bodhisattva ideal, which replaces that of Arahatta, or ranks

before it. Whereas the Arahat strives most earnestly for Nirvāna, the Bodhisattva as firmly refuses to accept the final release. "Forasmuch as there is the will that all sentient beings should be altogether made free, I will not forsake my fellow creatures." The Bodhisattva is he in whom the Bodhicitta or heart of wisdom is fully expanded. In a sense, we are all Bodhisattvas, and indeed all Buddhas, only that in us by reason of ignorance and imperfection in love the glory of the Bodhi-heart is not yet made manifest. But those are specially called Bodhisattvas who with specific determination dedicate all the activities of their future and present lives to the task of saving the world. They do not merely contemplate, but feel, all the sorrow of the world, and because of their love they cannot be idle, but expend their virtue with supernatural generosity. It is said of Gautama Buddha, for example, that there is no spot on earth where he has not in some past life sacrificed his life for the sake of others, while the whole story of his last incarnation related in the *Vessantara Jātaka* relates the same unstinting generosity, which does not shrink even from the giving away of wife and children. But Buddhahood once attained, according to the old school, it remains for others to work out their salvation alone: "Be ye lamps unto yourselves," in the last words of Gautama. According to the Mahāyāna, however, even the attainment of Buddhahood does not involve indifference to the sorrow of the world; the work of salvation is perpetually carried on by the Bodhisattva emanations of the supreme Buddhas, just as the work of the Father is done by Jesus.

The Bodhisattvas are specially distinguished from the Srāvakas (Arahats) and Pacceka-Buddhas or 'Private Buddhas,' who have become followers of the Buddha 'for the sake of their own complete Nirvāna': for the Bodhisattvas enter upon their course "out of compassion to the world, for the benefit, weal, and happiness of the world at large, both gods and men, for the sake of the complete Nirvāna of all beings. . . . Therefore they are called Bodhisattva Mahāsattva."

A doctrine specially associated with the Bodhisattva ideal is that of the *parivarta* or turning over of ethical merit to the advantage of others, which amounts very nearly to the doctrine of vicarious atonement. Whereas in early Buddhism it is emphasized that each life is entirely separate from every other (also a Jaina doctrine, and no doubt derived from the Sāmkhya conception of a plurality of Purushas), the Mahāyāna insists on the interdependence and even the identity of all life; and this position affords a logical basis for the view that the merit acquired by one may be devoted to the good of others. This is a peculiarly amiable feature in late Buddhism; we find, for example, that whoever accomplishes a good deed, such as a work of charity or a pilgrimage, adds the prayer that the merit may be shared by all sentient beings.

It will be seen that the doctrine of vicarious merit involves the interpretation of karma in the first and more general sense referred to previously. No man lives to himself alone, but we may regard the whole creation (which groaneth and travailleth together) as one life and therefore as sharing a common karma, to which every individual contributes for good or ill. Notwithstanding from the individualist standpoint it may appear both false and dangerous to limit the doctrine of purely individual responsibility, it is not so in fact; the good or evil of the individual also affects others, and rather increases his responsibility than lightens it. There is no mystery in karma; it is simply a phase of the law of cause and effect, and it holds as much for groups and communities as for individuals, if indeed, individuals are not also communities. Let us take a very simple example: if a single wise statesman by a generous treatment of a conquered race secures their loyalty at some future time of stress, that karma accrues not merely to himself but to the state for ever; and other members of the community, even those who would have dealt ungenerously in the first instance, benefit undeniably from the vicarious merit of a single man. Just in this sense it is possible for hero-souls to bear or share the burden of the karma of humanity. By this conception of the taking on of sin, or rather, the passing on of merit, the Mahāyāna has definitely emerged from the formula of psychic isolation which the Hīnayāna inherits from the Sāmkhya.

In other words, the great difficulty of imagining a particular karma passing from individual to individual, without the persistence even of a subtle body, is avoided by the conception of human beings, or indeed of the whole universe, as constituting one life or self. Thus it is from our ancestors that we receive our karma, and not merely from 'our own' past existences; and whatsoever karma we create will be inherited by humanity for ever.

The following account of karma is given by a modern Mahāyānist:

The aggregate actions of all sentient beings give birth to the varieties of mountains, rivers, countries, etc. They are caused by aggregate actions, and so are called aggregate fruits. Our present life is the reflection of past actions. Men consider these reflections as their real selves. Their eyes, noses, ears, tongues, and bodies—as well as their gardens, woods, farms, residences, servants, and maids—men imagine to be their own possessions; but, in fact, they are only results endlessly produced by innumerable actions. In tracing everything back to the ultimate limits of the past, we cannot find a beginning: hence it is said that death and birth have no beginning. Again, when seeking the ultimate limit of the future, we cannot find the end.

It may be pointed out here just how far the doctrine of karma is and is not fatalistic. It is fatalistic in the sense that the present is always determined by the past; but the future remains free. Every action we make depends on what we have come to be at the time. But what we are coming to be at any time depends on the direction of the will. The karmic law merely asserts that this direction cannot be altered suddenly by the forgiveness of sins, but must be changed by our own efforts. If ever the turning of the will appears to take place suddenly, that can only be due to the fruition of long accumulated latent tendencies (we constantly read that Gautama preached the Law to such and such a one, forasmuch as he saw that his or her intelligence was 'fully ripe,' and in these cases conversion immediately results). Thus, if we are not directly responsible for our present actions, we are always responsible for our character, on which future actions depend. On this account the object of Buddhist moral discipline is always the accumulation of merit (*punya*), that is to say the heaping up of grace, or simply the constant improvement of character. The Mahāyānist doctors recognize ten stations in the spiritual evolution of the Bodhisattva, beginning with the first awakening of the Wisdom-heart (Bodhicitta) in the warmth of compassion (karunā) and the light of divine knowledge (prajñā). These stations are those of 'joy,' 'purity,' 'effulgence,' 'burning,' 'hard to achieve,' 'showing the face,' 'going afar off,' 'not moving to and fro,' 'good intelligence,' and 'dharma-cloud.' It is in the first station that the Bodhisattva makes those pregnant resolutions (pranidhāna) which determine the course of his future lives. An example of such a vow is the resolution of Avalokiteśvara not to accept salvation until the least particle of dust shall have attained to Buddhahood before him.

It may be mentioned that the course (*cariyā*) of the Bodhisattva has this advantage, that he never comes to birth in any purgatory, nor in any unfavourable condition on earth. Nor is the Bodhisattva required to cultivate a disgust for the conditions of life; he does not practise a meditation on Foul Things, like the aspirant for Arahatta. The Bodhisattva simply recognizes that the conditions of life have come to be what they are, that it is in the nature (*tattva, bhutathā,* suchness) of things to be so, and he takes them accordingly for what they are worth. This position is nowhere more tersely summed up than in the well-known Japanese verselet—

> *Granted this dewdrop world be but a dewdrop world,*
> *This granted, yet . . .*

Thus the new Buddhist law was in no way puritanical, and did not inculcate an absolute detachment. Pleasure indeed is not to be sought as an end in itself, but it need not be rejected as it arises incidentally. The Bodhisattva shares in the life of the world; for example, he has a wife, that his supernatural generosity may be seen in the gift of wife and children, and for the same reason he may be the possessor of power and wealth. If by reason of attachment and this association with the world some venial sins are unavoidably committed, that is of little consequence, and such sins are wiped away in the love of others: the cardinal sins of hatred and self-thinking cannot be imagined in him in whom the heart of wisdom has been awakened. It must not, however, be supposed that the Mahāyāna in any way relaxes the rule of the Order; and even in the matter of the remission of sins of the laity it is only minor and inevitable shortcomings that are considered, and not deliberate deeds of evil. And if the Mahāyāna doctors preach the futility of remorse and discouragement, on the other hand they are by no means quietists, but advocate a mysticism fully as practical as that of Ruysbroeck.

The idea of the Bodhisattva corresponds to that of the Hero, the Superman, the Saviour and the Avatār of other systems. In this connexion it is interesting to note that legitimate pride—the will to power, conjoined with the bestowing virtue—is by no means alien to the Bodhisattva character, but on the contrary, "In respect of three things may pride be borne—man's works, his temptations, and his power," and the exposition follows:

The pride of works lies in the thought 'for me alone is the task.' This world, enslaved by passion, is powerless to accomplish its own weal; then must I do it for them, for I am not impotent like them. Shall another do a lowly task while I am standing by? If I in my pride will not do it, better it is that my pride perish. . . . Then with firm spirit I will undo the occasions of undoing; if I should be conquered by them, my ambition to conquer the threefold world would be a jest. I will conquer all; none shall conquer me. This is the pride that I will bear, for I am the son of the Conqueror Lions! . . . Surrounded by the troop of the passions man should become a thousand times prouder, and he as unconquerable to their hordes as a lion to flocks of deer . . . so, into whatever straits he may come, he will not fall into the power of the Passions. He will utterly give himself over to whatever task arrives, greedy for the work . . . how can he whose happiness is work itself be happy in doing no work? He will hold himself in readiness, so that even before a task comes to him he is prepared to turn to every course. As the seed of the cotton-tree is swayed at the coming and going of the wind, so will he be obedient to his resolution; and thus divine power is gained.

We may remark here an important distinction between the Mahāyāna and the Hīnayāna lies in the fact that the former is essentially mythical and unhistorical; the believer is, indeed, warned—precisely as the worshipper of Krishna is warned in the Vaishnava scriptures that the Krishna Līlā is not a history, but a process for ever unfolded in the heart of man—that matters of historical fact are without religious significance. On this account, notwithstanding its more popular form, the Mahāyāna has been justly called 'more philosophical' than the Hīnayāna, "because under the forms of religious or mystical imagery it expresses the universal, whereas the Hīnayāna cannot set itself free from the domination of the historical fact."

An important dogmatic distinction, the meaning of which will be made clear as we proceed, is also found in the new interpretation of the Three Refuges. In the Hīnayāna these are the Buddha, the Dhamma, and the Sangha; in the Mahāyāna they are the Buddhas, the Sons of the Buddhas (Bodhisattvas both in the special and in the wider sense), and the Dharmakāya.

## MAHĀYĀNA THEOLOGY

The Mahāyāna is thus distinguished by its mystical Buddha theology. This must not be confused with the popular and quite realistic theology of Sakka and Brahmā recognized in early Buddhism. The Mahāyāna Buddha theology, as remarked by Rhys Davids, "is the greatest possible contradiction to the Agnostic Atheism," which is the characteristic of Gautama's system of philosophy. But this opposition is simply the inevitable contrast of religion and philosophy, relative and absolute truth, and those who are interested in the science of theology, or are touched by art, will not be likely to agree in denouncing the Buddha gods as the inventions "of a sickly scholasticism, hollow abstractions without life or reality": in this contingent world we live every day by relative truths, and for all those who do not wish to avoid the world of Becoming at the earliest possible moment these relative truths are far from lacking in life or reality. The Mahā-yāna as a theistic faith is so only to the same extent as the Vedānta, that is to say it has an esoteric aspect which speaks in negative terms of a Suchness and a Void which cannot be known, while on the other it has an exoteric and more elaborate part in which the Absolute is seen through the glass of time and space, contracted and identified into variety. This development appears in the doctrine of the Trikāya, the Three Bodies of Buddha. These three are (1) the *Dharmakāya,* or Essence-body; (2) its heavenly manifestation in the *Sambhogakāya,* or Body of Bliss; and (3) the emanation, transformation, or projection thereof, called *Nirmānakāya,* apparent as the visible individual Buddha on earth. This is a system which hardly differs from what is implied in the Christian doctrine of Incarnation, and it is not unlikely that both Christianity and the Mahāyāna are inheritors from common Gnostic sources.

Thus the Dharmakāya may be compared to the Father; the Sambhogakāya to the figure of Christ in glory; the Nirmānakāya to the visible Jesus who announces in human speech that 'I and my Father are One.' Or again with the Vedānta: the Dharmakāya is the Brahman, timeless and unconditioned; the Sambhogakāya is realized in the forms of Īsvara; the Nirmānākaya in every avatār. The essence of all things, the one reality of which their fleeting shapes remind us, is the Dharmakāya. The Dharmakāya is not a personal being who reveals himself to us in a single in-carnation, but it is the all-pervading and traceless ground of the soul, which does not in fact suffer any modification but appears to us to assume a variety of forms: we read that though the Buddha (a term which we must here understand as impersonal) does not depart from his seat in the tower (state of Dharma-kāya), yet he may assume all and every form, whether of a Brahmā, a god, or a monk, or a physician, or a tradesman, or an artist; he may reveal himself in every form of art and industry, in cities or in villages: from the highest heaven to the lowest hell, there is the Dharmakāya, in which all sentient beings are one.

The Dharmakāya is the impersonal ground of Buddhahood from which the personal will, thought and love of innumerable Buddhas and Bodhisattvas ever proceed in response to the needs of those in whom the perfect nature is not yet realized. In some of the later phases of the Mahāyāna, however, the Dharmakāya is personified as Ādi-Buddha (sometimes Vairocana) who is then to be regarded as the Supreme Being, above all other Buddhas, and whose śakti is Prajñāpāramitā.

Dharmakāya is commonly translated 'Body of the Law,' but it must not be interpreted merely as equivalent to the sum of the scriptures. The fathomless being of Buddhahood, according to the Mahāyāna, is something more than the immortality of the individual in his doctrine; we must understand Dharma here as the *Om* or *Logos*. To understand the meaning of Dharmakāya more fully we must take into account also its synonyms, for example, *Svabhāvakāya*, or 'own-nature body' (like the Brāhmanical *svarūpa*, 'own-form'), *Tattva*, or 'suchness,' *Sunya*, 'the void' or 'abyss,' *Nirvāna*, 'the eternal liberty,' *Samādhikāya*, 'rapture-body,' *Bodhi*, 'wisdom,' *Prajñā*, 'divine knowledge,' *Tathāgatagarbha*, 'womb of those who attain.'

Some of these terms must be further considered. The 'Void,' for example, is not by any means 'naught,' but simply the absence of characteristics; the Dharmakāya is 'void' just as the Brahman is 'not so, not so,' and as Duns Scotus says that God 'is not improperly called Nothing.' It is precisely from the undetermined that evolution is imaginable; where there is nothing there is room for everything. The voidness of things is the non-existence of things-in-themselves, on which so much stress is rightly laid in early Buddhism. The phrase 'Own-nature body' emphasizes the thought 'I am that I am.' Bodhi is the 'wisdom-heart' which awakens with the determination to become a Buddha. 'Suchness' may be taken to mean inevitability, or spontaneity, that the highest cause of everything must needs be in the thing itself.

A special meaning attaches to the name Prajñā or Prajñāpāramitā, viz. Supreme Knowledge, Reason, Understanding, Sophia; for the name Prajñāpāramitā is applied to the chief of the Mahā-

yāna scriptures, or a group of scriptures, signifying the divine
knowledge which they embody, and she is also personified as a
feminine divinity. As one with the Dharmakāya she is the knowledge of the Abyss, the Buddhahood in which the individual
Bodhisattva passes away. But as Reason or Understanding she is
Tathāgata-garbha, the Womb or Mother of the Buddhas, and
the source from which issues the variety of things, both mental
and physical. In Hindu phraseology, she is the Śakti of the Supreme, the power of manifestation inseparable from that which
Manifests: she is Devī, *Māyā,* or *Prakriti,* the One who is also
the many. "In the root she is all-Brahman; in the stem she is
all-illusion; in the flower she is all-world; and in the fruit all-
liberation"—(*Tantra Tattva*).


## NIRVANA

The Mahāyāna doctrine of Nirvāna requires somewhat
lengthier consideration. We have seen that in earlier Buddhism
Nibbāna meant the dying out of the fires of passion, resentment,
and infatuation, and the dissolution of the individual personality,
but what more or less than this it meant metaphysically, Gautama
would not say, and he plainly condemns speculation as unedi-
fying.

Mahāyānists however do not hesitate to develop a far-reaching
idealism, similar to that of the Vedānta, and logically develop the
early Buddhism phenomenalism into a complete nihilism which,
as we have seen, declares that the whole world of becoming is
truly void and unreal.

This 'nihilism' is carried to its farthest extreme in works such
as the *Prajñāpāramitās* and the *Vajracchedika Sūtra*: we read,
for example, in the latter work:

And again, O Subhuti, a gift should not be given by a Bodhisattva,
while he still believes in the reality of objects; a gift should not be
given by him while he yet believes in anything; a gift should not be
given by him while he still believes in form; a gift should not be given
by him while he still believes in the special qualities of sound, smell,

taste, and touch. . . . And why? Because that Bodhisattva, O Subhuti, who gives a gift, without believing in anything, the measure of his stock of merit is not easy to learn!

And this denial of entity is carried to the logical extreme of denying the existence of scripture:

'Then what do you think, O Subhuti, is there any doctrine that was preached by the Tathāgata?' Subhuti said: 'Not so, indeed, O Worshipful, there is not anything that was preached by the Tathāgata.'

Even more striking is the famous 'Middle Path of Eight Noes' of Nāgārjuna:

There is no production (*utpāda*), no destruction (*uccheda*), no annihilation (*nirodha*), no persistence (*sāsvata*), no unity (*ekārtha*), no plurality (*nānārtha*), no coming in (*āgamana*), and no going forth (*nirgama*).

This view, however, is not properly to be understood as mere nihilism; it is constantly emphasized that things of all kinds neither exist nor do not exist. We may understand this 'middle view' in either of two ways: as the doctrine that of that which is other than phenomenal there cannot be any predication of existence or non-existence; or as the doctrine that from the standpoint of the Absolute, things have no existence, while from the standpoint of the Relative, they have a relative being.

## NĀGĀRJUNA

The latter view is distinctly maintained by Nāgārjuna, who, like Asvaghosa, must have been originally a Brāhman, and lived about the end of the second century A.D. The Middle View just mentioned is set forth by him in the *Mādhyamika sūtras*. And here Nāgārjuna gives a very clear answer to the objection that, if all be 'Void,' then the Four Ariyan Truths, the Order of Brethren, and Buddha himself must be considered to be and have been unreal: he meets the difficulty precisely as Sankarā-

cārya meets the inconsistencies of the Upanishads, by saying that
the Buddha speaks of two truths, the one Truth in the highest
sense, absolute, the other a conventional and relative truth; he
who does not comprehend the distinction of these cannot understand the deeper import of the teaching of the Buddha.

The Mahāyāna is thus far from affirming that Nirvāna is
non-existence pure and simple; it does not hesitate to say that to
lose our life is to save it. Nirvāna is positive, or positively is;
even for the individual it cannot be said to come to be, or to be
entered into; it merely comes to be realized, so soon as that
ignorance is overcome which obscures the knowledge of our
real freedom, which nothing has ever infringed, or ever can
infringe. Nirvāna is that which is not lacking, is not acquired,
is not intermittent, is not non-intermittent, is not subjet to destruction, and is not created, whose sign is the absence of signs,
which transcends alike non-Being and Being. The Mahāyāna
Nirvāna cannot be better explained than in the words of the
great Sūfī Al-Hujwīrī—"When a man becomes annihilated from
his attributes he attains to perfect subsistence, he is neither near
nor far, neither stranger nor intimate, neither sober nor intoxicated,
neither separated nor united; he has no name, or sign, or brand
or mark" (*Kashf al-Mahjūb*). It is the realization of the infinite
love and infinite wisdom, where knowledge and love alike proclaim identity, that constitute this Nirvāna. He in whom the
Heart of Wisdom awakes, however, does not shrink from future
rebirths, "but plunges himself into the ever rushing current of
Samsāra and sacrifices himself to save his fellow creatures from
being eternally drowned in it." He does not shrink from experience, for "just as the lotus-flowers do not grow on the dry
land, but spring from the dark and watery mud, so is it with
the Heart of Wisdom, it is by virtue of passion and sin that the
seeds and sprouts of Buddhahood are able to grow, and not from
inaction and eternal annihilation" (*Vimala-ķīrti Sūtra*).

Mahāyāna non-duality culminates in the magnificent paradox
of the identity of Nirvāna with the Samsāra, the non-distinction
of the unshown and the shown—"this our worldly life is an

activity of Nirvāna itself, not the slightest distinction exists between them"—(Nāgārjuna, *Mādhyamika Sāstra*). This view is
expressed with dramatic force in the aphorism, *'Yas klesas so
bodhi, yas samsāras tat nirvānam,'* That which is sin is also
Wisdom, the realm of Becoming is also Nirvāna. One and the
same is the heart of Suchness and the heart of Birth-and-Death—
'what is immortal and what is mortal are harmoniously blended,
for they are not one, nor are they separate'—(Asyaghosha). If
the truth is not to be found in our everyday experience, it will
not be found by searching elsewhere.

## MAHĀYĀNA MYSTICISM

It scarcely needs to be pointed out, though it is important to
realize, that this is the ultimate position to which the mystics of
every age and inheritance have ultimately returned. It is that of
Blake when he says that the notion that a man has a body distinct
from his soul must be expunged, and that it is only because the
doors of perception are closed—by ignorance—that we do not see
all things as they are, infinite. It is that of Kabīr when he says—
"in the home is reality; the home helps to attain Him who is
real—I behold His beauty everywhere"; and when he asks, "What
is the difference between the river and its waves; because it has
been named as wave, shall it no longer be considered water?"
It is that of Behmen when he says the Enochian life "is in this
world, yet as it were swallowed up in the Mystery; but it is not
altered in itself, it is only withdrawn from our sight and our
sense; for if our eyes were opened, we should see it": Paradise
is still upon earth, and only because of our self-thinking and self-
willing we do not see and hear God. It is that of Whitman,
when he says there "will never be any more perfection than there
is now, nor any more of heaven or hell than there is now," and
inquires, "Why should I wish to see God better than this day?"

> *Strange and hard that paradox true I give,*
> *Objects gross and the unseen soul are one.*

## THE BUDDHAS

In the realm of absolute (*paramārtha*) truth we may speak only of the Dharmakāya as void. But there exists also for us a realm of relative (*samvritti*) truth where the Absolute is made manifest by name and form; to the dwellers in heaven as Sambhogakāya, the Body of Bliss, and to those on earth as Nirmānakāya, the Body of Transformation.

The Sambhogakāya is the Buddha or Buddhas regarded as God in heaven, determined by name and form, but omniscient, omnipresent, and within the law of causality, omnipotent. A Buddha, in this sense, is identical with the Brāhmanical 'Īsvara,' who may be worshipped under various names (*e.g.* as Vishnu or as Siva), the worshipper attaining the heaven ruled by him whom he worships, though he knows that all of these forms are essentially one and the same. The Mahāyāna does in fact multiply the number of Buddhas indefinitely and quite logically, since it is the goal of every individual to become a Buddha. The nature of these Buddhas and their heavens will be best realized if we describe the most popular of all, whose name is Amitābha, or Amida.

Amitābha Buddha rules over the heaven Sukhāvati, the Pure Land or Western Paradise. With him are associated the historical Gautama as earthly emanation, and the Bodhisattva Avalokiteśvara as the Saviour. The history of Amitābha relates that many long ages ago he was a great king, who left his throne to become a wanderer, and he attained to Bodhisattvahood under the guidance of the Buddha, that is, the human Buddha then manifest; and he made a series of great vows, both to become a Buddha for sake of saving all living things, and to create a heaven where the souls of the blessed might enjoy an age-long state of happiness, wisdom and purity. The eighteenth of these vows is the chief source of the popular development of Amidism, as the belief of the worshippers of Amitābha is styled. This vow runs as follows:

When I become Buddha, let all living beings of the ten regions of the

universe maintain a confident and joyful faith in me; let them con-
centrate their longings on a rebirth in my Paradise; and let them call
upon my name, though it be only ten times or less: then, provided
only they have not been guilty of the five heinous sins, and have not
slandered or vilified the true religion, the desire of such beings to be
born in my Paradise will be surely fulfilled. If this be not so, may I
never receive the perfect enlightenment of Buddhahood.

This is a fully developed doctrine of salvation by faith. The
parallel with some forms of Christianity is very close. Amitābha
both 'draws' men to himself, and 'sent' his son Gautama to
lead men to him, and he is ever accessible through the holy
spirit of Avalokiteśvara. The efficacy of death-bed repentance is
admitted; and in any case the dying Amidist should contemplate
the glorious figure of Amitābha, just as the dying Catholic fixes
his eyes upon the Crucifix upheld by the priest who administers
extreme unction. The faithful Amidist is carried immediately
to heaven, and is there reborn with a spiritual body within the
calyx of one of the lotuses of the sacred lake. But those of less
virtue must wait long before their lotus expands, and until then
they cannot see God. Those who have committed one of the five
heinous sins, and yet have called on Amitābha's name, must
wait for countless ages, a period of time beyond conception,
before their flowers open; just as, according to Behmen, those
souls that depart from the body "without Christ's body, hanging
as it were by a thread," must wait for the last day, ere they come
forth. Another Mahāyānist idea, that the heaven of a Buddha is
coextensive with the universe, is also to be found in Behmen,
who, to the question, "Must not the soul leave the body at death,
and go either to heaven or hell?" answers, "There is verily no
such kind of entering in; forasmuch as heaven and hell are everywhere, being universally extended." Strictly speaking, the heaven
of Amitābha cannot be identified with Nirvāna, but is a 'Buddha-
field,' where preparation for Nirvāna is completed.
    The following Table will exhibit the complete scheme of
Mahāyāna Buddhology:

ĀDIBUDDHA

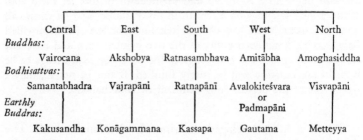

|               | Central        | East        | South          | West                      | North         |
|---------------|----------------|-------------|----------------|---------------------------|---------------|
| *Buddhas:*    | Vairocana      | Akshobya    | Ratnasambhava  | Amitābha                  | Amoghasiddha  |
| *Bodhisattvas:* | Samantabhadra | Vajrapāni  | Ratnapānī      | Avalokiteśvara or Padmapāni | Visvapāni    |
| *Earthly Buddras:* | Kakusandha | Konāgammana | Kassapa        | Gautama                   | Metteyya      |

The Mahāyāna pantheon, however, is extended far beyond this simple scheme, to include more than five hundred divinities: in the words of Lafcadio Hearn, "a most ancient shoreless sea of forms incomprehensibly interchanging and intermingling, but symbolizing the protean magic of that infinite Unknown that shapes and reshapes for ever all cosmic being." Of all these divinities some further account is given below, but there must be mentioned here Prajñāpāramitā, the Bodhisattvas Manjusrī and the Chinese Ti-tsang and Kwannon (Kwanyin), and also the Tārās or Saviouresses who are feminine divinities, recognized from about the sixth century A.D. as embodying the principle of Grace in the Bodhisattvas. The full development of this pantheon takes place during the first twelve centuries A.D., though its beginnings are earlier. Its final elaboration in Lamaistic Buddhism continues later.

We must now consider the Nirmānakāya, the plane of those Buddha-appearances which are emanated or projected from the Sambhogakāya as magical earthly apparitions, a doctrine of revelation in response to the spiritual needs of sentient beings. We have already seen that at an early stage of Buddhism Gautama is already made to affirm that he is not a man, but a Buddha; here, in a development similar to that of Christian Docetism, we find the view put forward that the earthly Buddhas are not living men, but ghosts or forms of thought, acting as vehicles of the saviour-will which led the Bodhisattva to the abyss of Buddhahood. In part, no doubt, this represents an attempt to get over

the logical difficulty presented by the continued survival of the
person Gautama for many years after the attainment of that
enlightenment which cuts the connecting bonds of the spiritual
compound known as personality; this continuance has also been
aptly compared to the continued spinning of the potter's wheel
for some time after the hand of the potter has been removed,
the final physical death of the body being likened to the subsequent stopping of the wheel.

## CONVENIENT MEANS

Intimately associated with the doctrine of emanation is that
of Convenient Means (*upāya*): "the Heart of Wisdom abiding
in the Unity creates particular means of salvation" (Nāgārjuna).
The knowledge of these means is one of the perfections of Buddhahood, and is the power of response to the infinite variety of
the spiritual needs of sentient beings. The various forms which
the divine Tathāgata assumes, revealing himself in the right
place, at the right time, and never missing the right opportunity
and the right word—these manifestations constitute the Nirmānakāya. To a certain extent the doctrine of upāya corresponds to
the ready wit of such teachers as Buddha or Christ, who with
little effort so effectually render aid to those who seek them,
and no less effectually confound their opponents: admirably
illustrated, for example, in Gautama's dealing with Gotamī the
Slender, and in many well-known anecdotes of Jesus. Of either it
may be said,

*He is the Answerer,*
*What can be answer'd he answers, and what cannot be answer'd*
*   he shows how it cannot be answer'd.*

This is also a doctrine of the graduation of truth: faiths are
not divided into the true and the false, but are so many rungs
of the ladder, so many separate ladders, that lead to One Unknown. The doctrine of upāya implies the perfect understanding
of human needs by that divine intelligence that knows no need

in itself, save that implied in the saying, *Eternity is in love with the productions of time*—the only reason we can allege for the desire of the One to become many. This perfect understanding, "as of father with son, comrade with comrade, lover with mistress," does not clash with the intellectual recognition of the gods as man-made, and this the Hindus have beautifully reconciled with the idea of Grace, in the adoration "Thou that doest take the forms imagined by Thy worshippers"—addressed, indeed, by Saivas to Siva, but no less appropriate to the thought of the Mahāyāna. The doctrine of upāya is comparable also with the thought, "He makes himself as we are, that we may be as He is." The arts and religions of the world are all so many upāyas—one source, one end, only with diversity of means.

# A. Mahayana Literature—Selections from *The Buddha Carita of Asvaghosha*

*Translated by E. B. Cowell*

## BOOK XVI

1. The omniscient lion of the Sâkyas then caused all the assembly, headed by those who belonged to the company of Maitrîya, to turn the wheel of the Law.

2. 'Listen, O company belonging to Maitrîya, ye who form one vast congregation,—as it was proclaimed by those past archsaints, so is it now proclaimed by Me.

3. 'These are the two extremes, O mendicants, in the self-control of the religious ascetic,—the one which is devoted to the joys of desire, vulgar and common,

4. 'And the other which is tormented by the excessive pursuit

Reprinted from E. B. Cowell, tr., *The Buddha Carita of Asvaghosha*, in *The Sacred Books of the East*, Vol. XLIX (1894).

of self-inflicted pain in the mortification of the soul's corruptions, —these are the two extremes of the religious ascetic, each devoted to that which is unworthy and useless.

5. 'These have nothing to do with true asceticism, renunciation of the world, or self-control, with true indifference or suppression of pain, or with any of the means of attaining deliverance.

6. 'They do not tend to the spiritual forms of knowledge, to wisdom, nor to Nirvâna; let him who is acquainted with the uselessness of inflicting pain and weariness on the body,

7. 'Who has lost his interest in any pleasure or pain of a visible nature, or in the future, and who follows this middle Path for the good of the world,—

8. 'Let him, the Tathâgata, the teacher of the world, proclaim the good Law, beginning that manifestation of the good Law which consists of the (four) noble truths,

9. 'And let the Buddha proclaim the Path with its eight divisions. I too who am now the perfectly wise, and the Tathâgata in the world,

10. 'Will proclaim the noble Law, beginning with those sublime truths and the eightfold Path which is the means to attain perfect knowledge.

11. 'Instructing all the world I will show to it Nirvâna; those four noble truths must be heard first and comprehended by the soul.

12. 'That must be understood and thoroughly realised by the true students of wisdom, which has been known here by me, through the favour of all the Buddhas.

13. 'Having known the noble eightfold Path, and embraced it as realised with joy,—thus I declare to you the first means for the attainment of liberation.

14. 'Having thus commenced the noble truths, I will describe the true self-control; this noble truth is the best of all holy laws.

15. 'Walk as long as existence lasts, holding fast the noble eightfold Path,—this noble truth is the highest law for the attainment of true liberation.

16. 'Having pondered and held fast the noble eightfold Path, walk in self-control; others, not understanding this, idle talkers full of self-conceit,

17. 'Say according to their own will that merit is the cause of corporeal existence, others maintain that the soul must be preserved (after death) for its merit is the cause of liberation.

18. 'Some say that everything comes spontaneously; others that the consequence was produced before; others talk loudly that all also depends on a Divine Lord.

19. 'If merit and demerit are produced by the good and evil fortune of the soul, how is it that good fortune does not always come to all embodied beings (at last), even in the absence of merit?

20. 'How is the difference accounted for, which we see in form, riches, happiness, and the rest,—if there are no previous actions, how do good and evil arise here?

21. 'If karma is said to be the cause of our actions, who would imagine cogency in this assumption? If all the world is produced spontaneously, who then would talk of the ownership of actions?

22. 'If good is caused by good, then evil will be the cause of evil,—how then could liberation from existence be produced by difficult penances?

23. 'Others unwisely talk of Îsvara as a cause,—how then is there not uniformity in the world if Îsvara be the uniformly acting cause?

24. 'Thus certain ignorant people, talking loudly "he is," "he is not,"—through the demerits of their false theories, are at last born wretched in the different hells.

25. 'Through the merits of good theories virtuous men, who understand noble knowledge, go to heavenly worlds, from their self-restraint as regards body, speech, and thought.

26. 'All those who are devoted to existence are tormented with the swarms of its evils, and being consumed by old age, diseases, and death, each one dies and is born again.

27. 'There are many wise men here who can discourse on the

laws of coming into being; but there is not even one who knows how the cessation of being is produced.

28. 'This body composed of the five skandhas, and produced from the five elements, is all empty and without soul, and arises from the action of the chain of causation.

29. 'This chain of causation is the cause of coming into existence, and the cessation of the series thereof is the cause of the state of cessation.

30. 'He who knowing this desires to promote the good of the world, let him hold fast the chain of causation, with his mind fixed on wisdom;

31. 'Let him embrace the vow of self-denial for the sake of wisdom, and practise the four perfections, and go through existence always doing good to all beings.

32. 'Then having become an Arhat and conquered all the wicked, even the hosts of Mâra, and attained the threefold wisdom, he shall enter Nirvâna.

33. 'Whosoever therefore has his mind indifferent and is void of all desire for any further form of existence, let him abolish one by one the several steps of the chain of causation.

34. 'When these effects of the chain of causation are thus one by one put an end to, he at last, being free from all stain and substratum, will pass into a blissful Nirvâna.

35. 'Listen all of you for your own happiness, with your minds free from stain,—I will declare to you step by step this chain of causation.

36. 'The idea of ignorance is what gives the root to the huge poison-tree of mundane existence with its trunk of pain.

37. 'The impressions are caused by this, which produce [the acts of] the body, voice, and mind; and consciousness arises from these impressions, which produces as its development the five senses and the mind (or internal sense).

38. 'The organism which is sometimes called sa*mgñ*â or sa*m*-dar*s*ana, springs from this; and from this arises the six organs of the senses, including mind.

39. 'The association of the six organs with their objects is

called "contact"; and the consciousness of these different contacts is called "sensation";

40. 'By this is produced thirst, which is the desire of being troubled by worldly objects; "attachment to continued existence," arising from this, sets itself in action towards pleasure and the rest;

41. 'From attachment springs continued existence, which is sensual, possessing form, or formless; and from existence arises birth through a returning to various wombs.

42. 'On birth is dependent the series of old age, death, sorrow and the like; by putting a stop to ignorance and what follows from it, all these successively surcease.

43. 'This is the chain of causation, having many turns, and whose sphere of action is created by ignorance,—this is to be meditated upon by you who enjoy the calm of dwelling tranquilly in lonely woods;

'He who knows it thoroughly reaches at last to absolute tenuity; and having become thus attenuated he becomes blissfully extinct.

44. 'When you have thus learned this, in order to be freed from the bond of existence, you must cut down with all your efforts the root of pain, ignorance.

45. 'Then, being set free from the bonds of the prison-house of existence, as Arhats, possessing natures perfectly pure, you shall attain Nirvâna.'

46. Having heard this lesson preached by the chief of saints, all the mendicants comprehended the course and the cessation of embodied existence.

47. As these five ascetics listened to his words, their intellectual eye was purified for the attainment of perfect wisdom:

48. The eye of dharma was purified in six hundred millions of gods, and the eye of wisdom in eight hundred millions of Brahmans.

49. The eye of dharma was purified in eighty thousand men, and even in all beings an ardour for the Law was made visible.

50. Everywhere all kinds of evil became tranquillised, and on

every side an ardour for all that helps on the good Law manifested itself.

51. In the heavens everywhere the heavenly beings with troops of Apsarases uttered forth great shouts, 'Even so, O noble being of boundless energy!'

52. Then Maitrîya addressed the holy one, 'O great mendicant, in what form has the wheel been turned by thee?'

53. Having heard this question asked by the great-souled Maitrîya, the holy one looked at him and thus addressed him:

54. 'The profound subtle wheel of the Law, so hard to be seen, has been turned by me, into which the disputatious Tîrthikas cannot penetrate.

55. 'The wheel of the Law has been turned, which has no extension, no origin, no birth, no home, isolated, and free from matter;

56. 'Having many divisions, and not being without divisions, having no cause, and susceptible of no definition,—that wheel, which is described as possessing perfect equilibrium, has been proclaimed by the Buddha.

57. 'Everything subject to successive causation is like a delusion, a mirage, or a dream, like the moon seen in water or an echo,—it lies stretched out on the surface, not to be extirpated, but not eternal.

58. 'The wheel of the Law has been described as that in which all false doctrines are extirpated; it is always like the pure ether, involving no doubts, ever bright.

59. 'The wheel of the Law is described as without end or middle, existing apart from "it is" or "it is not," separated from soul or soullessness.

60. 'The wheel of the Law has been here, set forth, with a description according to its real nature,—as it has a limit and as it has not a limit, in its actual quantity and quality.

61. 'The wheel of the Law has been here set forth, described as possessing unique attributes, apart from the power of the eye and so too as regards the sense of hearing or smell;

62. 'Apart from the tongue, the touch, or the mind,—without soul or exertion;

'Such is this wheel of the Law which has been turned by me;

63. 'He makes wise all the ignorant,—therefore is he called the Buddha; this knowledge of the laws of reality has been ascertained by me of myself,

64. 'Apart from all teaching by another, therefore is he called the self-existent,—having all laws under his control, therefore is he called the lord of Law.

65. 'He knows what is right (naya) and wrong (anaya) in laws, therefore is he called Nâyaka; he teaches unnumbered beings as they become fit to be taught.

66. 'He has reached the furthest limit of instruction, therefore is he called Vinâyaka, from his pointing out the best of good paths to beings who have lost their way.

67. 'He has reached the furthest limit of good teaching, he is the guide to all the Law,—attracting all beings by his knowledge of all the means of conciliation;

68. 'He has passed through the forest of mundane existence, therefore is he called the Leader of the Caravan; the absolute ruler over all law, therefore he is the Gina, the lord of Law.

69. 'From his turning the wheel of the Law he is the lord of all the sovereigns of Law; the master-giver of the Law, the teacher, the master of the Law, the lord of the world;

70. 'He who has offered the sacrifice, accomplished his end, fulfilled his hope, achieved his success, the consoler, the loving regarder, the hero, the champion, the victorious one in conflict;

71. 'He has come out from all conflict, released himself and the releaser of all,—he is become the light of the world, the illuminator of the knowledge of true wisdom;

72. 'The dispeller of the darkness of ignorance, the illuminer of the great torch, the great physician, the great seer, the healer of all evils,

73. 'The extractor of the barb of evil from all those who are wounded by evil,—he who is possessed of all distinctive marks and adorned with all signs,

74. 'With his body and limbs every way perfect, of pure conduct and perfectly clear mind, possessed of the ten powers, having great fortitude, learned with all learning,

75. 'Endowed with all the independent states, he who has attained the great Yâna, the lord of all Dharma, the ruler, the monarch of all worlds, the sovereign,

76. 'The lord of all wisdom, the wise, the destroyer of the pride of all disputers, the omniscient, the Arhat, possessed of the perfect knowledge, the great Buddha, the lord of saints;

77. 'The victorious triumphant overthrower of the insolence and pride of the evil Mâra, the perfect Buddha, the Sugata, the wise one, he who brings the desired end to all beings,

78. 'Ever cognisant of past acts, never speaking falsely, a mine of perfect excellence and of all good qualities, the destroyer of all evil ways, the guide in all good ways,

79. 'The ruler of the world, the bearer of the world, the master of the world, the sovereign of the world, the teacher of the world, the preceptor of the world, he who brings to the world the Law, virtue, and its true end,

80. 'The fount of an ambrosia which quenches the scorching of the flame of all pain, and the powerful luminary which dries up the great ocean of all pain,

81. 'He who brings all virtue and all true wealth, the possessor of perfect excellence and all good qualities, the guide on the road of wisdom, he who shows the way to Nirvâna,

82. 'The Tathâgata, without stain, without attachment, without uncertainty.—This is the compendious declaration in the turning of the wheel of the Law.

83. 'A concise manifestation of a Tathâgata's qualities is now declared by me; for a Buddha's knowledge is endless, unlimited like the ether;

84. 'A narrator might spend a Kalpa, but the virtues of the Buddha would not come to an end,—thus by me has the multitude of the virtues of the Buddha been described.

85. 'Having heard this and welcomed it with joy go on ever in happiness; this, Sirs, is the Mahâyâna, the instrument of the Law of the perfect Buddha, which is the establisher of the welfare of all beings, set forth by all the Buddhas.

86. 'In order that this methodical arrangement of the Law

may be always spread abroad, do you yourselves always proclaim it and hand it on.

87. 'Whosoever, Sirs, hears, sees, and welcomes with joy this methodical arrangement of the Law, which is a mine of happiness and prosperity, and honours it with folded hands,

88. 'Shall attain pre-eminent strength with a glorious form and limbs, and a retinue of the holy, and an intelligence of the highest reach,

89. 'And the happiness of perfect contemplation, with a deep calm of uninterrupted bliss, with his senses in their highest perfection, and illuminated by unclouded knowledge.

90. 'He shall assuredly attain these eight pre-eminent prefections, who hears and sees this Law with a serene soul and worships it with folded hands.

91. 'Whosoever in the midst of the assembly shall gladly offer a pulpit to the high-minded teacher of the great Law,

92. 'That virtuous man shall assuredly attain the seat of the most excellent, and also the seat of a householder, and the throne of a universal monarch;

93. 'He shall also attain the throne of one of the guardian-spirits of the world, and also the firm throne of Sakra, and also the throne of the Vasavartinah gods, aye, and the supreme throne of Brahman;

94. 'And also with the permission of the Bodhisattva who is seated on the Bodhi throne he shall obtain the throne of a teacher of the good Law who has risen to perfect knowledge.

95. 'These eight seats shall the pure-souled one attain who offers joyfully a seat to him who proclaims the Law.

96. 'Whosoever with a believing heart, after examination, shall utter applause to the pious man who proclaims this carefully arranged Law;

97. 'Shall become a truthful and pure speaker, and one whose words are to be accepted,—one whose utterances are welcome and delightful, whose voice is sweet and gentle;

98. 'Having a voice like a Kalaviṅka bird, with a deep and sweet tone, having also a pure voice like Brahman's, and a loud voice with a lion's sound.

99. 'He as an all-wise and truthful speaker shall obtain these eight excellences of speech, who utters applause to one who proclaims the good Law.

100. 'And whosoever, after writing this method of the Law in a book, shall set it in his house and always worship it and honour it with all reverential observances,

101. 'And uttering its praises shall hand the doctrine onward on every side, he, the very pious man, shall obtain a most excellent treasure of memory,

102. 'And a treasure of insight, and a treasure of prudence, and a treasure of good spells, and a treasure full of intelligence,

103. 'And a treasure of the highest wisdom, and the most excellent treasure of the Law, and a treasure of knowledge, the means to attain the excellences of the good Law,—

104. 'These eight treasures shall that high-minded man attain who joyfully writes this down and sets it in a sure place and always worships it.

105. 'And he who, himself holding this method of the Law in his mind, sets it going around him, shall obtain a complete supply for liberality for the good of the world,

106. 'Next, a complete supply of virtuous dispositions, a most excellent supply of sacred knowledge, a supply of perfect calmness, and that which is called spiritual insight,

107. 'A supply of the merit caused by the good Law, a most excellent supply of knowledge, a supply of boundless compassion, which is the means to attain the virtues of the perfect Buddha.

108. 'He, full of joy, shall obtain these eight supplies who himself holds this method of the Law in his mind and sets it going abroad.

109. 'And he who shall declare this method of the Law to others, shall have himself purified by great merit and shall be prosperous and possessed of supernatural powers.

110. 'He shall become a universal monarch, a king of kings, and even a ruler among the guardians of the world, an Indra ruler of the gods, and even the ruler of the Yâma heaven,

111. 'Yea, the ruler of the Tushita heaven, and the ruler of

the Sunirmitâ*h*, and the king of the Va*s*avartina*h*, and the lord of the Brahmaloka;

112. 'Yea, Mahâbrahman, the highest of Sages,—and in the end he shall even become a Buddha,—he, possessing a thoroughly pure intelligence, shall obtain these eight sublime rewards of merit.

113. 'And he who, thoroughly intent, with a believing heart, and filled with faith and devotion, shall hear this method of the Law as it is preached,

114. 'He shall have his intellect made perfectly pure, his mind calmed with boundless charity, and his soul happy with boundless compassion, and he shall be filled with boundless joy;

115. 'His soul constantly calm with universal indifference, rejoicing in the four contemplations, having reached the ecstatic state of absolute indifference, and with his senses abolished,

116. 'With the five transcendent faculties attained, and destroying the aggregate of latent impressions, he, endowed with supernatural powers, will attain the samâdhi called *Sûram*gama.

117. 'He, having his soul pure, will attain these eight forms of absolute spotlessness; yea, wherever this method of the Law will prevail universally,

118. 'There will be no fear of any disturbance in the kingdom, no fear of evil-minded thieves, nor fear of evil beasts;

119. 'There will be no fear of plagues, famines, or wildernesses; and no alarm shall spread, caused by quarrel or war;

120. 'There shall be no fear from the gods nor from Nâgas, Yakshas, and the like, nor shall there be anywhere any fear of any misfortune.

121. 'These eight fears shall not be found there where this Law extends; it is all briefly explained, my friends,—all that arises from holding it stedfastly.

122. 'A yet higher and most excellent merit is declared by all the Buddhas, even although all living beings were to practise complete self-restraint.

123. 'Let a man worship the Buddhas, honouring them always

with faith; from that comes this pre-eminent merit, as is declared by the Jinas.

124. 'And whosoever joyfully worships a Pratyeka-Buddha, they shall become themselves Pratyeka-Buddhas; therefore let every one worship them.

125. 'There is pre-eminent merit from the worship of one Bodhisattva, and they shall all themselves become Bodhisattvas, let every one worship them;

126. 'Therefore there is pre-eminent merit from the worship of one Buddha,—they shall all themselves become Jinas, let every one devoutly worship them; and he too shall obtain this pre-eminent merit who hears this or causes others to hear it.

127. 'And whosoever in days when the good Law is abolished abandons love for his own body and life and proclaims day and night these good words,—pre-eminent is his merit from this.

128. 'He who wishes to worship constantly the lords of saints, the Pratyeka-Buddhas and the Arhats, let him resolutely produce in his mind the idea of true wisdom and proclaim these good words and the Law.

129. 'This jewel of all good doctrines, which is uttered by the Buddhas for the good of all beings,—even one who lives in a house will be a Tathâgata for it, where this good doctrine prevails.

130. 'He obtains a glorious and endless splendour who teaches even one word thereof; he will not miss one consonant nor the meaning who gives this Sûtra to others.

131. 'He is the best of all guides of men, no other being is like unto him; he is like a jewel, of imperishable glory, who hears this Law with a pure heart.

132. 'Therefore let those who are endowed with lofty ambitions, always hear this Law which causes transcendent merit; let them hear it and gladly welcome it and lay it up in their minds and continually worship the three jewels with faith.'

## B. Mahayana Literature—
*The Diamond Cutter Sutra*

*Translated by F. Max Müller*

Adoration to the Blessed Ârya-pragñâ-pâramitâ (Perfection of Wisdom).

### I

Thus it was heard by me: At one time Bhagavat (the blessed Buddha) dwelt in Srâvastî, in the grove of Geta, in the garden of Anâthapindada, together with a large company of Bhikshus (mendicants), viz. with 1250 Bhikshus, with many noble-minded Bodhisattvas.

Then Bhagavat having in the forenoon put on his undergarment, and having taken his bowl and cloak, entered the great city of Srâvastî to collect alms. Then Bhagavat, after he had gone to the great city of Srâvastî to collect alms, performed the act of eating, and having returned from his round in the afternoon, he put away his bowl and cloak, washed his feet, and sat down on the seat intended for him, crossing his legs, holding his body upright, and turning his reflection upon himself. Then many Bhikshus approached to where Bhagavat was, saluted his feet with their heads, turned three times round him to the right, and sat down on one side. (1)

### II

At that time again the venerable Subhûti came to that assembly and sat down. Then rising from his seat and putting his robe

Reprinted from F. Max Müller, tr., *The Diamond Cutter Sutra*, in *The Sacred Books of the East*, Vol. XLIX (1894).

over one shoulder, kneeling on the earth with his right knee, he stretched out his folded hands towards Bhagavat and said to him: 'It is wonderful, O Bhagavat, it is exceedingly wonderful, O Sugata, how much the noble-minded Bodhisattvas have been favoured with the highest favour by the Tathâgata, the holy and fully enlightened! It is wonderful how much the noble-minded Bodhisattvas have been instructed with the highest instruction by the Tathâgata, the holy and fully enlightened! How then, O Bhagavat, should the son or the daughter of a good family, after having entered on the path of the Bodhisattvas, behave, how should he advance, and how should he restrain his thoughts?'

After the venerable Subhûti had thus spoken, Bhagavat said to him: 'Well said, well said, Subhûti! So it is, Subhûti, so it is, as you say. The noble-minded Bodhisattvas have been favoured with the highest favour by the Tathâgata, the noble-minded Bodhisattvas have been instructed with the highest instruction by the Tathâgata. Therefore, O Subhûti, listen and take it to heart, well and rightly. I shall tell you, how any one who has entered on the path of Bodhisattvas should behave, how he should advance, and how he should restrain his thoughts.' Then the venerable Subhûti answered the Bhagavat and said: 'So be it, O Bhagavat.' (2)

## III

Then the Bhagavat thus spoke to him: 'Any one, O Subhûti, who has entered here on the path of the Bodhisattvas must thus frame his thought: As many beings as there are in this world of beings, comprehended under the term of beings (either born of eggs, or from the womb, or from moisture, or miraculously), with form or without form, with name or without name, or neither with nor without name, as far as any known world of beings is known, all these must be delivered by me in the perfect world of Nirvâna. And yet, after I have thus delivered immeasurable beings, not one single being has been delivered. And why? If, O Subhûti, a Bodhisattva had any idea of (belief in) a being, he could not be called a Bodhisattva (one who is fit to become a Buddha). And why? Because, O Subhûti, no one is to be called a Bodhisattva, for whom there should exist the idea of a being, the idea of a living being, or the idea of a person.' (3)

## IV

'And again, O Subhûti, a gift should not be given by a Bodhisattva, while he believes in objects; a gift should not be given by him, while he believes in anything; a gift should not be given by him, while he believes in form; a gift should not be given by him, while he believes in the special qualities of sound, smell, taste, and touch. For thus, O Subhûti, should a gift be given by a noble-minded Bodhisattva, that he should not believe even in the idea of cause. And why? Because that Bodhisattva, O Subhûti, who gives a gift, without believing in anything, the measure of his stock of merit is not easy to learn.'—'What do you think, O Subhûti, is it easy to learn the measure of space in the eastern quarter?' Subhûti said: 'Not indeed, O Bhagavat.'—Bhagavat said: 'In like manner, is it easy to learn the measure of space in the southern, western, northern quarters, below and above (nadir and zenith), in quarters and subquarters, in the ten quarters all round?' Subhûti said: 'Not indeed, O Bhagavat.' Bhagavat said: 'In the same manner, O Subhûti, the measure of the stock of merit of a Bodhisattva, who gives a gift without believing in anything, is not easy to learn. And thus indeed, O Subhûti, should one who has entered on the path of Bodhisattvas give a gift, that he should not believe even in the idea of cause.' (4)

## V

'Now, what do you think, O Subhûti, should a Tathâgata be seen (known) by the possession of signs?' Subhûti said: 'Not indeed, O Bhagavat, a Tathâgata is not to be seen (known) by the possession of signs. And why? Because what has been preached by the Tathâgata as the possession of signs, that is indeed the possession of no-signs.'

After this, Bhagavat spoke thus to the venerable Subhûti: 'Wherever there is, O Subhûti, the possession of signs, there is falsehood; wherever there is no possession of signs, there is no falsehood. Hence the Tathâgata is to be seen (known) from no-signs as signs.' (5)

## VI

After this, the venerable Subhûti spoke thus to the Bhagavat: 'Forsooth, O Bhagavat, will there be any beings in the future, in the last time, in the last moment, in the last 500 years, during the time of the decay of the good Law, who, when these very words of the Sûtras are being preached, will frame a true idea?' The Bhagavat said: 'Do not speak thus, Subhûti. Yes, there will be some beings in the future, in the last time, in the last moment, in the last 500 years, during the decay of the good Law, who will frame a true idea when these very words are being preached.

'And again, O Subhûti, there will be noble-minded Bodhi-sattvas, in the future, in the last time, in the last moment, in the last 500 years, during the decay of the good Law, there will be strong and good and wise beings, who, when these very words of the Sûtras are being preached, will frame a true idea. But those noble-minded Bodhisattvas, O Subhûti, will not have served one Buddha only, and the stock of their merit will not have been accumulated under one Buddha only; on the contrary, O Subhûti, those noble-minded Bodhisattvas will have served many hundred thousands of Buddhas, and the stock of their merit will have been accumulated under many hundred thousands of Buddhas; and they, when these very words of the Sûtras are being preached, will obtain one and the same faith. They are known, O Subhûti, by the Tathâgata through his Buddha-knowledge; they are seen, O Subhûti, by the Tathâgata through his Buddha-eye; they are understood, O Subhûti, by the Tathâgata. All these, O Subhûti, will produce and will hold fast an immeasurable and innumerable stock of merit. And why? Because, O Subhûti, there does not exist in those noble-minded Bodhisattvas the idea of self,

there does not exist the idea of a being, the idea of a living being, the idea of a person. Nor does there exist, O Subhûti, for these noble-minded Bodhisattvas the idea of quality (dharma), nor of no-quality. Neither does there exist, O Subhûti, any idea (sa*mgñ*â) or no-idea. And why? Because, O Subhûti, if there existed for these noble-minded Bodhisattvas the idea of quality, then they would believe in a self, they would believe in a being, they would believe in a living being, they would believe in a person. And if there existed for them the idea of no-quality, even then they would believe in a self, they would believe in a being, they would believe in a living being, they would believe in a person. And why? Because, O Subhûti, neither quality nor no-quality is to be accepted by a noble-minded Bodhisattva. Therefore this hidden saying has been preached by the Tathâgata: "By those who know the teaching of the Law, as like unto a raft, all qualities indeed must be abandoned; much more no-qualities." '
(6)


## VII

And again Bhagavat spoke thus to the venerable Subhûti: 'What do you think, O Subhûti, is there anything (dharma) that was known by the Tathâgata under the name of the highest perfect knowledge, or anything that was taught by the Tathâgata?'

After these words, the venerable Subhûti spoke thus to Bhagavat: 'As I, O Bhagavat, understand the meaning of the preaching of the Bhagavat, there is nothing that was known by the Tathâgata under the name of the highest perfect knowledge, nor is there anything that is taught by the Tathâgata. And why? Because that thing which was known or taught by the Tathâgata is incomprehensible and inexpressible. It is neither a thing nor no-thing. And why? Because the holy persons are of imperfect power.' (7)

## VIII

Bhagavat said: 'What do you think, O Subhûti, if a son or daughter of a good family filled this sphere of a million millions of worlds with the seven gems or treasures, and gave it as a gift to the holy and enlightened Tathâgatas, would that son or daughter of a good family on the strength of this produce a large stock of merit? Subhûti said: 'Yes, O Bhagavat, yes, O Sugata, that son or daughter of a good family would on the strength of this produce a large stock of merit. And why? Because, O Bhagavat, what was preached by the Tathâgata as the stock of merit, that was preached by the Tathâgata as no-stock of merit. Therefore the Tathâgata preaches: "A stock of merit, a stock of merit indeed!"' Bhagavat said: 'And if, O Subhûti, the son or daughter of a good family should fill this sphere of a million millions of worlds with the seven treasures and should give it as a gift to the holy and enlightened Tathâgatas, and if another after taking from this treatise of the Law one Gâthâ of four lines only should fully teach others and explain it, he indeed would on the strength of this produce a larger stock of merit immeasurable and innumerable. And why? Because, O Subhûti, the highest perfect knowledge of the holy and enlightened Tathâgatas is produced from it; the blessed Buddhas are produced from it. And why? Because, O Subhûti, when the Tathâgata preached: "The qualities of Buddha, the qualities of Buddha indeed!" they were preached by him as no-qualities of Buddha. Therefore they are called the qualities of Buddha.' (8)

## IX

Bhagavat said: 'Now, what do you think, O Subhûti, does a Srota-âpanna think in this wise: The fruit of Srota-âpatti has been obtained by me?' Subhûti said: 'Not indeed, O Bhagavat, a Srota-âpanna does not think in this wise: The fruit of Srota-âpatti has been obtained by me. And why? Because, O Bhagavat, he has not obtained any particular state (dharma). Therefore he

is called a Srota-âpanna. He has not obtained any form, nor
sounds, nor smells, nor tastes, nor things that can be touched.
Therefore he is called a Srota-âpanna. If, O Bhagavat, a Srota-
âpanna were to think in this wise: The fruit of Srota-âpatti has
been obtained by me, he would believe in a self, he would believe
in a being, he would believe in a living being, he would believe
in a person.'

Bhagavat said: 'What do you think, O Subhûti, does a Sakridâgâmin think in this wise: The fruit of a Sakridâgâmin has been
obtained by me?' Subhûti said: 'Not indeed, O Bhagavat, a Sakridâgâmin does not think in this wise: The fruit of a Sakridâgâmin
has been obtained by me. And why? Because he is not an individual being (dharma), who has obtained the state of a Sakridâgâmin. Therefore he is called a Sakridâgâmin.'

Bhagavat said: 'What do you think, O Subhûti, does an Anâgâmin think in this wise: The fruit of an Anâgâmin has been
obtained by me?' Subhûti said: 'Not indeed, O Bhagavat, an
Anâgâmin does not think in this wise: The fruit of an Anâgâmin
has been obtained by me. And why? Because he is not an individual being, who has obtained the state of an Anâgâmin. Therefore he is called an Anâgâmin.'

Bhagavat said: 'What do you think, O Subhûti, does an Arhat
think in this wise: The fruit of an Arhat has been obtained by
me?' Subhûti said: 'Not indeed, O Bhagavat, an Arhat does not
think in this wise: The fruit of an Arhat has been obtained by
me. And why? Because he is not an individual being, who is
called an Arhat. Therefore he is called an Arhat. And if, O
Bhagavat, an Arhat were to think in this wise: The state of an
Arhat has been obtained by me, he would believe in a self, he
would believe in a being, he would believe in a living being, he
would believe in a person.

'And why? I have been pointed out, O Bhagavat, by the holy
and fully enlightened Tathâgata, as the foremost of those who
dwell in virtue. I, O Bhagavat, am an Arhat, freed from passion.
And yet, O Bhagavat, I do not think in this wise: I am an Arhat,
I am freed from passion. If, O Bhagavat, I should think in this
wise, that the state of an Arhat has been obtained by me, then

the Tathâgata would not have truly prophesied of me, saying:
"Subhûti, the son of a good family, the foremost of those dwelling in virtue, does not dwell anywhere, and therefore he is called
a dweller in virtue, a dweller in virtue indeed!" ' (9)

## X

Bhagavat said: 'What do you think, O Subhûti, is there anything (dharma) which the Tathâgata has adopted from the
Tathâgata Dîpankara, the holy and fully enlightened?' Subhûti
said: 'Not indeed, O Bhagavat: there is not anything which the
Tathâgata has adopted from the Tathâgata Dîpankara, the holy
and fully enlightened.'

Bhagavat said: 'If, O Subhûti, a Bodhisattva should say: "I
shall create numbers of worlds," he would say what is untrue.
And why? Because, O Subhûti, when the Tathâgata preached:
"Numbers of worlds, numbers of worlds indeed!" they were
preached by him as no-numbers. Therefore they are called numbers of worlds.

'Therefore, O Subhûti, a noble-minded Bodhisattva should in
this wise frame an independent mind, which is to be framed as a
mind not believing in anything, not believing in form, not believing in sound, smell, taste, and anything that can be touched.
Now, for instance, O Subhûti, a man might have a body and a
large body, so that his size should be as large as the king of
mountains, Sumeru. Do you think then, O Subhûti, that his
selfhood (he himself) would be large?' Subhûti said: 'Yes, O
Bhagavat, yes, O Sugata, his selfhood would be large. And why?
Because, O Bhagavat, when the Tathâgata preached: "Selfhood,
selfhood indeed!" it was preached by him as no-selfhood. Therefore it is called selfhood.' (10)

## XI

Bhagavat said: 'What do you think, O Subhûti, if there were
as many Gangâ rivers as there are grains of sand in the large
river Gangâ, would the grains of sand be many?' Subhûti said:

'Those Gaṅgâ rivers would indeed be many, much more the grains of sand in those Gaṅgâ rivers.' Bhagavat said: 'I tell you, O Subhûti, I announce to you, If a woman or man were to fill with the seven treasures as many worlds as there would be grains of sand in those Gaṅgâ rivers and present them as a gift to the holy and fully enlightened Tathâgatas—What do you think, O Subhûti, would that woman or man on the strength of this produce a large stock of merit?' Subhûti said: 'Yes, O Bhagavat, yes, O Sugata, that woman or man would on the strength of this produce a large stock of merit, immeasurable and innumerable.' Bhagavat said: 'And if, O Subhûti, a woman or man having filled so many worlds with the seven treasures should give them as a gift to the holy and enlightened Tathâgatas, and if another son or daughter of a good family, after taking from this treatise of the Law one Gâthâ of four lines only, should fully teach others and explain it, he, indeed, would on the strength of this produce a larger stock of merit, immeasurable and innumerable.' (11)

## XII

'Then again, O Subhûti, that part of the world in which, after taking from this treatise of the Law one Gâthâ of four lines only, it should be preached or explained, would be like a Kaitya (holy shrine) for the whole world of gods, men, and spirits; what should we say then of those who learn the whole of this treatise of the Law to the end, who repeat it, understand it, and fully explain it to others? They, O Subhûti, will be endowed with the highest wonder. And in that place, O Subhûti, there dwells the teacher, or one after another holding the place of the wise preceptor.' (12)

## XIII

After these words, the venerable Subhûti spoke thus to Bhagavat: 'O Bhagavat, how is this treatise of the Law called, and how can I learn it?' After this, Bhagavat spoke thus to the venerable Subhûti: 'This treatise of the Law, O Subhûti, is called the Pragñâ-pâramitâ (Transcendent wisdom), and you should learn it by that name. And why? Because, O Subhûti, what was preached by the Tathâgata as the Pragñâ-pâramitâ, that was preached by the Tathâgata as no-Pâramitâ. Therefore it is called the Pragñâ-pâramitâ.

'Then, what do you think, O Subhûti, is there anything (dharma) that was preached by the Tathâgata?' Subhûti said: 'Not indeed, O Bhagavat, there is not anything that was preached by the Tathâgata.'

Bhagavat said: 'What do you think then, O Subhûti,—the dust of the earth which is found in this sphere of a million millions of worlds, is that much?' Subhûti said: 'Yes, O Bhagavat, yes, O Sugata, that dust of the earth would be much. And why? Because, O Bhagavat, what was preached by the Tathâgata as the dust of the earth, that was preached by the Tathâgata as no-dust. Therefore it is called the dust of the earth. And what was preached by the Tathâgata as the sphere of worlds, that was preached by the Tathâgata as no-sphere. Therefore it is called the sphere of worlds.'

Bhagavat said: 'What do you think, O Subhûti, is a holy and fully enlightened Tathâgata to be seen (known) by the thirty-two signs of a hero?' Subhûti said: 'No indeed, O Bhagavat; a holy and fully enlightened Tathâgata is not to be seen (known) by the thirty-two signs of a hero. And why? Because what was preached by the Tathâgata as the thirty-two signs of a hero, that was preached by the Tathâgata as no-signs. Therefore they are called the thirty-two signs of a hero.'

Bhagavat said: 'If, O Subhûti, a woman or man should day by day sacrifice his life (selfhood) as many times as there are grains of sand in the river Gangâ, and if he should thus sacrifice his life for as many kalpas as there are grains of sand in the river Gangâ, and if another man, after taking from this treatise of the Law one Gâthâ of four lines only, should fully teach others and explain it, he indeed would on the strength of this produce a larger stock of merit, immeasurable and innumerable.' (13)

## XIV

At that time, the venerable Subhûti was moved by the power of the Law, shed tears, and having wiped his tears, he thus spoke to Bhagavat: 'It is wonderful, O Bhagavat, it is exceedingly wonderful, O Sugata, how fully this teaching of the Law has been preached by the Tathâgata for the benefit of those beings who entered on the foremost path (the path that leads to Nirvâna), and who entered on the best path, from whence, O Bhagavat, knowledge has been produced in me. Never indeed, O Bhagavat, has such a teaching of the Law been heard by me before. Those Bodhisattvas, O Bhagavat, will be endowed with the highest wonder, who when this Sûtra is being preached hear it and will frame to themselves a true idea. And why? Because what is a true idea is not a true idea. Therefore the Tathâgata preaches: "A true idea, a true idea indeed!"

'It is no wonder to me, O Bhagavat, that I accept and believe this treatise of the Law, which has been preached. And those beings also, O Bhagavat, who will exist in the future, in the last time, in the last moment, in the last 500 years, during the time of the decay of the good Law, who will learn this treatise of the Law, O Bhagavat, remember it, recite it, understand it, and fully explain it to others, they will indeed be endowed with the highest wonder.

'But, O Bhagavat, there will not arise in them any idea of a self, any idea of a being, of a living being, or a person, nor does there exist for them any idea or no-idea. And why? Because, O Bhagavat, the idea of a self is no-idea, and the idea of a being, or a living being, or a person is no-idea. And why? Because the blessed Buddhas are freed from all ideas.'

After these words, Bhagavat thus spoke to the venerable Subhûti: 'So it is, O Subhûti, so it is. Those beings, O Subhûti, who when this Sûtra was being recited here will not be disturbed or frightened or become alarmed, will be endowed with the highest wonder. And why? Because, O Subhûti, this was preached by the Tathâgata, as the Parama-pâramitâ, which is no-Pâramitâ.

And, O Subhûti, what the Tathâgata preaches as the Parama-pâramitâ, that was preached also by immeasurable blessed Buddhas. Therefore it is called the Parama-pâramitâ.

'And, O Subhûti, the Pâramitâ or the highest perfection of endurance (kshânti) belonging to a Tathâgata, that also is no-Pâramitâ. And why? Because, O Subhûti, at the time when the king of Kalinga cut my flesh from every limb, I had no idea of a self, of a being, of a living being, or of a person; I had neither an idea nor no-idea. And why? Because, O Subhûti, if I at that time had had an idea of a self, I should also have had an idea of malevolence. If I had had an idea of a being, or of a living being, or of a person, I should also have had an idea of malevolence. And why? Because, O Subhûti, I remember the past 500 births, when I was the *Ri*shi Kshântivâdin (preacher of endurance). At that time also, I had no idea of a self, of a being, of a living being, of a person. Therefore then, O Subhûti, a noble-minded Bodhisattva, after putting aside all ideas, should raise his mind to the highest perfect knowledge. He should frame his mind so as not to believe (depend) in form, sound, smell, taste, or anything that can be touched, in something (dharma), in nothing or anything. And why? Because what is believed is not believed (not to be depended on). Therefore the Tathâgata preaches: "A gift should not be given by a Bodhisattva who believes in anything, it should not be given by one who believes in form, sound, smell, taste, or anything that can be touched."

'And again, O Subhûti, a Bodhisattva should in such wise give his gift for the benefit of all beings. And why? Because, O Subhûti, the idea of a being is no-idea. And those who are thus spoken of by the Tathâgata as all beings are indeed no-beings. And why? Because, O Subhûti, a Tathâgata says what is real, says what is true, says the things as they are; a Tathâgata does not speak untruth.

'But again, O Subhûti, whatever doctrine has been perceived, taught, and meditated on by a Tathâgata, in it there is neither truth nor falsehood. And as a man who has entered the darkness would not see anything, thus a Bodhisattva is to be considered who is immersed in objects, and who being immersed in objects gives a gift. But as a man who has eyes would, when the night becomes light, and the sun has risen, see many things, thus a Bodhisattva is to be considered who is not immersed in objects, and who not being immersed in objects gives a gift.

'And again, O Subhûti, if any sons or daughters of good families will learn this treatise of the Law, will remember, recite, and understand it, and fully explain it to others, they, O Subhûti, are known by the Tathâgata through his Buddha-knowledge, they are seen, O Subhûti, by the Tathâgata through his Buddha-eye. All these beings, O Subhûti, will produce and hold fast an immeasurable and innumerable stock of merit.' (14)


## XV

'And if, O Subhûti, a woman or man sacrificed in the morning as many lives as there are grains of sand in the river Gangâ and did the same at noon and the same in the evening, and if in this way they sacrificed their lives for a hundred thousands of niyutas of koṭîs of ages, and if another, after hearing this treatise of the Law, should not oppose it, then the latter would on the strength of this produce a larger stock of merit, immeasurable and innumerable. What should we say then of him who after having written it, learns it, remembers it, understands it, and fully explains it to others?

'And again, O Subhûti, this treatise of the Law is incomprehensible and incomparable. And this treatise of the Law has been preached by the Tathâgata for the benefit of those beings who entered on the foremost path (the path that leads to Nirvâna), and who entered on the best path. And those who will learn this treatise of the Law, who will remember it, recite it, understand it, and fully explain it to others, they are known, O Subhûti, by the Tathâgata through his Buddha-knowledge, they are seen, O Subhûti, by the Tathâgata through his Buddha-eye. All these beings, O Subhûti, will be endowed with an immeasurable stock of merit, they will be endowed with an incomprehensible, incomparable, immeasurable and unmeasured stock of merit. All these beings, O Subhûti, will equally remember the Bodhi (the highest Buddha-knowledge), will recite it, and understand it. And why? Because it is not possible, O Subhûti, that this treatise of the Law should be heard by beings of little faith, by those who believe in self, in beings, in living beings, and in persons. It is impossible that this treatise of the Law should be heard by beings who have not acquired the knowledge of Bodhisattvas, or that it should be learned, remembered, recited, and understood by them. The thing is impossible.

'And again, O Subhûti, that part of the world in which this Sûtra will be propounded, will have to be honoured by the whole world of gods, men, and evil spirits, will have to be worshipped, and will become like a Kaitya (a holy sepulchre).' (15)

## XVI

'And, O Subhûti, sons or daughters of a good family who will learn these very Sûtras, who will remember them, recite them, understand them, thoroughly take them to heart, and fully explain them to others, they will be overcome, they will be greatly overcome. And why? Because, O Subhûti, whatever evil deeds these beings have done in a former birth, deeds that must lead to suffering, those deeds these beings, owing to their being overcome, after they have seen the Law, will destroy, and they will obtain the knowledge of Buddha.

'I remember, O Subhûti, in the past, before innumerable and more than innumerable kalpas, there were eighty-four hundred thousands of niyutas of koṭis of Buddhas following after the venerable and fully enlightened Tathâgata Dîpaṅkara, who were pleased by me, and after being pleased were not displeased. And if, O Subhûti, these blessed Buddhas were pleased by me, and after being pleased were not displeased, and if on the other hand people at the last time, at the last moment, in the last 500 years, during the time of the decay of the good Law, will learn these very Sûtras, remember them, recite them, understand them, and

fully explain them to others, then, O Subhûti, in comparison with
their stock of merit that former stock of merit will not come to
one hundredth part, nay, not to one thousandth part, not to a
hundred thousandth part, not to a ten millionth part, not to a
hundred millionth part, not to a hundred thousand ten millionth
part, not to a hundred thousands of niyutas ten millionth part.
It will not bear number, nor fraction, nor counting, nor comparison, nor approach, nor analogy.

'And if, O Subhûti, I were to tell you the stock of merit of
those sons or daughters of good families, and how large a stock
of merit those sons or daughters of good families will produce,
and hold fast at that time, people would become distracted and
their thoughts would become bewildered. And again, O Subhûti,
as this treatise of the Law preached by the Tathâgata is incomprehensible and incomparable, its rewards also must be expected
(to be) incomprehensible.' (16)


# XVII

At that time the venerable Subhûti thus spoke to the Bhagavat:
'How should a person, after having entered on the path of the
Bodhisattvas, behave, how should he advance, and how should
he restrain his thoughts?' Bhagavat said: 'He who has entered on
the path of the Bodhisattvas should thus frame his thought: All
beings must be delivered by me in the perfect world of Nirvâna;
and yet after I have thus delivered these beings, no being has
been delivered. And why? Because, O Subhûti, if a Bodhisattva
had any idea of beings, he could not be called a Bodhisattva, and
so on from the idea of a living being to the idea of a person; if
he had any such idea, he could not be called a Bodhisattva. And
why? Because, O Subhûti, there is no such thing (dharma) as
one who has entered on the path of the Bodhisattvas.

'What do you think, O Subhûti, is there anything which the
Tathâgata has adopted from the Tathâgata Dîpankara with re-
gard to the highest perfect knowledge?' After this, the venerable
Subhûti spoke thus to the Bhagavat: 'As far as I, O Bhagavat,

understand the meaning of the preaching of the Bhagavat, there is nothing which has been adopted by the Tathâgata from the holy and fully enlightened Tathâgata Dîpankara with regard to the highest perfect knowledge.' After this, Bhagavat thus spoke to the venerable Subhûti: 'So it is, Subhûti, so it is. There is not, O Subhûti, anything which has been adopted by the Tathâgata from the holy and fully enlightened Tathâgata Dîpankara with regard to the highest perfect knowledge. And if, O Subhûti, anything had been adopted by the Tathâgata, the Tathâgata Dîpankara would not have prophesied of me, saying: "Thou, O boy, wilt be in the future the holy and fully enlightened Tathâgata called Sâkyamuni." Because then, O Subhûti, there is nothing that has been adopted by the holy and fully enlightened Tathâgata with regard to the highest perfect knowledge, therefore I was prophesied by the Tathâgata Dîpankara, saying: "Thou, boy, wilt be in the future the holy and fully enlightened Tathâgata called Sâkyamuni."

'And why, O Subhûti, the name of Tathâgata? It expresses true suchness. And why Tathâgata, O Subhûti? It expresses that he had no origin. And why Tathâgata, O Subhûti? It expresses the destruction of all qualities. And why Tathâgata, O Subhûti? It expresses one who had no origin whatever. And why this? Because, O Subhûti, no-origin is the highest goal.

'And whosoever, O Subhûti, should say that, by the holy and fully enlightened Tathâgata, the highest perfect knowledge has been known, he would speak an untruth, and would slander me, O Subhûti, with some untruth that he has learned. And why? Because there is no such thing, O Subhûti, as has been known by the Tathâgata with regard to the highest perfect knowledge. And in that, O Subhûti, which has been known and taught by the Tathâgata, there is neither truth nor falsehood. Therefore the Tathâgata preaches: "All things are Buddha-things." And why? Because what was preached by the Tathâgata, O Subhûti, as all things, that was preached as no-things; and therefore all things are called Buddha-things.

'Now, O Subhûti, a man might have a body and a large body.'

The venerable Subhûti said: 'That man who was spoken of by the Tathâgata as a man with a body, with a large body, he, O Bhagavat, was spoken of by the Tathâgata as without a body, and therefore he is called a man with a body and with a large body.'

Bhagavat said: 'So it is, O Subhûti; and if a Bodhisattva were to say: "I shall deliver all beings," he ought not to be called a Bodhisattva. And why? Is there anything, O Subhûti, that is called a Bodhisattva?' Subhûti said: 'Not indeed, Bhagavat, there is nothing which is called a Bodhisattva.' Bhagavat said: 'Those who were spoken of as beings, beings indeed, O Subhûti, they were spoken of as no-beings by the Tathâgata, and therefore they are called beings. Therefore the Tathâgata says: "All beings are without self, all beings are without life, without manhood, without a personality."

'If, O Subhûti, a Bodhisattva were to say: "I shall create numbers of worlds," he would say what is untrue. And why? Because, what were spoken of as numbers of worlds, numbers of worlds indeed, O Subhûti, these were spoken of as no-numbers by the Tathâgata, and therefore they are called numbers of worlds.

'A Bodhisattva, O Subhûti, who believes that all things are without self, that all things are without self, he has faith, he is called a noble-minded Bodhisattva by the holy and fully enlightened Tathâgata.' (17)


XVIII

Bhagavat said: 'What do you think, O Subhûti, has the Tathâgata the bodily eye?' Subhûti said: 'So it is, O Bhagavat, the Tathâgata has the bodily eye.'

Bhagavat said: 'What do you think, O Subhûti, has the Tathâgata the heavenly eye?' Subhûti said: 'So it is, O Bhagavat, the Tathâgata has the heavenly eye.'

Bhagavat said: 'What do you think, O Subhûti, has the Tathâgata the eye of knowledge?' Subhûti said: 'So it is, O Bhagavat, the Tathâgata has the eye of knowledge.'

Bhagavat said: 'What do you think, O Subhûti, has the Tathâ-gata the eye of the Law?' Subhûti said: 'So it is, O Bhagavat, the Tathâgata has the eye of the Law.'

Bhagavat said: 'What do you think, O Subhûti, has the Tathâ-gata the eye of Buddha?' Subhûti said: 'So it is, O Bhagavat, the Tathâgata has the eye of Buddha.'

Bhagavat said: 'What do you think, O Subhûti, as many grains of sand as there are in the great river Gangâ—were they preached by the Tathâgata as grains of sand?' Subhûti said: 'So it is, O Bhagavat, so it is, O Sugata, they were preached as grains of sand by the Tathâgata.' Bhagavat said: 'What do you think, O Subhûti, if there were as many Gangâ rivers as there are grains of sand in the great river Gangâ; and, if there were as many worlds as there are grains of sand in these, would these worlds be many?' Subhûti said: 'So it is, O Bhagavat, so it is, O Sugata, these worlds would be many.' Bhagavat said: 'As many beings as there are in all those worlds, I know the manifold trains of thought of them all. And why? Because what was preached as the train of thoughts, the train of thoughts indeed, O Subhûti, that was preached by the Tathâgata as no-train of thoughts, and therefore it is called the train of thoughts. And why? Because, O Subhûti, a past thought is not perceived, a future thought is not perceived, and the present thought is not perceived.' (18)

## XIX

'What do you think, O Subhûti, if a son or a daughter of a good family should fill this sphere of a million millions of worlds with the seven treasures, and give it as a gift to holy and fully enlightened Buddhas, would that son or daughter of a good family produce on the strength of this a large stock of merit?' Subhûti said: 'Yes, a large one.' Bhagavat said: 'So it is, Subhûti, so it is; that son or daughter of a good family would produce on the strength of this a large stock of merit, immeasurable and innumerable. And why? Because what was preached as a stock of merit, a stock of merit indeed, O Subhûti, that was preached as no-stock of merit by the Tathâgata, and therefore it is called a stock of merit. If, O Subhûti, there existed a stock of merit, the Tathâgata would not have preached: "A stock of merit, a stock of merit indeed!" ' (19)

## XX

'What do you think then, O Subhûti, is a Tathâgata to be seen (known) by the shape of his visible body?' Subhûti said: 'Not indeed, O Bhagavat, a Tathâgata is not to be seen (known) by the shape of his visible body. And why? Because, what was preached, O Bhagavat, as the shape of the visible body, the shape of the visible body indeed, that was preached by the Tathâgata as no-shape of the visible body, and therefore it is called the shape of the visible body.'

Bhagavat said: 'What do you think, O Subhûti, should a Tathâgata be seen (known) by the possession of signs?' Subhûti said: 'Not indeed, O Bhagavat, a Tathâgata is not to be seen (known) by the possession of signs. And why? Because, what was preached by the Tathâgata as the possession of signs, that was preached as no-possession of signs by the Tathâgata, and therefore it is called the possession of signs.' (20)

## XXI

Bhagavat said: 'What do you think, O Subhûti, does the Tathâgata think in this wise: The Law has been taught by me?' Subhûti said: 'Not indeed, O Bhagavat, does the Tathâgata think in this wise: The Law has been taught by me.' Bhagavat said: 'If a man should say that the Law has been taught by the Tathâgata, he would say what is not true; he would slander me with untruth which he has learned. And why? Because, O Subhûti, it is said the teaching of the Law, the teaching of the Law indeed. O Subhûti, there is nothing that can be perceived by the name of the teaching of the Law.'

After this, the venerable Subhûti spoke thus to the Bhagavat:

'Forsooth, O Bhagavat, will there be any beings in the future, in the last time, in the last moment, in the last 500 years, during the time of the decay of the good Law, who, when they have heard these very Laws, will believe?' Bhagavat said: 'These, O Subhûti, are neither beings nor no-beings. And why? Because, O Subhûti, those who were preached as beings, beings indeed, they were preached as no-beings by the Tathâgata, and therefore they are called beings.' (21)

## XXII

'What do you think then, O Subhûti, is there anything which has been known by the Tathâgata in the form of the highest perfect knowledge?' The venerable Subhûti said: 'Not indeed, O Bhagavat, there is nothing, O Bhagavat, that has been known by the Tathâgata in the form of the highest perfect knowledge.' Bhagavat said: 'So it is, Subhûti, so it is. Even the smallest thing is not known or perceived there, therefore it is called the highest perfect knowledge.' (22)

## XXIII

'Also, Subhûti, all is the same there, there is no difference there, and therefore it is called the highest perfect knowledge. Free from self, free from being, free from life, free from personality, that highest perfect knowledge is always the same, and thus known with all good things. And why? Because, what were preached as good things, good things indeed, O Subhûti, they were preached as no-things by the Tathâgata, and therefore they are called good things.' (23)

## XXIV

'And if, O Subhûti, a woman or man, putting together as many heaps of the seven treasures as there are Sumerus, kings of mountains, in the sphere of a million millions of worlds,

should give them as a gift to holy and fully enlightened Tathâgatas; and, if a son or a daughter of a good family, after taking
from this treatise of the Law, this Pragñâpâramitâ, one Gâthâ of
four lines only, should teach it to others, then, O Subhûti, compared with his stock of merit, the former stock of merit would
not come to the one hundredth part,' &c., till 'it will not bear
an approach.' (24)


## XXV

'What do you think then, O Subhûti, does a Tathâgata think
in this wise: Beings have been delivered by me? You should not
think so, O Subhûti. And why? Because there is no being, O
Subhûti, that has been delivered by the Tathâgata. And, if there
were a being, O Subhûti, that has been delivered by the Tathâgata, then the Tathâgata would believe in self, believe in a being,
believe in a living being, and believe in a person. And what is
called a belief in self, O Subhûti, that is preached as no-belief by
the Tathâgata. And this is learned by children and ignorant
persons; and they who were preached as children and ignorant
persons, O Subhûti, were preached as no-persons by the Tathâgata, and therefore they are called children and ignorant persons.' (25)


## XXVI

'What do you think then, O Subhûti, is the Tathâgata to be
seen (known) by the possession of signs?' Subhûti said: 'Not
indeed, O Bhagavat. So far as I know the meaning of the preaching of the Bhagavat, the Tathâgata is not to be seen (known) by
the possession of signs.' Bhagavat said: 'Good, good, Subhûti, so
it is, Subhûti; so it is, as you say; a Tathâgata is not to be seen
(known) by the possession of signs. And why? Because, O
Subhûti, if the Tathâgata were to be seen (known) by the
possession of signs, a wheel-turning king also would be a Tathâgata; therefore a Tathâgata is not to be seen (known) by the

possession of signs.' The venerable Subhûti spoke thus to the Bhagavat: 'As I understand the meaning of the preaching of the Bhagavat, a Tathâgata is not to be seen (known) by the possession of signs.' Then the Bhagavat at that moment preached these two Gâthâs:

They who saw me by form, and they who heard me by sound,
They engaged in false endeavours, will not see me.
A Buddha is to be seen (known) from the Law; for the Lords
   (Buddhas) have the Law-body;
And the nature of the Law cannot be understood, nor can it
   be made to be understood. (26)

## XXVII

'What do you think then, O Subhûti, has the highest perfect knowledge been known by the Tathâgata through the possession of signs? You should not think so, O Subhûti. And why? Because, O Subhûti, the highest perfect knowledge would not be known by the Tathâgata through the possession of signs. Nor should anybody, O Subhûti, say to you that the destruction or annihilation of any thing is proclaimed by those who have entered on the path of the Bodhisattvas.' (27)

## XXVIII

'And if, O Subhûti, a son or a daughter of a good family were to fill worlds equal to the number of grains of sand of the river Gangâ with the seven treasures, and give them as a gift to holy and fully enlightened Tathâgatas; and if a Bodhisattva acquired endurance in selfless and uncreated things, then the latter will on the strength of this produce a larger stock of merit, immeasurable and innumerable.

'But, O Subhûti, a stock of merit should not be appropriated by a noble-minded Bodhisattva.' The venerable Subhûti said: 'Should a stock of merit, O Bhagavat, not be appropriated by a Bodhisattva?' Bhagavat said: 'It should be appropriated, O Subhûti; it should not be appropriated; and therefore it is said: It should be appropriated.' (28)

## XXIX

'And again, O Subhûti, if anybody were to say that the Tathâgata goes, or comes, or stands, or sits, or lies down, he, O Subhûti, does not understand the meaning of my preaching. And why? Because the word Tathâgata means one who does not go to anywhere, and does not come from anywhere; and therefore he is called the Tathâgata (truly come), holy and fully enlightened.' (29)

## XXX

'And again, O Subhûti, if a son or a daughter of a good family were to take as many worlds as there are grains of earth-dust in this sphere of a million millions of worlds, and reduce them to such fine dust as can be made with immeasurable strength, like what is called a mass of the smallest atoms, do you think, O Subhûti, would that be a mass of many atoms?' Subhûti said: 'Yes, Bhagavat, yes, Sugata, that would be a mass of many atoms. And why? Because, O Bhagavat, if it were a mass of many atoms, Bhagavat would not call it a mass of many atoms. And why? Because, what was preached as a mass of many atoms by the Tathâgata, that was preached as no-mass of atoms by the Tathâgata; and therefore it is called a mass of many atoms. And what was preached by the Tathâgata as the sphere of a million millions of worlds, that was preached by the Tathâgata as no-sphere of worlds; and therefore it is called the sphere of a million millions of worlds. And why? Because, O Bhagavat, if there were a sphere of worlds, there would exist a belief in matter; and what was preached as a belief in matter by the Tathâgata, that was preached as no-belief by the Tathâgata; and therefore it is called a belief in matter.' Bhagavat said: 'And a belief in matter itself, O Subhûti, is unmentionable and inexpressible; it is neither a thing nor no-thing, and this is known by children and ignorant persons.' (30)

## XXXI

'And why? Because, O Subhûti, if a man were to say that belief in self, belief in a being, belief in life, belief in personality had been preached by the Tathâgata, would he be speaking truly?' Subhûti said: 'Not indeed, Bhagavat, not indeed, Sugata; he would not be speaking truly. And why? Because, O Bhagavat, what was preached by the Tathâgata as a belief in self, that was preached by the Tathâgata as no-belief; therefore it is called belief in self.'

Bhagavat said: 'Thus then, O Subhûti, are all things to be perceived, to be looked upon, and to be believed by one who has entered on the path of the Bodhisattvas. And in this wise are they to be perceived, to be looked upon, and to be believed, that a man should believe neither in the idea of a thing nor in the idea of a no-thing. And why? Because, by saying: The idea of a thing, the idea of a thing indeed, it has been preached by the Tathâgata as no-idea of a thing.' (31)

## XXXII

'And, O Subhûti, if a noble-minded Bodhisattva were to fill immeasurable and innumerable spheres of worlds with the seven treasures, and give them as a gift to holy and fully enlightened Tathâgatas; and if a son or a daughter of a good family, after taking from this treatise of the Law, this Pragñâpâramitâ, one Gâthâ of four lines only, should learn it, repeat it, understand it, and fully explain it to others, then the latter would on the strength of this produce a larger stock of merit, immeasurable and innumerable. And how should he explain it? As in the sky:

Stars, darkness, a lamp, a phantom, dew, a bubble.
A dream, a flash of lightning, and a cloud—thus we should look upon the world (all that was made).

Thus he should explain; therefore it is said: He should explain.'

Thus spoke the Bhagavat enraptured. The elder Subhûti, and the friars, nuns, the faithful laymen and women, and the Bodhisattvas also, and the whole world of gods, men, evil spirits and fairies, praised the preaching of the Bhagavat. (32)

# C. Mahayana Literature—Selections from *The Lotus of the True Law*

*Translated by H. Kern*

### PARABLE OF THE BURNING HOUSE

Let us suppose the following case, Sâriputra. In a certain village, town, borough, province, kingdom, or capital, there was a certain housekeeper, old, aged, decrepit, very advanced in years, rich, wealthy, opulent; he had a great house, high, spacious, built a long time ago and old, inhabited by some two, three, four, or five hundred living beings. The house had but one door, and a thatch; its terraces were tottering, the bases of its pillars rotten, the coverings and plaster of the walls loose. On a sudden the whole house was from every side put in conflagration by a mass of fire. Let us suppose that the man had many little boys, say five, or ten, or even twenty, and that he himself had come out of the house.

Now, Sâriputra, that man, on seeing the house from every side wrapt in a blaze by a great mass of fire, got afraid, frightened, anxious in his mind, and made the following reflection: I myself am able to come out from the burning house through the door, quickly and safely, without being touched or scorched by that great mass of fire; but my children, those young boys, are staying

Reprinted from H. Kern, tr., *Saddharma-Puṇḍarika,* in *The Sacred Books of the East,* Vol. XXI (1884).

in the burning house, playing, amusing, and diverting themselves with all sorts of sports. They do not perceive, nor know, nor understand, nor mind that the house is on fire, and do not get afraid. Though scorched by that great mass of fire, and affected with such a mass of pain, they do not mind the pain, nor do they conceive the idea of escaping.

The man, Sâriputra, is strong, has powerful arms, and (so) he makes this reflection: I am strong, and have powerful arms; why, let me gather all my little boys and take them to my breast to effect their escape from the house. A second reflection then presented itself to his mind: This house has but one opening; the door is shut; and those boys, fickle, unsteady, and childlike as they are, will, it is to be feared, run hither and thither, and come to grief and disaster in this mass of fire. Therefore I will warn them. So resolved, he calls to the boys: Come, my children; the house is burning with a mass of fire; come, lest ye be burnt in that mass of fire, and come to grief and disaster. But the ignorant boys do not heed the words of him who is their well-wisher; they are not afraid, not alarmed, and feel no misgiving; they do not care, nor fly, nor even know nor understand the purport of the word 'burning'; on the contrary, they run hither and thither, walk about, and repeatedly look at their father; all, because they are so ignorant.

Then the man is going to reflect thus: The house is burning, is blazing by a mass of fire. It is to be feared that myself as well as my children will come to grief and disaster. Let me therefore by some skilful means get the boys out of the house. The man knows the disposition of the boys, and has a clear perception of their inclinations. Now these boys happen to have many and manifold toys to play with, pretty, nice, pleasant, dear, amusing, and precious. The man, knowing the disposition of the boys, says to them: My children, your toys, which are so pretty, precious, and admirable, which you are so loth to miss, which are so various and multifarious, (such as) bullock-carts, goat-carts, deer-carts, which are so pretty, nice, dear, and precious to you, have all been put by me outside the house-door for you to play with. Come, run out, leave the house; to each of you I shall give what he wants. Come soon; come out for the sake of these toys. And the boys, on hearing the names mentioned of such playthings as they like and desire, so agreeable to their taste, so pretty, dear, and delightful, quickly rush out from the burning house, with eager effort and great alacrity, one having no time to wait for the other, and pushing each other on with the cry of 'Who shall arrive first, the very first?'

The man, seeing that his children have safely and happily escaped, and knowing that they are free from danger, goes and sits down in the open air on the square of the village, his heart filled with joy and delight, released from trouble and hindrance, quite at ease. The boys go up to the place where their father is sitting, and say: 'Father, give us those toys to play with, those bullock-carts, goat-carts, and deer-carts.' Then, Sâriputra, the man gives to his sons, who run swift as the wind, bullock-carts only, made of seven precious substances, provided with benches, hung with a multitude of small bells, lofty, adorned with rare and wonderful jewels, embellished with jewel wreaths, decorated with garlands of flowers, carpeted with cotton mattresses and woollen coverlets, covered with white cloth and silk, having on both sides rosy cushions, yoked with white, very fair and fleet bullocks, led by a multitude of men. To each of his children he gives several bullock-carts of one appearance and one kind, provided with flags, and swift as the wind. That man does so, Sâriputra, because being rich, wealthy, and in possession of many treasures and granaries, he rightly thinks: Why should I give these boys inferior carts, all these boys being my own children, dear and precious? I have got such great vehicles, and ought to treat all the boys equally and without partiality. As I own many treasures and granaries, I could give such great vehicles to all beings, how much more then to my own children. Meanwhile the boys are mounting the vehicles with feelings of astonishment and wonder. Now, Sâriputra, what is thy opinion? Has that man made himself guilty of a falsehood by first holding out to his children the prospect of three vehicles and afterwards giving to each of them the greatest vehicles only, the most magnificent vehicles?

Sâriputra answered: By no means, Lord; by no means, Sugata. That is not sufficient, O Lord, to qualify the man as a speaker of falsehood, since it only was a skilful device to persuade his children to go out of the burning house and save their lives. Nay, besides recovering their very body, O Lord, they have received all those toys. If that man, O Lord, had given no single cart, even then he would not have been a speaker of falsehood, for he had previously been meditating on saving the little boys from a great mass of pain by some able device. Even in this case, O Lord, the man would not have been guilty of falsehood, and far less now that he, considering his having plenty of treasures and prompted by no other motive but the love of his children, gives to all, to coax them, vehicles of one kind, and those the greatest vehicles. That man, Lord, is not guilty of falsehood.

The venerable Sâriputra having thus spoken, the Lord said to him: Very well, very well, Sâriputra, quite so; it is even as thou sayest. So, too, Sâriputra, the Tathâgata, &c., is free from all dangers, wholly exempt from all misfortune, despondency, calamity, pain, grief, the thick enveloping dark mists of ignorance. He, the Tathâgata, endowed with Buddha-knowledge, forces, absence of hesitation, uncommon properties, and mighty by magical power, is the father of the world, who has reached the highest perfection in the knowledge of skilful means, who is most merciful, long-suffering, benevolent, compassionate, He appears in this triple world; which is like a house the roof and shelter whereof are decayed, (a house) burning by a mass of misery, in order to deliver from affection, hatred, and delusion the beings subject to birth, old age, disease, death, grief, wailing, pain, melancholy, despondency, the dark enveloping mists of ignorance, in order to rouse them to supreme and perfect enlightenment. Once born, he sees how the creatures are burnt, tormented, vexed, distressed by birth, old age, disease, death, grief, wailing, pain, melancholy, despondency; how for the sake of enjoyments, and prompted by sensual desires, they severally suffer various pains. In consequence both of what in this world they are seeking and what they have acquired, they will in a future state suffer various pains, in hell, in the brute creation, in the realm of Yama; suffer such pains as poverty in the world of gods or men, union with hateful persons or things, and separation from the beloved ones. And whilst incessantly whirling in that mass of evils they are sporting, playing, diverting themselves; they do not fear, nor dread, nor are they seized with terror; they do not know, nor mind; they are not startled, do not try to escape, but are enjoying themselves in that triple world which is like unto a burning house, and run hither and thither. Though overwhelmed by that mass of evil, they do not conceive the idea that they must beware of it.

Under such circumstances, Sâriputra, the Tathâgata reflects thus: Verily, I am the father of these beings; I must have them from this mass of evil, and bestow on them the immense, inconceivable bliss of Buddha-knowledge, wherewith they shall sport, play, and divert themselves, wherein they shall find their rest.

Then, Sâriputra, the Tathâgata reflects thus: If, in the conviction of my possessing the power of knowledge and magical faculties, I manifest to these beings the knowledge, forces, and absence of hesitation of the Tathâgata, without availing myself of some device, these beings will not escape. For they are attached to the pleasures of the five senses, to worldly pleasures; they will not be freed from birth, old age, disease, death, grief, wailing, pain, melancholy, despondency, by which they are burnt, tormented, vexed, distressed. Unless they are forced to leave the triple world which is like a house the shelter and roof whereof is in a blaze, how are they to get acquainted with Buddha-knowledge?

Now, Sâriputra, even as that man with powerful arms, without using the strength of his arms, attracts his children out of the burning house by an able device, and afterwards gives them magnificent, great carts, so, Sâriputra, the Tathâgata, the Arhat, &c., possessed of knowledge and freedom from all hesitation, without using them, in order to attract the creatures out of the triple world which is like a burning house with decayed roof and shelter, shows, by his knowledge of able devices, three vehicles, viz. the vehicle of the disciples, the vehicle of the Pratyekabuddhas, and the vehicle of the Bodhisattvas. By means of these three vehicles he attracts the creatures and speaks to them thus: Do not delight in this triple world, which is like a burning house, in these miserable forms, sounds, odours, flavours, and contacts. For in delighting in this triple world ye are burnt, heated, inflamed with the thirst inseparable from the pleasures of the five senses. Fly from this triple world; betake yourselves to the three vehicles: the vehicle of the disciples, the vehicle of the Pratyekabuddhas, the vehicle of the Bodhisattvas. I give you my pledge for it, that I shall give you these three vehicles; make an effort to run out of this triple world. And to attract them I say: These vehicles are grand, praised by the Âryas, and provided with most pleasant things; with such you are to sport, play, and divert yourselves in a noble manner. Ye will feel the great delight of the faculties, powers, constituents of Bodhi, meditations, the (eight) degrees of emancipation, self-concentration, and the results of self-concentration, and ye will become greatly happy and cheerful.

Now, Sâriputra, the beings who have become wise have faith in the Tathâgata, the father of the world, and consequently apply themselves to his commandments. Amongst them there are some who, wishing to follow the dictate of an authoritative voice, apply themselves to the commandment of the Tathâgata to acquire the knowledge of the four great truths, for the sake of their own complete Nirvâna. These one may say to be those who, coveting the vehicle of the disciples, fly from the triple world, just as some of the boys will fly from that burning house, prompted by a desire of getting a cart yoked with deer. Other beings desirous of the science without a master, of self-restraint and tranquillity, apply themselves to the commandment of the Tathâgata to learn to understand causes and effects, for the sake of their own complete Nirvâna. These one may say to be those who, coveting the vehicle of the Pratyekabuddhas, fly from the triple world, just as some of the boys fly from the burning house, prompted by the desire of getting a cart yoked with goats. Others again desirous of the knowledge of the all-knowing, the knowledge of Buddha, the knowledge of the self-born one, the science without a master, apply themselves to the commandment of the Tathâgata to learn to understand the knowledge, powers, and freedom from hesitation of the Tathâgata, for the sake of the common weal and happiness, out of compassion to the world, for the benefit, weal, and happiness of the world at large, both gods and men, for the sake of the complete Nirvâna of all beings. These one may say to be those who, coveting the great vehicle, fly from the triple world. Therefore they are called Bodhisattvas Mahâsattvas. They may be likened to those among the boys who have fled from the burning house prompted by the desire of getting a cart yoked with bullocks.

In the same manner, Sâriputra, as that man, on seeing his children escaped from the burning house and knowing them safely and happily rescued and out of danger, in the consciousness of his great wealth, gives the boys one single grand cart; so, too, Sâriputra, the Tathâgata, the Arhat, &c., on seeing many kotis of beings recovered from the triple world, released from sorrow, fear, terror, and calamity, having escaped owing to the command of the Tathâgata, delivered from all fears, calamities, and difficulties, and having reached the bliss of Nirvâna, so, too, Sâriputra, the Tathâgata, the Arhat, &c., considering that he possesses great wealth of knowledge, power, and absence of hesitation, and that all beings are his children, leads them by no other vehicle but the Buddha-vehicle to full development. But he does not teach a particular Nirvâna for each being; he causes all beings to reach complete Nirvâna by means of the complete Nirvâna of the Tathâgata. And those beings, Sâriputra, who are delivered from the triple world, to them the Tathâgata gives as toys to amuse themselves with the lofty pleasures of the Âryas, the pleasures of meditation, emancipation, self-concentration, and its results; (toys) all of the same kind. Even as that man, Sâriputra, cannot be said to have told a falsehood for having held out to those boys the prospect of three vehicles and given to all of them but one great vehicle, a magnificent vehicle made of seven precious substances, decorated with all sorts of ornaments, a vehicle of one kind, the most egregious of all, so, too, Sâriputra, the Tathâgata, the Arhat, &c., tells no falsehood when by an able device he first holds forth three vehicles and afterwards leads all to complete Nirvâna by the one great vehicle. For the Tathâgata, Sâriputra, who is rich in treasures and storehouses of abundant knowledge, powers, and absence of hesitation, is able to teach all beings the law which is connected with the knowledge of the all-knowing. In this way, Sâriputra, one has to understand how the Tathâgata by an able device and direction shows but one vehicle, the great vehicle.

## PARABLE OF THE BLIND MAN

Lord, if there are not three vehicles, for what reason then is the designation of disciples (Srâvakas), Buddhas, and Bodhisattvas kept up in the present times?

On this speech the Lord answered the venerable Mahâ-Kâsyapa as follows: It is, Kâsyapa, as if a potter made different vessels out of the same clay. Some of those pots are to contain sugar, others ghee, others curds and milk; others, of inferior quality, are vessels of impurity. There is no diversity in the clay used; no, the diversity of the pots is only due to the substances which are put into each of them. In like manner, Kâsyapa, is there but one vehicle, viz. the Buddha-vehicle; there is no second vehicle, no third.

The Lord having thus spoken, the venerable Mahâ-Kâsyapa said: Lord, if the beings are of different disposition, will there be for those who have left the triple world one Nirvâna, or two, or three? The Lord replied: Nirvâna, Kâsyapa, is a consequence of understanding that all laws (things) are equal. Hence there is but one Nirvâna, not two, not three. Therefore, Kâsyapa, I will tell thee a parable, for men of good understanding will generally readily enough catch the meaning of what is taught under the shape of a parable.

It is a case, Kâsyapa, similar to that of a certain blind-born man, who says: There are no handsome or ugly shapes; there are no men able to see handsome or ugly shapes; there exists no sun nor moon; there are no asterisms nor planets; there are no men able to see planets. But other persons say to the blind-born: There are handsome and ugly shapes; there are men able to see handsome and ugly shapes; there is a sun and moon; there are asterisms and planets; there are men able to see planets. But the blind-born does not believe them, nor accept what they say. Now there is a physician who knows all diseases. He sees that blind-born man and makes to himself this reflection: The disease of this man originates in his sinful actions in former times. All diseases possible to arise are fourfold: rheumatical, cholerical, phlegmatical, and caused by a complication of the (corrupted) humours. The physician, after thinking again and again on a means to cure the disease, makes to himself this reflection: Surely, with the drugs in common use it is impossible to cure this disease, but there are in the Himâlaya, the king of mountains, four herbs, to wit: first, one called Possessed-of-all-sorts-of-colours-and-flavours; second Delivering-from-all-diseases; third, Delivering-from-all-poisons; fourth, Procuring-happiness-to-those-standing-in-the-right-place. As the physician feels compassion for the blind-born man he contrives some device to get to the Himâlaya, the king of mountains. There he goes up and down and across to search. In doing so he finds the four herbs. One he gives after chewing it with the teeth; another after pounding; another after having it mixed with another drug and boiled; another after having it mixed with a raw drug; another after piercing with a lancet somewhere a vein; another after singeing it in fire; another after combining it with various other substances so as to enter in a compound potion, food, &c. Owing to these means being applied the blind-born recovers his eyesight, and in consequence of that recovery he sees outwardly and inwardly, far and near, the shine of sun and moon, the asterisms, planets, and all phenom-

ena. Then he says: O how foolish was I that I did not believe
what they told me, nor accepted what they affirmed. Now I see
all; I am delivered from my blindness and have recovered my
eyesight; there is none in the world who could surpass me. And
at the same moment Seers of the five transcendent faculties,
strong in the divine sight and hearing, in the knowledge of
others' minds, in the memory of former abodes, in magical
science and intuition, speak to the man thus: Good man, thou
hast just recovered thine eyesight, nothing more, and dost not
know yet anything. Whence comes this conceitedness to thee?
Thou hast no wisdom, nor art thou a clever man. Further they
say to him: Good man, when sitting in the interior of thy room,
thou canst not see nor distinguish forms outside, nor discern
which beings are animated with kind feelings and which with
hostile feelings; thou canst not distinguish nor hear at the distance
of five yoganas the voice of a man or the sound of a drum, conch
trumpet, and the like; thou canst not even walk as far as a kos
without lifting up thy feet; thou hast been produced and developed in thy mother's womb without remembering the fact;
how then wouldst thou be clever, and how canst thou say: I see
all? Good man, thou takest darkness for light, and takest light
for darkness.

Whereupon the Seers are asked by the man: By what means
and by what good work shall I acquire such wisdom and with
your favour acquire those good qualities (or virtues)? And the
Seers say to that man: If that be thy wish, go and live in the
wilderness or take thine abode in mountain caves, to meditate on
the law and cast off evil passions. So shalt thou become endowed with the virtues of an ascetic and acquire the transcendent
faculties. The man catches their meaning and becomes an ascetic.
Living in the wilderness, the mind intent upon one sole object,
he shakes off worldly desires, and acquires the five transcendent
faculties. After that acquisition he reflects thus: Formerly I did
not do the right thing; hence no good accrued to me. Now, however, I can go whither my mind prompts me; formerly I was
ignorant, of little understanding, in fact, a blind man.

Such, Kâsyapa, is the parable I have invented to make thee understand my meaning. The moral to be drawn from it is as follows. The word 'blind-born,' Kâsyapa, is a designation for the creatures staying in the whirl of the world with its six states; the creatures who do not know the true law and are heaping up the thick darkness of evil passions. Those are blind from ignorance, and in consequence of it they build up conceptions; in consequence of the latter name-and-form, and so forth, up to the genesis of this whole huge mass of evils.

So the creatures blind from ignorance remain in the whirl of life, but the Tathâgata, who is out of the triple world, feels compassion, prompted by which, like a father for his dear and only son, he appears in the triple world and sees with his eye of wisdom that the creatures are revolving in the circle of the mundane whirl, and are toiling without finding the right means to escape from the rotation. And on seeing this he comes to the conclusion: Yon beings, according to the good works they have done in former states, have feeble aversions and strong attachments; (or) feeble attachments and strong aversions; some have little wisdom, others are clever; some have soundly developed views, others have unsound views. To all of them the Tathâgata skilfully shows three vehicles.

The Seers in the parable, those possessing the five transcendent faculties and clear-sight, are the Bodhisattvas who produce enlightened thought, and by the acquirement of acquiescence in the eternal law awake us to supreme, perfect enlightenment.

The great physician in the parable is the Tathâgata. To the blind-born may be likened the creatures blind with infatuation. Attachment, aversion, and infatuation are likened to rheum, bile, and phlegm. The sixty-two false theories also must be looked upon as such (i. e. as doshas, 'humours and corrupted humours of the body,' 'faults and corruptions'). The four herbs are like vanity (or voidness), causelessness (or purposelessness), unfixedness, and reaching Nirvâna. Just as by using different drugs different diseases are healed, so by developing the idea of vanity (or voidness), purposelessness, unfixedness, (which are) the principles of emancipation, is ignorance suppressed; the suppression of ignorance is succeeded by the suppression of conceptions (or fancies); and so forth, up to the suppression of the whole huge mass of evils. And thus one's mind will dwell no more on good nor on evil.

To the man who recovers his eyesight is likened the votary of the vehicle of the disciples and of Pratyekabuddhas. He rends the ties of evil passion in the whirl of the world; freed from those ties he is released from the triple world with its six states of existence. Therefore the votary of the vehicle of the disciples may think and speak thus: There are no more laws to be penetrated; I have reached Nirvâna. Then the Tathâgata preaches to him: How can he who has not penetrated all laws have reached Nirvâna? The Lord rouses him to enlightenment, and the disciple, when the consciousness of enlightenment has been awakened in him, no longer stays in the mundane whirl, but at the same time has not yet reached Nirvâna. As he has arrived at true insight, he looks upon this triple world in every direction as void, resembling the produce of magic, similar to a dream, a mirage, an echo. He sees that all laws (and phenomena) are unborn and undestroyed, not bound and not loose, not dark and not bright. He who views the profound laws in such a light, sees, as if he were not seeing, the whole triple world full of beings of contrary and omnifarious fancies and dispositions.

And on that occasion, in order to more amply explain the same subject, the Lord uttered the following stanzas:

45. As the rays of the sun and moon descend alike on all men, good and bad, without deficiency (in one case) or surplus (in the other);

46. So the wisdom of the Tathâgata shines like the sun and moon, leading all beings without partiality.

47. As the potter, making clay vessels, produces from the same clay pots for sugar, milk, ghee, or water;

48. Some for impurities, others for curdled milk, the clay used by the artificer for the vessels being of but one sort;

49. As a vessel is made to receive all its distinguishing qualities

according to the quality of the substance laid into it, so the Tathâgatas, on account of the diversity of taste,

50. Mention a diversity of vehicles, though the Buddha-vehicle be the only indisputable one. He who ignores the rotation of mundane existence, has no perception of blessed rest;

51. But he who understands that all laws are void and without reality (and without individual character) penetrates the enlightenment of the perfectly enlightened Lords in its very essence.

52. One who occupies a middle position of wisdom is called a Pratyekagina (i. e. Pratyekabuddha); one lacking the insight of voidness is termed a disciple.

53. But after understanding all laws one is called a perfectly-enlightened one; such a one is assiduous in preaching the law to living beings by means of hundreds of devices.

54. It is as if some blind-born man, because he sees no sun, moon, planets, and stars, in his blind ignorance (should say): There are no visible things at all.

55. But a great physician taking compassion on the blind man, goes to the Himâlaya, where (seeking) across, up and down,

56. He fetches from the mountain four plants; the herb Of-all-colours-flavours-and-cases, and others. These he intends to apply.

57. He applies them in this manner: one he gives to the blind man after chewing it, another after pounding, again another by introducing it with the point of a needle into the man's body.

58. The man having got his eyesight, sees the sun, moon, planets, and stars, and arrives at the conclusion that it was from sheer ignorance that he spoke thus as he had formerly done.

59. In the same way do people of great ignorance, blind from their birth, move in the turmoil of the world, because they do not know the wheel of causes and effects, the path of toils.

60. In the world so blinded by ignorance appears the highest of those who know all, the Tathâgata, the great physician, of compassionate nature.

61. As an able teacher he shows the true law; he reveals supreme Buddha-enlightenment to him who is most advanced.

62. To those of middling wisdom the Leader preaches a middling enlightenment; again another enlightenment he recommends to him who is afraid of the mundane whirl.

63. The disciple who by his discrimination has escaped from the triple world thinks he has reached pure, blest Nirvâna, but it is only by knowing all laws (and the universal laws) that the immortal Nirvâna is reached.

64. In that case it is as if the great Seers, moved by compassion, said to him: Thou art mistaken; do not be proud of thy knowledge.

65. When thou art in the interior of thy room, thou canst not perceive what is going on without, fool as thou art.

66. Thou who, when staying within, dost not perceive even now what people outside are doing or not doing, how wouldst thou be wise, fool as thou art?

67. Thou art not able to hear a sound at a distance of but five yoganas, far less at a greater distance.

68. Thou canst not discern who are malevolent or benevolent towards thee. Whence then comes that pride to thee?

69. If thou hast to walk so far as a kos, thou canst not go without a beaten track; and what happened to thee when in thy mother's womb thou hast immediately forgotten.

70. In this world he is called all-knowing who possesses the five transcendent faculties, but when thou who knowest nothing pretendest to be all-knowing, it is an effect of infatuation.

71. If thou art desirous of omniscience, direct thy attention to transcendent wisdom; then betake thyself to the wilderness and meditate on the pure law; by it thou shalt acquire the transcendent faculties.

72. The man catches the meaning, goes to the wilderness, meditates with the greatest attention, and, as he is endowed with good qualities, ere long acquires the five transcendent faculties.

73. Similarly all disciples fancy having reached Nirvâna, but

the *G*ina instructs them (by saying): This is a (temporary) repose, no final rest.

74. It is an artifice of the Buddhas to enunciate this dogma. There is no (real) Nirvâ*n*a without all-knowingness; try to reach this.

75. The boundless knowledge of the three paths (of time), the six utmost perfections (Pâramitâs), voidness, the absence of purpose (or object), the absence of finiteness;

76. The idea of enlightenment and the other laws leading to Nirvâ*n*a, both such as are mixed with imperfection and such as are exempt from it, such as are tranquil and comparable to ethereal space;

77. The four Brahmavihâras and the four Sa*n*grahas, as well as the laws sanctioned by eminent sages for the education of creatures;

78. (He who knows these things) and that all phenomena have the nature of illusion and dreams, that they are pithless as the stem of the plantain, and similar to an echo;

79. And who knows that the triple world throughout is of that nature, not fast and not loose, he knows rest.

80. He who considers all laws to be alike, void, devoid of particularity and individuality, not derived from an intelligent cause; nay, who discerns that nothingness is law;

81. Such a one has great wisdom and sees the whole of the law entirely. There are no three vehicles by any means; there is but one vehicle in this world.

82. All laws (or the laws of all) are alike, equal, for all, and ever alike. Knowing this, one understands immortal, blest Nirvâ*n*a.

## CHAPTER VIII

# Zen Buddhism

### D. T. Suzuki

## Introduction

Zen in its essence is the art of seeing into the nature of one's own being, and it points the way from bondage to freedom. By making us drink right from the fountain of life, it liberates us from all the yokes under which we finite beings are usually suffering in this world. We can say that Zen liberates all the energies properly and naturally stored in each of us, which are in ordinary circumstances cramped and distorted so that they find no adequate channel for activity.

This body of ours is something like an electric battery in which a mysterious power latently lies. When this power is not properly brought into operation, it either grows mouldy and withers away or is warped and expresses itself abnormally. It is the object of Zen, therefore, to save us from going crazy or being crippled. This is what I mean by freedom, giving free play to all the creative and benevolent impulses inherently lying in our hearts. Generally, we are blind to this fact, that we are in possession of all the necessary faculties that will make us happy and loving towards one another. All the struggles that we see around us come from this ignorance. Zen, therefore, wants us to open a "third eye," as Buddhists call it, to the hitherto undreamed-of region shut away from us through our own ignorance. When the cloud of ignorance disappears, the infinity of the heavens is manifested, where we see for the first time into the nature of our

Reprinted from D. T. Suzuki, *Essays in Zen Buddhism* (1st Series) (London: Rider & Company, 1916; New York, Grove Press, Inc., 1961), pages (Rider edition) 11-19, 227-233, 236-245, 256-264. Used by permission of Hutchinson Publishing Group, Ltd., and Grove Press, Inc.

own being. We now know the signification of life, we know that it is not blind striving, nor is it a mere display of brutal forces, but that while we know not definitely what the ultimate purport of life is, there is something in it that makes us feel infinitely blessed in the living of it and remain quite contented with it in all its evolution, without raising questions or entertaining pessimistic doubts.

When we are full of vitality and not yet awakened to the knowledge of life, we cannot comprehend the seriousness of all the conflicts involved in it which are apparently for the moment in a state of quiescence. But sooner or later the time will come when we have to face life squarely and solve its most perplexing and most pressing riddles. Says Confucius, "At fifteen my mind was directed to study, and at thirty I knew where to stand." This is one of the wisest sayings of the Chinese sage. Psychologists will all agree to this statement of his; for, generally speaking, fifteen is about the age youth begins to look around seriously and inquire into the meaning of life. All the spiritual powers until now securely hidden in the subconscious part of the mind break out almost simultaneously. And when this breaking out is too precipitous and violent, the mind may lose its balance more or less permanently; in fact, so many cases of nervous prostration reported during adolescence are chiefly due to this loss of the mental equilibrium. In most cases the effect is not very grave and the crisis may pass without leaving deep marks. But in some characters, either through their inherent tendencies or on account of the influence of environment upon their plastic constitution, the spiritual awakening stirs them up to the very depths of their personality. This is the time you will be asked to choose between the "Everlasting No" and the "Everlasting Yea." This choosing is what Confucius means by "study"; it is not studying the classics, but deeply delving into the mysteries of life.

Normally, the outcome of the struggle is the "Everlasting Yea," or "Let thy will be done"; for life is after all a form of affirmation, however negatively it might be conceived by the pessimists. But we cannot deny the fact that there are many things in this world which will turn our too sensitive minds towards the other direction and make us exclaim with Andreyev in "The Life of Man": "I curse everything that you have given. I curse the day on which I was born. I curse the day on which I shall die. I curse the whole of my life. I fling everything back at your cruel face, senseless Fate! Be accursed, be forever accursed! With my curses I conquer you. What else can you do to me? . . . With my last thought I will shout into your asinine ears: Be accursed, be accursed!" This is a terrible indictment of life, it is a complete negation of life, it is a most dismal picture of the destiny of man on earth. "Leaving no trace" is quite true, for we know nothing of our future except that we all pass away, including the very earth from which we have come. There are certainly things justifying pessimism.

Life, as most of us live it, is suffering. There is no denying the fact. As long as life is a form of struggle, it cannot be anything but pain. Does not a struggle mean the impact of two conflicting forces, each trying to get the upper hand of the other? If the battle is lost, the outcome is death, and death is the fearsomest thing in the world. Even when death is conquered, one is left alone, and the loneliness is sometimes more unbearable than the struggle itself. One may not be conscious of all this, and may go on indulging in those momentary pleasures that are afforded by the senses. But this being unconscious does not in the least alter the facts of life. However insistently the blind may deny the existence of the sun, they cannot annihilate it. The tropical heat will mercilessly scorch them, and if they do not take proper care they will all be wiped away from the surface of the earth.

The Buddha was perfectly right when he propounded his "Fourfold Noble Truth," the first of which is that life is pain. Did not everyone of us come to this world screaming and in a way protesting? To come out into cold and prohibitive surroundings after a soft, warm motherly womb was surely a painful incident, to say the least. Growth is always attended with pain. Teething is more or less a painful process. Puberty is usually accompanied by a mental as well as a physical disturbance. The growth of the organism called society is also marked with painful cataclysms, and we are at present witnessing one of its birth-throes. We may calmly reason and say that this is all inevitable, that inasmuch as every reconstruction means the destruction of the old regime, we cannot help going through a painful operation. But this cold intellectual analysis does not alleviate whatever harrowing feelings we have to undergo. The pain heartlessly inflicted on our nerves is ineradicable. Life is, after all arguing, a painful struggle.

This, however, is providential. For the more you suffer the deeper grows your character, and with the deepening of your character you read the more penetratingly into the secrets of life. All great artists, all great religious leaders, and all great social reformers have come out of the intensest struggles which they fought bravely, quite frequently in tears and with bleeding hearts. Unless you eat your bread in sorrow, you cannot taste of real life. Mencius is right when he says that when Heaven wants to perfect a great man it tries him in every possible way until he comes out triumphantly from all his painful experiences.

To me Oscar Wilde seems always posing or striving for an effect; he may be a great artist, but there is something in him that turns me away from him. Yet he exclaims in his *De Profundis*: "During the last few months I have, after terrible difficulties and struggles, been able to comprehend some of the lessons hidden in the heart of pain. Clergymen and people who use phrases without wisdom sometimes talk of suffering as a mystery. It is really a revelation. One discerns things one never discerned before. One approaches the whole of history from a different standpoint." You will observe here what sanctifying effects his prison life produced on his character. If he had had to go through a similar trial in the beginning of his career, he might have been able to produce far greater works than those we have of him at present.

We are too ego-centred. The ego-shell in which we live is the hardest thing to outgrow. We seem to carry it all the time from childhood up to the time we finally pass away. We are, however, given many chances to break through this shell, and the first and greatest of them is when we reach adolescence. This is the first time the ego really comes to recognize the "other." I mean the awakening of sexual love. An ego, entire and undivided, now begins to feel a sort of split in itself. Love hitherto dormant deep in his heart lifts its head and causes a great commotion in it. For the love now stirred demands at once the assertion of the ego and its annihilation. Love makes the ego lose itself in the object it loves, and yet at the same time it wants to have the object as its own. This is a contradiction, and a great tragedy of life. This elemental feeling must be one of the divine agencies whereby man is urged to advance in his upward walk. God gives tragedies to perfect man. The greatest bulk of literature ever produced in this world is but the harping on the same string of love, and we never seem to grow weary of it. But this is not the topic we are concerned with here. What I want to emphasize in this connection is this: that through the awakening of love we get a glimpse into the infinity of things, and that this glimpse urges youth to Romanticism or to Rationalism according to his temperament and environment and education.

When the ego-shell is broken and the "other" is taken into its own body, we can say that the ego has denied itself or that the ego has taken its first steps towards the infinite. Religiously, here ensues an intense struggle between the finite and the infinite, between the intellect and a higher power, or, more plainly, between the flesh and the spirit. This is the problem of problems that has driven many a youth into the hands of Satan. When a grown-up man looks back to these youthful days he cannot but feel a sort of shudder going through his entire frame. The struggle to be fought in sincerity may go on up to the age of thirty, when Confucius states that he knew where to stand. The religious consciousness is now fully awakened, and all the possible ways of escaping from the struggle or bringing it to an end are most earnestly sought in every direction. Books are read, lectures are attended, sermons are greedily taken in, and various religious exercises or disciplines are tried. And naturally Zen too comes to be inquired into.

How does Zen solve the problem of problems?

In the first place, Zen proposes its solution by directly appealing to facts of personal experience and not to book-knowledge. The nature of one's own being where apparently rages the struggle between the finite and the infinite is to be grasped by a higher faculty than the intellect. For Zen says it is the latter that first made us raise the question which it could not answer by itself, and that therefore it is to be put aside to make room for something higher and more enlightening. For the intellect has a peculiarly disquieting quality in it. Though it raises questions enough to disturb the serenity of the mind, it is too frequently unable to give satisfactory answers to them. It upsets the blissful peace of ignorance and yet it does not restore the former state of things by offering something else. Because it points out ignorance, it is often considered illuminating, whereas the fact is that it disturbs, not necessarily always bringing light on its path. It is not final, it waits for something higher than itself for the solution of all the questions it will raise regardless of consequences. If it were able to bring a new order into the disturbance and settle it once for all, there would have been no need for philosophy after it had been first systematized by a great thinker, by an Aristotle or by a Hegel. But the history of thought proves that each new structure raised by a man of extraordinary intellect is sure to be pulled down by the succeeding ones. This constant pulling down and building up is all right as far as philosophy itself is concerned; for the inherent nature of the intellect, as I take it, demands it and we cannot put a stop to the progress of philosophical inquiries any more than to our breathing. But when it comes to the question of life itself we cannot wait for the ultimate solution to be offered by the intellect, even if it could do so. We cannot suspend even for a moment our life-activity for philosophy to unravel its mysteries. Let the mysteries remain as they are, but live we must. The hungry cannot wait until a complete analysis of food is obtained and the nourishing value of each element is determined. For the dead the scientific knowledge of food will be of no use whatever. Zen therefore does not rely on the intellect for the solution of its deepest problems.

By personal experience it is meant to get at the fact at first hand and not through any intermediary, whatever this may be. Its favourite analogy is: to point at the moon a finger is needed, but woe to those who take the finger for the moon; a basket is welcome to carry our fish home, but when the fish are safely on the table why should we eternally bother ourselves with the basket? Here stands the fact, and let us grasp it with the naked hands lest it should slip away—this is what Zen proposes to do. As nature abhors a vacuum, Zen abhors anything coming between the fact and ourselves. According to Zen there is no struggle in the fact itself such as between the finite and the infinite, between the flesh and the spirit. These are idle distinctions fictitiously designed by the intellect for its own interest. Those who take them too seriously or those who try to read them into the very fact of life are those who take the finger for the moon. When we are hungry we eat; when we are sleepy we lay ourselves down; and where does the infinite or the finite come in here? Are not we complete in ourselves and each in himself? Life as it is lived suffices. It is only when the disquieting intellect steps in and tries to murder it that we stop to live and imagine ourselves to be short of or in something. Let the intellect alone, it has its usefulness in its proper sphere, but let it not interfere with the flowing of the life-stream. If you are at all tempted to look into it, do so while letting it flow. The fact of flowing must under no circumstances be arrested or meddled with; for the moment your hands are dipped into it, its transparency is disturbed, it ceases to reflect your image which you have had from the very beginning and will continue to have to the end of time.

Almost corresponding to the "Four Maxims" of the Nichiren Sect, Zen has its own four statements:

A special transmission outside the Scriptures;
No dependence upon words and letters;
Direct pointing to the soul of man;
Seeing into one's nature and the attainment of Buddhahood.

This sums up all that is claimed by Zen as religion. Of course we must not forget that there is a historical background to this bold pronunciamento. At the time of the introduction of Zen into China, most of the Buddhists were addicted to the discussion of highly metaphysical questions, or satisfied with the merely observing of the ethical precepts laid down by the Buddha or with the leading of a lethargic life entirely absorbed in the contemplation of the evanescence of things worldly. They all missed apprehending the great fact of life itself, which flows altogether outside of these vain exercises of the intellect or of the imagination. Bodhi-Dharma and his successors recognized this pitiful state of affairs. Hence their proclamation of "The Four Great Statements" of Zen as above cited. In a word, they mean that Zen has its own way of pointing to the nature of one's own being, and that when this is done one attains to Buddhahood, in which all the contradictions and disturbances caused by the intellect are entirely harmonized in a unity of higher order.

For this reason Zen never explains but indicates, it does not appeal to circumlocution, nor does it generalize. It always deals with facts, concrete and tangible. Logically considered, Zen may be full of contradictions and repetitions. But as it stands above all things, it goes serenely on its own way. As a Zen master aptly puts it, "carrying his home-made cane on the shoulder, he goes right on among the mountains one rising above another." It does not challenge logic, it simply walks its path of facts, leaving all the rest to their own fates. It is only when logic neglecting its proper functions tries to step into the track of Zen that it loudly proclaims its principles and forcibly drives out the intruder. Zen is not an enemy of anything. There is no reason why it should antagonize the intellect which may sometimes be utilized for the cause of Zen itself. To show some examples of Zen's direct dealing with the fundamental facts of existence, the following are selected:

Rinzai[1] (Lin-chi) once delivered a sermon, saying: "Over a

---

[1] The founder of the Rinzai School of Zen Buddhism, died 867.

mass of reddish flesh there sits a true man who has no title; he is all the time coming in and out from your sense-organs. If you have not yet testified to the fact, Look! Look!" A monk came forward and asked, "Who is this true man of no title?" Rinzai came right down from his straw chair and taking hold of the monk exclaimed: "Speak! Speak!" The monk remained irresolute, not knowing what to say, whereupon the master, letting him go, remarked, "What worthless stuff is this true man of no title!" Rinzai then went straight back to his room.

Rinzai was noted for his "rough" and direct treatment of his disciples. He never liked those roundabout dealings which generally characterized the methods of a lukewarm master. He must have got this directness from his own teacher Obaku (Huang-nieh), by whom he was struck three times for asking what the fundamental principle of Buddhism was. It goes without saying that Zen has nothing to do with mere striking or roughly shaking the questioner. If you take this as constituting the essentials of Zen, you would commit the same gross error as one who took the finger for the moon. As in everything else, but most particularly in Zen, all its outward manifestations or demonstrations must never be regarded as final. They just indicate the way where to look for the facts. . . .

## ON SATORI—THE REVELATION OF A NEW TRUTH
## IN ZEN BUDDHISM

### I

The essence of Zen Buddhism consists in acquiring a new viewpoint of looking at life and things generally. By this I mean that if we want to get into the inmost life of Zen, we must forgo all our ordinary habits of thinking which control our everyday life, we must try to see if there is any other way of judging things, or rather if our ordinary way is always sufficient to give us the ultimate satisfaction of our spiritual needs. If we feel dissatisfied somehow with this life, if there is something in our ordinary way of living that deprives us of freedom in its most sanctified sense, we must endeavour to find a way somewhere which gives us a sense of finality and contentment. Zen proposes to do this for us and assures us of the acquirement of a new point of view in which life assumes a fresher, deeper, and more satisfying aspect. This acquirement, however, is really and naturally the greatest mental cataclysm one can go through with in life. It is no easy task, it is a kind of fiery baptism, and one has to go through the storm, the earthquake, the overthrowing of the mountains, and the breaking in pieces of the rocks.

This acquiring of a new point of view in our dealings with life and the world is popularly called by Japanese Zen students "satori" (*wu* in Chinese). It is really another name for Enlightenment (*anuttara-samyak-sambodhi*), which is the word used by the Buddha and his Indian followers ever since his realization under the Bodhi-tree by the River Nairanjana. There are several other phrases in Chinese designating this spiritual experience, each of which has a special connotation, showing tentatively how this phenomenon is interpreted. At all events there is no Zen without satori, which is indeed the Alpha and Omega of Zen Buddhism. Zen devoid of satori is like a sun without its light and heat. Zen may lose all its literature, all its monasteries, and all its paraphernalia; but as long as there is satori in it it will survive to eternity. I want to emphasize this most fundamental fact concerning the very life of Zen; for there are some even among the students of Zen themselves who are blind to this central fact and are apt to think when Zen has been explained away logically or psychologically, or as one of the Buddhist philosophies which can be summed up by using highly technical and conceptual Buddhist phrases, Zen is exhausted, and there remains nothing in it that makes it what it is. But my contention is, the life of Zen begins with the opening of satori (*kai wu* in Chinese).

Satori may be defined as an intuitive looking into the nature of things in contradistinction to the analytical or logical understanding of it. Practically, it means the unfolding of a new world hitherto unperceived in the confusion of a dualistically-trained mind. Or we may say that with satori our entire surroundings are viewed from quite an unexpected angle of perception. Whatever this is, the world for those who have gained a satori is no more the old world as it used to be; even with all its flowing streams and burning fires, it is never the same one again. Logically stated, all its opposites and contradictions are united and harmonized into a consistent organic whole. This is a mystery and a miracle, but according to the Zen masters such is being performed every day. Satori can thus be had only through our once personally experiencing it.

Its semblance or analogy in a more or less feeble and fragmentary way is gained when a difficult mathematical problem is solved, or when a great discovery is made, or when a sudden means of escape is realized in the midst of most desperate complications; in short, when one exclaims "Eureka! Eureka!" But this refers only to the intellectual aspect of satori, which is therefore necessarily partial and incomplete and does not touch the very foundations of life considered one indivisible whole. Satori as the Zen experience must be concerned with the entirety of life. For what Zen proposes to do is the revolution, and the revaluation as well, of oneself as a spiritual unity. The solving of a mathematical problem ends with the solution, it does not affect one's whole life. So with all other particular questions, practical or scientific, they do not enter the basic life-tone of the individual concerned. But the opening of satori is the remaking of life itself. When it is genuine—for there are many simulacra of it—its effects on one's moral and spiritual life are revolutionary, and they are so enhancing, purifying, as well as exacting. When a master was asked what constituted Buddhahood, he answered, "The bottom of a pail is broken through." From this we can see what a complete revolution is produced by this spiritual experience. The birth of a new man is really cataclysmic.

In the psychology of religion this spiritual enhancement of one's whole life is called "conversion." But as the term is generally used by Christian converts, it cannot be applied in its strict sense to the Buddhist experience, especially to that of the

Zen followers; the term has too affective or emotional a shade to take the place of satori, which is above all noetic. The general tendency of Buddhism is, as we know, more intellectual than emotional, and its doctrine of Enlightenment distinguishes it sharply from the Christian view of salvation; Zen as one of the Mahayana schools naturally shares a large amount of what we may call transcendental intellectualism, which does not issue in logical dualism. When poetically or figuratively expressed, satori is "the opening of the mind-flower," or "the removing of the bar," or "the brightening up of the mind-works."

All these tend to mean the clearing up of a passage which has been somehow blocked, preventing the free, unobstructed operation of a machine or a full display of the inner works. With the removal of the obstruction, a new vista opens before one, boundless in expanse and reaching the end of time. As life thus feels quite free in its activity, which was not the case before the awakening, it now enjoys itself to the fullest extent of its possibilities, to attain which is the object of Zen discipline. This is often taken to be equivalent to "vacuity of interest and poverty of purpose." But according to the Zen masters the doctrine of non-achievement concerns itself with the subjective attitude of mind which goes beyond the limitations of thought. It does not deny ethical ideals, nor does it transcend them; it is simply an inner state of consciousness without reference to its objective consequences.

## II

The coming of Bodhi-Dharma (Bodai-daruma in Japanese, P'u-ti Ta-mo in Chinese) to China early in the sixth century was simply to introduce this satori element into the body of Buddhism, whose advocates were then so engrossed in subtleties of philosophical discussion or in the mere literary observance of rituals and disciplinary rules. By the "absolute transmission of the spiritual seal," which was claimed by the first patriarch, is meant the opening of satori, obtaining an eye to see into the spirit of the Buddhist teaching.

The sixth patriarch, Yeno (Hui-neng), was distinguished because of his upholding the satori aspect of dhyana against the mere mental tranquilization of the Northern school of Zen under the leadership of Jinshu (Shen-hsiu). Baso (Ma-tsu), Obaku (Huan-po), Rinzai (Lin-chi), and all the other stars illuminating the early days of Zen in the T'ang dynasty were advocates of satori. Their life-activities were unceasingly directed towards the advancement of this; and as one can readily recognize, they so differed from those merely absorbed in contemplation or the practising of dhyana so called. They were strongly against quietism, declaring its adherents to be purblind and living in the cave of darkness. Before we go on it is advisable, therefore, to have this point clearly understood so that we leave no doubt as to the ultimate purport of Zen, which is by no means wasting one's life away in a trance-inducing practice, but consists in seeing into the life of one's being or opening an eye of satori.

There is in Japan a book going under the title of *Six Essays by Shoshitsu* (that is, by Bodhi-Dharma, the first patriarch of Zen); the book contains no doubt some of the sayings of Dharma, but most of the Essays are not his; they were probably composed during the T'ang dynasty when Zen Buddhism began to make its influence more generally felt among the Chinese Buddhists. The spirit, however, pervading the book is in perfect accord with the principle of Zen. One of the Essays entitled "Kechimyaku-ron," or "Treatise on the Lineage of Faith," discusses the question of *Chien-hsing,*[2] or satori, which, according to the author, con-

---

[2] *Hsing* means nature, character, essence, soul, or what is innate to one. "Seeing into one's Nature" is one of the set phrases used by the Zen masters, and is in fact the avowed object of all Zen discipline. Satori is its more popular expression. When one gets into the inwardness of things, there is satori. This latter, however, being a broad term, can be used to designate any kind of a thorough understanding, and it is only in Zen that it has a restricted meaning. In this article I have used the term as the most essential thing in the study of Zen; for "seeing into one's Nature" suggests the idea that Zen has something concrete and substantial which requires being seen into by us. This is misleading, though satori too I admit is a vague and naturally ambiguous word. For ordinary purposes, not too strictly philosophical, satori will answer, and whenever *chien-hsing* is referred to it means this: the opening of the mental eye.

stitutes the essence of Zen Buddhism. The following passages are extracts.

"If you wish to seek the Buddha, you ought to see into your own Nature (*hsing*); for this Nature is the Buddha himself. If you have not seen into your own Nature, what is the use of thinking of the Buddha, reciting the Sutras, observing a fast, or keeping the precepts? By thinking of the Buddha, your cause [i.e. meritorious deed] may bear fruit; by reciting the Sutras your intelligence may grow brighter; by keeping the precepts you may be born in the heavens; by practising charity you may be rewarded abundantly; but as to seeking the Buddha, you are far away from him. If your Self is not yet clearly comprehended, you ought to see a wise teacher and get a thorough understanding as to the root of birth-and-death. One who has not seen into one's own Nature is not to be called a wise teacher.

"When this [seeing into one's own Nature] is not attained, one cannot escape from the transmigration of birth-and-death, however well one may be versed in the study of the sacred scriptures in twelve divisions. No time will ever come to one to get out of the sufferings of the triple world. Anciently there was a Bhikshu Zensho who was capable of reciting all the twelve divisions of scriptures, yet he could not save himself from transmigration, because he had no insight into his own Nature. If this was the case even with Zensho, how about those moderners who, being able to discourse only on a few Sutras and Sastras, regard themselves as exponents of Buddhism? They are truly simple-minded ones. When Mind is not understood it is absolutely of no avail to recite and discourse on idle literature. If you want to seek the Buddha, you ought to see into your own Nature, which is the Buddha himself. The Buddha is a free man—a man who neither works nor achieves. If, instead of seeing into your own Nature, you turn away and seek the Buddha in external things, you will never get at him.

"The Buddha is your own Mind, make no mistake to bow [to external objects]. 'Buddha' is a Western word, and in this country it means 'enlightened nature'; and by 'enlightened' is meant 'spiritually enlightened.' It is one's own spiritual Nature in enlightenment that responds to the external world, comes in contact with objects, raises the eyebrows, winks the eyelids, and moves the hands and legs. This Nature is the Mind, and the Mind is the Buddha, and the Buddha is the Way, and the Way is Zen. This simple word, Zen, is beyond the comprehension both of the wise and the ignorant. To see directly into one's original Nature, that is Zen. Even if you are well learned in hundreds of the Sutras and Sastras, you still remain an ignoramus in Buddhism when you have not yet seen into your original Nature. Buddhism is not there [in mere learning]. The highest truth is unfathomably deep, is not an object of talk or discussion, and even the canonical texts have no way to bring it within our reach. Let us once see into our own original Nature and we have the truth, even when we are quite illiterate, not knowing a word. . . .

"Those who have not seen into their own Nature may read the Sutras, think of the Buddha, study long, work hard, practise religion throughout the six periods of the day, sit for a long time and never lie down for sleep, and may be wide in learning and well informed in all things; and they may believe that all this is Buddhism. All the Buddhas in successive ages only talk of seeing into one's Nature. All things are impermanent, until you get an insight into your Nature, do not say 'I have perfect knowledge.' Such is really committing a very grave crime. Ananda, one of the ten great disciples of the Buddha was known for his wide information, but did not have any insight into Buddhahood, because he was so bent on gaining information only. . . ."

## III

The records quoted below do not always give the whole history of the mental development leading up to a satori; that is, from the first moment when the disciple came to the master until the last moment of realization, with all the intermittent psychological vicissitudes which he had to go through. The examples are just to show that the whole Zen discipline gains meaning when there takes place this turning of the mental hinge to a wider and deeper world. For when this wise and deeper world opens, everyday life, even the most trivial thing of it, grows loaded with the truths of Zen. On the one hand, therefore, satori is a most prosaic and matter-of-fact thing, but on the other hand, when it is not understood it is something of a mystery. But after all, is not life itself filled with wonders, mysteries, and unfathomabilities, far beyond our discursive understanding?

A monk asked Joshu (Chao-chou Tsung-shen, 778–897) to be instructed in Zen. Said the master, "Have you had your breakfast or not?" "Yes, master, I have," answered the monk. "If so, have your dishes washed," was an immediate response, which, it is said, at once opened the monk's mind to the truth of Zen.

This is enough to show what a commonplace thing satori is; but to see what an important role this most trivial incident of life plays in Zen, it will be necessary to add some remarks which were made by the masters, and through these the reader may have a glimpse into the content of satori. Ummon (Yun-men Wen-yen, died 949), who lived a little later than Joshu, commented on him: "Was there any special instruction in the remark of Joshu, or not? If there was, what was it? If there was not, what satori was it that the monk attained?" Later, Umpo Monyetsu (Yun-feng Wen-yueh, 997–1062) made a retort, saying: "The great master Ummon does not know what is what, hence this comment of his. It was altogether unnecessary, it was like painting legs to the snake and growing a beard to the eunuch. My view differs from his: that monk who seems to have attained a satori goes to hell as straight as an arrow!"

Now, what does this all mean—Joshu's remark about washing the dishes, the monk's attainment of satori, Ummon's alternatives, and Monyetsu's assurance? Are they speaking against each other? Is this much ado about nothing? This is where Zen is difficult to grasp and at the same time difficult to explain. Let me add a few more queries. How did Joshu make the monk's eye open by such a prosaic remark? Did the remark have any hidden meaning, however, which happened to coincide with the mental tone of the monk? How was the monk so mentally prepared for the final stroke of the master, whose service was just pressing the button, as it were? Nothing of satori is so far gleaned from washing the dishes; we have to look somewhere else for the truth of Zen. At any rate, we could not say that Joshu had nothing to do with the monk's realization. Hence Ummon's remark, which is somewhat enigmatic, yet to the point. As to Monyetsu's comment, it is what is technically known as *Nenro,* "handling and playing," or "playful criticism." He appears to be making a disparaging remark about Ummon, but in truth he is joining hands with his predecessors.

Tokusan (Teh-shan Hsuan-chien, 779–865) was a great scholar of the *Diamond Sutra* (*Vajracchedika*). Learning that there was such a thing as Zen ignoring all the written scriptures and directly laying hands on one's soul, he came to Ryutan (Lung-t'an) to be instructed in the doctrine. One day Tokusan was sitting outside trying to see into the mystery of Zen. Ryutan said, "Why don't you come in?" Replied Tokusan, "It is pitch dark." A candle was lighted and handed over to Tokusan. When the latter was at the point of taking it, Ryutan suddenly blew the light out, whereupon the mind of Tokusan was opened.

Hyakujo (Pai-chang Huai-hai, 724–814) one day went out attending his master Baso (Ma-tsu). A flock of wild geese was seen flying and Baso asked:

"What are they?"

"They are wild geese, sir."

"Whither are they flying?"

"They have flown away, sir."

Baso abruptly taking hold of Hyakujo's nose gave it a twist. Overcome with pain, Hyakujo cried aloud: "Oh! Oh!"

"You say they have flown away," Baso said, "but all the same they have been here from the very beginning."

This made Hyakujo's back wet with cold perspiration. He had satori.

Is there any connection in any possible way between the washing of the dishes and the blowing out of a candle and the twisting of the nose? We must say with Ummon: If there is none, how could they all come to the realization of the truth of Zen? If there is, what inner relationship is there? What is this satori? What new point of viewing things is this? So long as our observation is limited to those conditions which preceded the opening of a disciple's eye we cannot perhaps fully comprehend where lies the ultimate issue. They are matters of everyday occurrence, and if Zen lies objectively among them, every one of us is a master before we are told of it. This is partly true inasmuch as there is nothing artificially constructed in Zen, but if the nose is to be really twisted or the candle blown out in order to take the scale off the eye, our attention must be directed inwardly to the working of our minds, and it will be there where we are to take hold of the hidden relation existing between the flying geese and the washed dishes and the blown-out candle and any other happenings that weave out infinitely variegated patterns of human life.

Under Daiye (Tai-hui, 1089–1163), the great Zen teacher of the Sung dynasty, there was a monk named Doken (Tao-ch'ien) who had spent many years in the study of Zen, but who had not yet delved into its secrets, if there were any. He was discouraged when he was sent on an errand to a distant city. A trip requiring half a year to finish would surely be a hindrance rather than a help to his study. Sogen (Tsung-yuan), one of his fellow-monks, took pity on him and said: "I will accompany you on this trip and do all that I can for you. There is no reason why you cannot go on with your meditation even while travelling." They started together.

One evening Doken despairingly implored his friend to assist him in the solution of the mystery of life. The friend said: "I am willing to help you in every way, but there are five things in which I cannot be of any help to you. These you must look after yourself." Doken expressed the desire to know what they were. "For instance," said the friend, "when you are hungry or thirsty, my eating of food or drinking does not fill your stomach. You must drink and eat yourself. When you want to respond to the calls of nature, you must take care of them yourself, for I cannot be of any use to you. And then it will be nobody else but your-self that will carry this corpse of yours [i.e. the body] along this highway." This remark at once opened the mind of the truth-seeking monk, who, transported with his discovery, did not know how to express his joy. Sogen now told him that his work was done and that his further companionship would have no mean-ing after this. So they parted company and Doken was left alone to continue the trip. After the half-year, Doken came back to his own monastery. Daiye, his teacher, happened to meet him on his way down the mountain, and made the following remark, "This time he knows it all." What was it, one may remark, that flashed through Doken's mind when his friend gave him such matter-of-fact advice?

Kyogen (Hsian-yen) was a disciple of Hyakujo. After the master's death he went to Yisan (Wei-shan, 771–853), who was a senior disciple of Hyakujo. Yisan asked him: "I am told that you have been under my late master Hyakujo, and also that you have remarkable intelligence; but the understanding of Zen through this medium necessarily ends in intellectual and ana-lytical comprehension, which is not of much use. Yet you may have had an insight into the truth of Zen. Let me have your view as to the reason of birth-and-death; that is, as to your own being before your parents gave birth to you."

Thus asked, Kyogen did not know how to reply. He retired into his own room and assiduously made research among his notes which he had taken of the sermons given by his late master. He failed to come across a suitable passage he might present as his own view. He returned to Yisan and implored him to teach in the faith of Zen. But Yisan said: "I really have nothing to impart to you, and if I tried to do so you may have occasion to make me an object of ridicule later on. Besides, whatever I can instruct you is my own and will never be yours." Kyogen was disappointed and considered his senior disciple unkind. Finally he came to the decision to burn up all his notes and memoran-dums which were of no help to his spiritual welfare, and, retiring altogether from the world, to spend the rest of his life in solitude and simplicity in accordance with the Buddhist rules. He reasoned: "What is the use of studying Buddhism, so difficult to comprehend and too subtle to receive instructions from another? I shall be a plain homeless monk, troubled with no desire to master things too deep for thought." He left Yisan and built a hut near the tomb of Chu (Hui-chung), the National Master, at Nan-yang. One day he was weeding and sweeping the ground, and when a piece of rock brushed away struck a bamboo, the sound produced by the percussion unexpectedly elevated his mind to a state of satori. The question proposed by Yisan became transparent; his joy was boundless, he felt as if meeting again his lost parent. Besides, he came to realize the kindness of his abandoned senior brother monk who refused him instruction. For he now knew that this would not have happened to him if Yisan had been unkind enough to explain things for him.

Below is the verse he composed soon after his achievement, from which we may get an idea of his satori:

One stroke has made me forget all my previous knowledge,
No artificial discipline is at all needed;
In every movement I uphold the ancient way,
And never fall into the rut of mere quietism;
Wherever I walk no traces are left,
And my senses are not fettered by rules of conduct;
Everywhere those who have attained to the truth,
All declare this to be of the highest order.

## IV

There is something, we must admit, in Zen that defies explanation, and to which no master however ingenious can lead his disciples through intellectual analysis. Kyogen or Tokusan had enough knowledge of the canonical teachings or of the master's expository discourses; but when the real thing was demanded of them they significantly failed to produce it either to their inner satisfaction or for the master's approval. The satori, after all, is not a thing to be gained through the understanding. But once the key is within one's grasp, everything seems to be laid bare

before him; the entire world assumes then a different aspect. By
those who know, this inner change is recognized. The Doken
before he started on his mission and the Doken after the realization were apparently the same person; but as soon as Daiye saw
him he knew what had taken place in him, even when he uttered
not a word. Baso twisted Hyakujo's nose, and the latter turned
into such a wild soul as to have the audacity to roll up the matting
before his master's discourse had hardly begun. The experience they have gone through within themselves is not a very
elaborate, complicated, and intellectually demonstrable thing;
for none of them ever try to expound it by a series of learned
discourses; they do just this thing or that, or utter a single phrase
unintelligible to outsiders, and the whole affair proves most satisfactory both to the master and to the disciple. The satori cannot
be a phantasm, empty and contentless, and lacking in real value,
while it must be the simplest possible experience perhaps because
it is the very foundation of all experiences.

As to the opening of satori, all that Zen can do is to indicate
the way and leave the rest all to one's own experience; that is to
say, following up the indication and arriving at the goal—this is
to be done by oneself and without another's help. With all that
the master can do, he is helpless to make the disciple take hold
of the thing unless the latter is inwardly fully prepared for it.
Just as we cannot make a horse drink against his will, the taking
hold of the ultimate reality is to be done by oneself. Just as the
flower blooms out of its inner necessity, the looking into one's
own nature must be the outcome of one's own inner overflowing.
This is where Zen is so personal and subjective, in the sense of
being inner and creative. In the Agama or Nikaya literature we
encounter so frequently such phrases as "Atta-dipa viharatha atta
sarana ananna-sarana," or "sayam abhinna," or "Dittha-dhammo
patta-dhammo vidita-dhammo pariyogalha-dhammo aparappac-
cayo satthu sasane"; they show that Enlightenment is the awakening, within oneself and not depending on others, of an inner
sense in one's consciousness, enabling one to create a world of
eternal harmony and beauty—the home of Nirvana.

I said that Zen does not give us any intellectual assistance, nor does it waste time in arguing the point with us; but it merely suggests or indicates, not because it wants to be indefinite, but because that is really the only thing it can do for us. If it could, it would do anything to help us come to an understanding. In fact Zen is exhausting every possible means to do that, as we can see in all the great masters' attitudes towards their disciples. When they are actually knocking them down, their kindheartedness is never to be doubted. They are just waiting for the time when their pupils' minds get all ripened for the final moment. When this is come, the opportunity of opening an eye to the truth of Zen lies everywhere. One can pick it up in the hearing of an inarticulate sound, or listening to an unintelligible remark, or in the observation of a flower blooming, or in the encountering of any trivial everyday incident such as stumbling, rolling up a screen, using a fan, etc. These are all sufficient conditions that will awaken one's inner sense. Evidently a most insignificant happening, and yet its effect on the mind infinitely surpasses all that one could expect of it. A light touch of an ignited wire, and an explosion shaking the very foundations of the earth. In fact, all the causes of satori are in the mind. That is why when the clock clicks, all that has been lying there bursts up like a volcanic eruption or flashes out like a bolt of lightning. Zen calls this "returning to one's own home"; for its followers will declare: "You have now found yourself; from the very beginning nothing has been kept away from you. It was yourself that closed the eye to the fact. In Zen there is nothing to explain, nothing to teach, that will add to your knowledge. Unless it grows out of yourself, no knowledge is really of value to you, a borrowed plumage never grows."

Kozankoku (Huang San-ku), a Confucian poet and statesman, came to Kwaido (Hui-t'ang, 1024–1100) to be initiated into Zen. Said the Zen master: "There is a passage in the text you are so thoroughly familiar with which fitly describes the teaching of Zen. Did not Confucius declare: 'Do you think I am holding back something from you, O my disciples? Indeed, I have held nothing back from you'?" Kozankoku tried to answer, but Kwaido immediately made him keep silence by saying, "No, no!" The Confucian disciple felt troubled in mind, and did not know how to express himself. Some time later they were having a walk in the mountains. The wild laurel was in full bloom and the air was redolent. Asked the Zen master, "Do you smell it?" When the Confucian answered affirmatively, Kwaido said, "There, I have kept nothing back from you!" This suggestion from the teacher at once led to the opening of Kozankoku's mind. Is it not evident now that satori is not a thing to be imposed upon another, but that it is self-growing from within? Though nothing is kept away from us, it is through a satori that we become cognizant of the fact, being convinced that we are all sufficient unto ourselves. All that therefore Zen contrives is to assert that there is such a thing as self-revelation, or the opening of satori.

## V

As satori strikes at the primary fact of existence, its attainment marks a turning-point in one's life. The attainment, however, must be thorough-going and clear-cut in order to produce a satisfactory result. To deserve the name "satori" the mental revolution must be so complete as to make one really and sincerely feel that there took place a fiery baptism of the spirit. The intensity of this feeling is proportional to the amount of effort the opener of satori has put into the achievement. For there is a gradation in satori as to its intensity, as in all our mental activity. The possessor of a lukewarm satori may suffer no such spiritual revolution as Rinzai, or Bukko (Fo-kuang), whose case is quoted below. Zen is a matter of character and not of the intellect, which means that Zen grows out of the will as the first principle of life. A brilliant intellect may fail to unravel all the mysteries of Zen, but a strong soul will drink deep of the inexhaustible fountain. I do not know if the intellect is superficial and touches only the fringe of one's personality, but the fact is that the will is the man himself, and Zen appeals to it. When one becomes penetratingly conscious of the working of this agency, there is the opening of satori and the understanding of Zen. As they say, the snake has now grown into the dragon; or, more graphically, a common cur —a most miserable creature wagging its tail for food and sympathy, and kicked about by the street boys so mercilessly—has now turned into a golden-haired lion whose roar frightens to death all the feeble-minded.

Therefore, when Rinzai was meekly submitting to the "thirty blows" of Obaku, he was a pitiable sight; as soon as he attained satori he was quite a different personage, and his first exclamation was, "There is not much after all in the Buddhism of Obaku." And when he saw the reproachful Obaku again, he returned his favour by giving him a slap on the face. "What an arrogance, what an impudence!" Obaku exclaimed; but there was reason in Rinzai's rudeness, and the old master could not but be pleased with this treatment from his former tearful Rinzai.

When Tokusan gained an insight into the truth of Zen he immediately took up all his commentaries on the *Diamond Sutra,* once so valued and considered indispensable that he had to carry them wherever he went; he now set fire to them, reducing all the manuscripts to nothingness. He exclaimed, "However deep your knowledge of abstruse philosophy, it is like a piece of hair placed in the vastness of space; and however important your experience in things worldly, it is like a drop of water thrown into an unfathomable abyss." . . .

## VIII

These cases will be sufficient to show what mental process one has to go through before the opening of satori takes place. Of course these are prominent examples and highly accentuated, and every satori is not preceded by such an extraordinary degree of concentration. But an experience more or less like these must be the necessary antecedent to all satori, especially to that which is to be gone through at the outset of the study. The mirror of mind or the field of consciousness then seems to be so thoroughly swept clean as not to leave a particle of dust on it.

When thus all mentation is temporarily suspended, even the consciousness of an effort to keep an idea focused at the centre of attention is gone—that is, when, as the Zen followers say, the mind is so completely possessed or identified with its object of thought that even the consciousness of identity is lost as when one mirror reflects another, the subject feels as if living in a crystal palace, all transparent, refreshing, buoyant, and royal. But the end has not yet been reached, this being merely the preliminary condition leading to the consummation called satori. If the mind remains in this state of fixation, there will be no occasion for its being awakened to the truth of Zen. The state of "Great Doubt" (tai-gi), as it is technically known, is the antecedent. It must be broken up and exploded into the next stage, which is looking into one's nature or the opening of satori.

The explosion, as it is nothing else, generally takes place when this finely balanced equilibrium tilts for one reason or another. A stone is thrown into a sheet of water in perfect stillness, and the disturbance at once spreads all over the surface. It is somewhat like this. A sound knocks at the gate of consciousness so tightly closed, and it at once reverberates through the entire being of the individual. He is awakened in the most vivid sense of the word. He comes out baptized in the fire of creation. He has seen the work of God in his very workshop. The occasion may not necessarily be the hearing of a temple bell, it may be reading a stanza, or seeing something moving, or the sense of touch irritated, when a most highly accentuated state of concentration bursts out into a satori.

The concentration, however, may not be kept up to such an almost abnormal degree as in the case of Bukko. It may last just a second or two, and if it is the right kind of concentration, and rightly handled by the master, the inevitable opening of the mind will follow. When the monk Jo (Ting) asked Rinzai "What is the ultimate principle of Buddhism?" the master came right down from his seat, took hold of the monk, slapped him with his hand, and pushed him away from him. The monk stood stupefied. A bystander suggested, "Why don't you make a bow?"

Obeying the order, Jo was about to bow, when he abruptly awoke to the truth of Zen.

In this case Jo's self-absorption or concentration did not seemingly last very long; the bowing was the turning-point, it broke up the spell and restored him to sense, not to an ordinary sense of awareness, but to the inward consciousness of his own being. Generally we have no records of the inner working prior to a satori, and may pass lightly over the event as a merely happy incident or some intellectual trick having no deeper background. When we read such records, we have to supply from our own experience, whatever this is, all the necessary antecedent conditions for breaking up into a satori.

# IX

So far the phenomenon called satori in Zen Buddhism has been treated as constituting the essence of Zen, as the turning-point in one's life which opens the mind to a wider and deeper world, as something to be gleaned even from a most trivial incident of everyday life; and then it was explained how satori is to come out of one's inner life, and not by any outside help except as merely indicating the way to it. Next I proceeded to describe what a change satori brings in one's idea of things—that is, how it all upsets the former valuation of things generally, making one stand now entirely on a different footing. For illustrations, some verses were quoted which were composed by the masters at the moment of their attainment of satori. They are mostly descriptive of the feelings they experienced, such as those by Bukko and Yodainen and Yengo and others are typical of this class, as they have almost no intellectual elements in them. If one tries to pick up something from these verses by a mere analytical process, one will be greatly disappointed. The psychological side of satori, which is minutely narrated by Hakuin and others, will be of great interest to those who are desirous of making a psychological inquiry into Zen. Of course these narratives alone will not do, for there are many other things one has to consider in order to study it thoroughly, among which I may mention the general Buddhist attitude towards life and the world and the historical atmosphere in which the students of Zen find themselves.

I wish to close this Essay by making a few general remarks in the way of recapitulation on the Buddhist experience known as satori.

1. People often imagine that the discipline of Zen is to induce a state of self-suggestion through meditation. This is not quite right. As we can see from the various instances above cited, satori does not consist in producing a certain premeditated condition by intensely thinking of it. It is the growing conscious of a new power in the mind, which enabled it to judge things from a new point of view. Even since the unfoldment of consciousness we have been led to respond to the inner and outer conditions in a certain conceptual and analytical manner. The discipline of Zen consists in upsetting this artificially constructed framework once for all and in remodelling it on an entirely new basis. The older frame is called "Ignorance" (*avidya*) and the new one "Enlightenment" (*sambodhi*). It is evident therefore that meditating on a metaphysical or symbolical statement which is a product of our relative consciousness plays no part in Zen, as I have touched on this in the Introduction.

2. Without the attainment of satori no one can enter into the mystery of Zen. It is the sudden flashing of a new truth hitherto altogether undreamed of. It is a sort of mental catastrophe taking place all at once after so much piling of matters intellectual and demonstrative. The piling has reached its limit and the whole edifice has now come to the ground, when behold a new heaven is opened to your full survey. Water freezes suddenly when it reaches a certain point, the liquid has turned into a solidity, and it no more flows. Satori comes upon you unawares when you feel you have exhausted your whole being. Religiously this is a new birth, and, morally, the revaluation of one's relationship to the world. The latter now appears to be dressed in a different garment which covers up all the ugliness of dualism, which is called in Buddhist phraseology delusion (*maya*) born of reasoning (*tarka*) and error (*vikalpa*).

3. Satori is the *raison d'être* of Zen, and without which Zen is no Zen. Therefore every contrivance (*upaya*), disciplinary or doctrinal, is directed toward the attainment of satori. Zen masters could not remain patient for satori to come by itself; that is, to come sporadically and at its own pleasure. They earnestly seek out some way to make people deliberately or systematically realize the truth of Zen. Their manifestly enigmatical presentations of it were mostly to create a state of mind in their disciples, which would pave the way to the enlightenment of Zen. All the intellectual demonstrations and exhortatory persuasions so far carried out by most religious and philosophical leaders failed to produce the desired effect. The disciples were led further and further astray. Especially when Buddhism was introduced into China with all its Indian equipments, with its highly metaphysical abstractions, and in a most complicated system of moral discipline, the Chinese were at a loss how to grasp the central point of the doctrine of Buddhism. Daruma, Yeno, Baso, and other masters noticed the fact. The natural outcome was the proclamation of Zen; satori was placed above Sutra-reading and scholarly discussion of the Sastras, and it came to be identified with Zen. Zen therefore without satori is like pepper without its pungency. But at the same time we must not forget that there is such a thing as too much satori, which is indeed to be detested.

4. This emphasizing in Zen of satori above everything else makes the fact quite significant that Zen is not a system of dhyana as practised in India and by other schools of Buddhism than the Zen. By dhyana is understood popularly a kind of meditation or contemplation; that is, fixing of thought, especially in Mahayana Buddhism, on the doctrine of emptiness (*sunyata*). When the mind is so trained as to be able to realize the state of perfect void in which there is not a trace of consciousness left, even the sense of being unconscious having departed—in other words, when all forms of mental activity are swept clean from the field of consciousness, which is now like a sky devoid of every speck of cloud, a mere broad expanse of blue—dhyana is said to have reached its perfection. This may be called ecstasy or trance, but it is not Zen. In Zen there must be a satori; there must

be a general mental upheaval which destroys the old accumulations of intellectuality and lays down a foundation for a new faith; there must be the awakening of a new sense which will review the old things from an angle of perception entirely and most refreshingly new. In dhyana there are none of these things, for it is merely a quieting exercise of the mind. As such it has doubtless its own merits, but Zen ought not to be identified with such dhyanas. The Buddha therefore got dissatisfied with his two Sankhya teachers, in whose teaching the meditations were so many stages of self-abstraction or thought-annihilation.

5. Satori is not seeing God as he is, as may be contended by some Christian mystics. Zen has from the very beginning made clear its principal thesis, which is to see into the work of creation and not interview the creator himself. The latter may be found then busy moulding his universe, but Zen can go along with its own work even when he is not found there. It is not depending on his support. When it grasps the reason of living a life, it is satisfied. Hoyen, of Gosozan, used to produce his own hand and asked his disciples why it is called a hand. When one knows the reason, there is satori and one has Zen. Whereas with the God of mysticism there is the grasping of a definite object, and when you have God, what is not God is excluded. This is self-limiting. Zen wants absolute freedom, even from God. "No abiding place" means that; "Cleanse your mouth even when you utter the word 'Buddha'" amounts to the same thing. It is not that Zen wants to be morbidly unholy and godless, but that it knows the incompleteness of a name. Therefore when Yakusan (Yueh-shan) was asked to give a lecture, he did not say a word, but instead came down from the pulpit and went off to his own room. Hyakujo (Pai-chang) merely walked forward a few steps, stood still, and opened his arms—which was his exposition of the great principle of Buddhism.

6. Satori is the most intimate individual experience and therefore cannot be expressed in words or described in any manner. All that one can do in the way of communicating the experience to others is to suggest or indicate, and this only tentatively. The

one who has had it understands readily enough when such indications are given, but when we try to have a glimpse of it
through the indices given we utterly fail. We are then like the
man who says that he loves the most beautiful woman in the
world and yet who knows nothing of her pedigree or social position, of her personal name or family name, knows nothing of
her individuality physical as well as moral. We are again like
the man who puts up a staircase in a place where four crossroads
meet, to mount up thereby into the upper story of a mansion,
and yet who knows not just where that mansion is, in the East
or West, in the North or South. The Buddha was quite to the
point when he thus derided all those philosophers and vain talkers
of his day, who merely dealt in abstractions, empty hearsays, and
fruitless indications. Zen therefore wants us to build the staircase
right at the front of the very palace into whose upper story we
are to mount up. When we can say "This is the very personality,
this is the very house," we have the satori interviewed face to
face and realized by oneself. (*Ditthe va dhamme sayam abhinna
sacchikatva.*)

7. Satori is not a morbid state of mind, a fit subject for abnormal psychology. If anything it is a perfectly normal state of
mind. When I speak of a mental upheaval, one may be led to
consider Zen something to be shunned by ordinary people. This
is a mistaken view of Zen, unfortunately often held by prejudiced
critics. As Nansen (Nan-ch'uan) declared, it is your "everyday
thought." When later a monk asked a master what was meant
by "everyday thought," he said,

> Drinking tea, eating rice,
> I pass my time as it comes;
> Looking down at the stream, looking up at the mountains,
> How serene and relaxed I feel indeed!

It all depends upon the adjustment of the hinge whether the
door opens in or out. Even in the twinkling of an eye, the whole
affair is changed, and you have Zen, and you are as perfect and
normal as ever. More than that, you have in the meantime ac-

quired something altogether new. All your mental activities are now working to a different key, which is more satisfying, more peaceful, and fuller of joy than anything you ever had. The tone of your life is altered. There is something rejuvenating in it. The spring flowers look prettier, and the mountain stream runs cooler and more transparent. The subjective revolution that brings out this state of things cannot be called abnormal. When life becomes more enjoyable and its expanse is as broad as the universe itself, there must be something in satori quite healthy and worth one's striving after its attainment.

8. We are supposedly living in the same world, but who can tell the thing we popularly call a stone lying before this window is the same thing to all of us? According to the way we look at it, to some the stone ceases to be a stone, while to others it forever remains a worthless specimen of geological product. And this initial divergence of views calls forth an endless series of divergencies later in our moral and spiritual lives. Just a little twisting, as it were, in our modes of thinking, and yet what a world of difference will grow up eventually between one another! So with Zen, satori is this twisting, or rather screwing, not in the wrong way, but in a deeper and fuller sense, and the result is the revelation of a world of entirely new values.

Again, you and I sip a cup of tea. The act is apparently alike, but who can tell what a wide gap there is subjectively between you and me? In your drinking there may be no Zen, while mine is brim full of it. The reason is, the one moves in the logical circle and the other is out of it; that is to say, in one case rigid rules of intellection so called are asserting themselves, and the actor even when acting is unable to unfetter himself from these intellectual bonds; while in the other case the subject has struck a new path and is not at all conscious of the duality of his act; in him life is not split into object and subject or into acting and acted. The drinking at the moment to him means the whole fact, the whole world. Zen lives and is therefore free, whereas our "ordinary" life is in bondage; satori is the first step to freedom.

9. Satori is Enlightenment (*sambodhi*). So long as Buddhism

is the doctrine of Enlightenment, as we know it to be, from its earliest as well as from its later literature, and so long as Zen asserts satori to be its culmination, satori must be said to represent the very spirit of the Buddhist teaching. When it announces itself to be the transmission of the Buddha-citta (*fo-hsin*) not dependent upon the logical and discursive exposition in the canonical writings, either Hinayana or Mahayana, it is by no means exaggerating its fundamental characteristic as distinguished from the other schools of Buddhism that have grown up in Japan and China. Whatever this may be, there is no doubt that Zen is one of the most precious and in many respects the most remarkable spiritual possessions bequeathed to Eastern people. Even when it is considered the Buddhist form of speculative mysticism not unknown to the West in the philosophy of Plotinus, Eckhart, and their followers, its complete literature alone since the sixth patriarch, Yeno (Hui-neng, 638–713), so well preserved, is worth the serious study of scholars and truth-seekers. And then the whole body of the ko-ans systematically grading the progress of the spiritual awakening is the wonderful treasure in the hands of the Zen monks in Japan at present.

# Glossary

| | |
|---|---|
| Adi-Buddha. | Primordial Buddha Spirit. Source of all future Buddha-beings. |
| ahamkara. | Pride over personal individuality, egoism. |
| anatta. | Doctrine of not-self, nonego. |
| annica. | Transience, impermanence. |
| Arhat (Arahat). | Ideal man of Hinayana. Being who has achieved Buddhahood. Saint who has realized highest fruit of ascetic-monastic life. |
| asravas. | Literally, "flowings." Sources of desire, becoming. |
| atman. | Ego or selfhood. In Hinduism, Atman, the absolute and unconditioned divine Reality. |
| atta. | Person, soul. Permanent unity of personality. |
| avidya. | Ignorance, which sees Oneness (Suchness) as variety. |
| bhakti. | Devotional or sacrificial living or worship. |
| bhikku. | Buddhist monk. |

| | |
|---|---|
| bhutatathata. | Spontaneity of being. Primal ground. Inevitability of things. |
| bodhi. | Wisdom, inner light. |
| bodhi-citta. | Divine spark of Buddha-nature within. Heart-of-Wisdom. Grace. |
| Bodhisattva. | Enlightened being. Gotama, just prior to enlightenment. Potential Buddha. Ideal man of Mahayana. A person or deity dedicated to salvation of all sentient beings. |
| Brahman. | Unconditioned Reality. Unity of all being. In Hinduism, usually identified with Atman. |
| Brahmin (Brahman). | Man born into priestly caste in Hindu society. |
| Buddha. | Enlightened. Siddhartha Gotama after achieving enlightenment. One who has achieved Nirvana. |
| citta. | Heart. |
| dhamma (dharma). | Law of righteousness. Norm of Buddhist conduct. Core of Buddhist religion and morality. |
| Dharmakaya. | Absolute knowledge. Ground of all being. Supreme state of Buddhahood. |
| dhyana. | Concentration of mind and spirit by disciplined meditation. |
| Hinayana. | The "smaller vehicle" or "career." Appelation given by Mahayanists to doctrines of early Buddhism. |

| | |
|---|---|
| Jaina (Jina). | A follower of Mahavira. Literally, "conqueror." |
| jataka. | Legendary materials relating stories of Buddha's birth and former existences. |
| jnana. | Knowledge. |
| kama. | Love, lust. |
| karma. | Deeds, acts, law of causality, law of ethical consequence. |
| karuna. | Compassion, a chief quality of a Bodhisattva. |
| koan. | Utterances used in Zen to express or provoke enlightenment. |
| ksaya. | Act of extinguishing all worldly attachments, or the state of such extinction. |
| Madhyamika. | School of Mahayana Buddhism founded by Nagarjuna. |
| Mahayana. | "Larger vehicle" or "career." A major division of Buddhism, sometimes referred to as the Northern school. |
| mana. | Pride, egotistical action. |
| manas. | Ego characteristics, personality traits. |
| Mara. | Enemy of righteousness. Personification of evil. Tempter. |
| marga (magga). | Way or path. |
| maya. | Illusion. Power creating manifold events and beings. |
| moha. | Folly, confusion. |

Nirvana (Nibbana).          Highest good. Stillness-Bliss, Peace, Void, Nothingness. Full enlightenment. Realization of truth. Release from wheel of rebirth, suffering, and ignorance.

paramita.                   Transcendental perfection.

pari-Nirvana.               Final release.

Prajna-Paramita.            Literally, "wisdom gone beyond." Supreme Knowledge.

punya.                      Store of merit.

samadhi.                    Tranquillity, rapture, detached calmness. State of supraconsciousness. Detached awareness and equanimity achieved by enlightened being.

samana.                     Wandering ascetic.

samsara.                    Literally, "circling on." World of becoming and change. Round of evil, suffering, death, rebirth. Conditioned existence.

samskara.                   Dispositions to act resulting from previous deeds. Conformity of actions, past, present, future.

Sangha.                     Buddhist monastic order.

satori.                     Zen term referring to enlightenment, final illumination.

sattva.                     Being.

skandha.                    Collections of aggregates making up consciousness.

sunyata.                    Emptiness, Void, Reality.

Sutra (Sutta).          Literally, "thread." Literary form of Buddhist scripture. The Buddha's words strung together in sermons or dialogues.

tapas.                  Dispositional structures leading to striving and world involvement.

Tara.                   Feminine counterpart of Bodhisattva.

Tathagata.              Literally, "Thus gone" or "Thus come." Refers to an enlightened Buddha. One who has attained perfection.

tathagata-garbha.       Germ of Buddha residing in all living things.

Theravada.              "Words of the elders." The way Hinayanists characterize the sacred Pali texts.

Tri-ratna.              "Three jewels." In Hinayana: Buddha, dhamma, sangha. In Mahayana: Buddha, Sons of Buddha, Dharmakaya.

upadhi.                 Literally, "attributes" that are superimposed by mind upon Unconditioned Reality, thereby giving rise to the conditioned world.

Vinaya.                 Rules of Buddhist monastic discipline.

Yogacara.               School of Mahayana Buddhism, associated with Asanga.

# Selected
# Bibliography

Carus, Paul, *The Gospel of Buddhism*. The Open Court Publishing Company, 1921.

Conze, Edward, *Buddhism: Its Essence and Development*. Philosophical Library, 1954. Also Harper Torchbook.

Coomaraswamy, Ananda K., *Buddha and the Gospel of Buddhism*. London: George G. Harrap, 1916. Also Harper Torchbook.

Rhys Davids, Thomas W., *Buddhism: Its History and Literature*. G. P. Putnam's Sons, 1926.

Eliot, Charles, *Hinduism and Buddhism: An Historical Sketch*. London: Routledge & Kegan Paul, Ltd., 1921. 3 vols.

Gard, Richard A., *Buddhism*. Washington Square Press, Inc., 1963.

Humphreys, Christmas, *Buddhism*. Harmondsworth: Penguin Books, Ltd., 1951.

McGovern, William, *Introduction to Mahayana Buddhism*. London: Kegan Paul, Trench, Trubner & Co., Ltd., 1922.

Pratt, James B., *The Pilgrimage of Buddhism and a Buddhist Pilgrimage*. The Macmillan Company, 1928.

Ross, Nancy Wilson (ed.), *The World of Zen*. Vintage Book, Random House, Inc., 1960.

Suzuki, D. T., *Essays in Zen Buddhism (First Series)*. Grove Press, Inc., 1961.

—— *Outlines of Mahayana Buddhism*. Schocken Books, Inc., 1963.

Thomas, Edward J., *History of Buddhist Thought*. London:

George Routledge & Sons, Ltd., and Kegan Paul, Trench, Trubner & Co., Ltd., 1933.

Zimmer, Heinrich, *Philosophies of India,* ed. by Joseph Campbell. Bollingen Series XXVI, Pantheon Books, 1951.